THE MOTOR BIKE BOOK

THE MOTOR BIKE BOOK

THE DEFINITIVE VISUAL HISTORY

LONDON, NEW YORK, MELBOURNE, MUNICH, AND DELHI

DORLING KINDERSLEY

Senior Project Editor Jemima Dunne
Senior Art Editor Helen Spencer
Editors David Summers, Alison Sturgeon, Sam Atkinson, Victoria Wiggins
Designers Amy Orsborne, Paul Drislane, Philip Fitzgerald, Richard Horsford, Steve Woosnam-Savage
Photographers Gary Ombler, James Mann, Simon K. Fielder, Deepak Aggarwal
Picture Research Nic Dean
DK Picture Library Claire Bowers, Emma Shepherd, Laura Evans
Jacket Designer Steve Woosnam-Savage
Database David Roberts, Peter Cook
Production Editors Tony Phipps, Ben Marcus
Production Controller Linda Dare
Managing Editor Esther Ripley
Managing Art Editor Karen Self
Publisher Laura Buller
Art Director Phil Ormerod
Associate Publishing Director Liz Wheeler
Publishing Director Jonathan Metcalf

DK INDIA

Senior Editor Monica Saigal
Senior Art Editor Sudakshina Basu
Editors Suparna Sengupta, Sreshtha Bhattacharya
Assistant Editor Gaurav Joshi
Art Editors Shriya Parameswaran, Pallavi Narain, Nico Alba
Assistant Art Editors Jomin Johny, Neha Sharma, Niyati Gosain, Nidhi Mehra
Production Manager Pankaj Sharma
DTP Manager Balwant Singh
DTP Designers Nand Kishor Acharya, Dheeraj Arora, Mohammad Usman, Vishal Bhatia, Jaypal Singh Chauhan
Deputy Managing Editor Pakshalika Jayaprakash Sinha
Managing Art Editor Arunesh Talapatra

Editor-in-chief Mick Duckworth
Contributors Phil Hunt, Malcolm McKay, Hugo Wilson, James Robinson

First published in Great Britain in 2012 by
Dorling Kindersley Limited,
80 Strand, London WC2R 0RL

A Penguin Company

Copyright © 2012 Dorling Kindersley Limited

2 4 6 8 10 9 7 5 3
002 – 182744 – 04/12

A CIP catalogue record for this book is available from the British Library.

ISBN: 978-1-4053-9440-6

Printed and bound in China by Leo Paper Products

Discover more at
www.dk.com

Contents

BEFORE 1920

Gottlieb Daimler's gas-powered engine on a bicycle set fire to the seat on its maiden voyage, but it heralded the birth of the motorcycle. The new century saw rapid progress in design, durability, and performance.

THE 1920s

After World War I there were bikes for the masses and sports machines capable of covering the ground faster than any other vehicle. Mighty V-twins were built for speed or for hauling a sidecar laden with the family.

THE 1930s

Through the Great Depression, the emphasis switched from speed to economy but machines became more sophisticated in appearance and performance. Racing continued to test out new technology.

THE 1940s

While the world was at war, motorcyle development was put on hold with military bikes from BSA, Triumph, and DKW becoming workhorses throughout the conflict. After the war everyone needed a motorcycle.

THE 1950s

With cars still a luxury, simple two-strokes were the obvious choice, although powerful twin cylinders were aimed at the prosperous US market. The scooter was on the rise, the ubiquitous Honda Super Cub was launched, and the Japanese made their first Grand Prix appearance.

THE 1960S

The rise of the car hit the motorcycle industry hard but new niche markets included scooters for mods and powerful bikes for Café Racers. Beautifully engineered Japanese machines with six gears and push-button starting began to infiltrate European and US markets.

THE 1970S

Classic marques like Norton and Royal Enfield went to the wall, unable to compete with the superbike offerings from Japanese manufacturers. Motocross bikes were launched for the young, and trailbikes for US adventurers.

THE 1980S

Although the motorcycle industry had little to celebrate in the economic boom, bikes were refined and updated with water-cooled engines, electronic ignition, improved aerodynamics, and better handling and braking power. Interest in classic bikes also influenced the design of new machines. Bikes became more specialized, from race replicas and fully equipped tourers to rugged off-roaders.

THE 1990s

A period of sales growth saw an increased demarcation of product classes, and a revival of several defunct marques, the most successful being Triumph in the UK. Stylish and economic scooters gained a new generation of fans, faced with rising fuel costs and traffic congestion.

FROM 2000

Motorbike riders in the new millenium are rewarded with remarkable sophistication – anti-lock brakes, power-reduction at the flick of a switch, exotically styled lightweight frames, luxury, and comfort. There is even an effective electric motorcycle on offer.

THE ENGINE

Engines: A single engine size has been given in cubic centimetres (cc) for each catalogue entry. Engine sizes can be converted to cubic inches (cu in) by multiplying the cubic centimetres (cc) figure by 0.061.

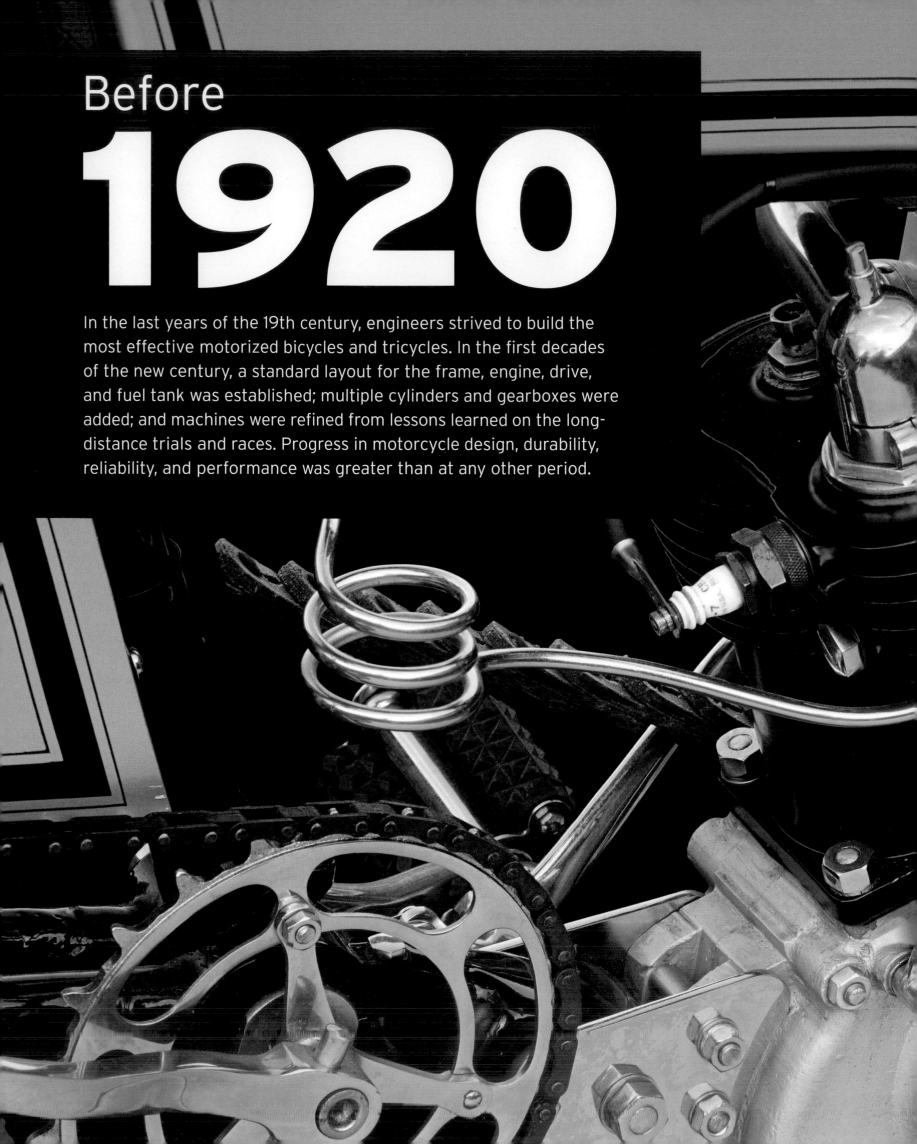

Before
1920

In the last years of the 19th century, engineers strived to build the most effective motorized bicycles and tricycles. In the first decades of the new century, a standard layout for the frame, engine, drive, and fuel tank was established; multiple cylinders and gearboxes were added; and machines were refined from lessons learned on the long-distance trials and races. Progress in motorcycle design, durability, reliability, and performance was greater than at any other period.

Early Pioneers

Bicycles had reached an advanced stage of development by the 1880s, most of them closely resembling machines we still ride today. As soon as a small internal combustion engine had been invented, it was a logical step to attach it to a bicycle, creating the first motorcycles. Almost all early development took place in Europe and the brilliance of some designs – and impracticality of others – was breathtaking.

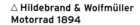

△ Hildebrand & Wolfmüller Motorrad 1894

Origin Germany

Engine 1,489 cc, in-line twin

Top speed 28 mph (45 km/h)

The world's first production motorcycle used the rear wheel as its flywheel/crankshaft with a direct drive from the two connecting rods, and the rear mudguard to carry water.

◁ Gaillardet Gaillardette 1899

Origin France

Engine 800 cc, single-cylinder

Top speed 27 mph (43 km/h)

Frédéric Gaillardet was involved with several pioneering French tricycles. His engine design was a side-valve with easily changeable valves, mounted behind the rear axle.

▽ Perks Birch Motorwheel 1900

Origin UK

Engine 222 cc, single-cylinder

Top speed 22 mph (35 km/h)

This brilliant design by Edwin Perks and Frank Birch incorporated an engine, fuel tank, carburettor, and magneto within a two-sided, cast alloy wheel.

▽ Daimler Reitwagen 1885

Origin Germany

Engine 264 cc, single-cylinder

Top speed 7 mph (11 km/h)

Gottlieb Daimler and Wilhelm Maybach were inspired pioneers, designing a high-revving (600 rpm), benzine-fuelled engine that they fitted to this "riding car" in 1885.

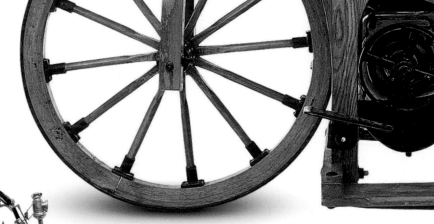

◁ Singer 200 1901

Origin UK

Engine 208 cc, single-cylinder

Top speed 28 mph (45 km/h)

Singer purchased the rights to build the Perks Birch Motorwheel in 1901 and fitted it in both the rear of bicycles and front of tricycles until 1904.

▷ Werner 1901

Origin France

Engine 262 cc, single-cylinder

Top speed 40 mph (64 km/h)

Franco-Russian pioneers Michel and Eugène Werner patented this influential motorcycle layout in 1902, with the engine incorporated into the bottom of the frame.

◁ **Ormonde 1901**

Origin UK

Engine 220 cc, single-cylinder

Top speed 28 mph (45 km/h)

Ormonde used Belgian Kelecom engines in this well-designed motor bicycle layout, which was to become an ancestor of the Velocette marque.

▷ **Cyklon 1901**

Origin Germany

Engine 300 cc, single-cylinder

Top speed 22 mph (35 km/h)

Cyklon used the French Werner engine, mounted on the front forks and driving the front wheel by a belt, placing the rider rather close to noise and fumes.

◁ **H. Collier & Sons Silent Matchless 1902**

Origin UK

Engine 160 cc, single-cylinder

Top speed 25 mph (40 km/h)

London bicycle-maker Henry Collier & Sons built its first motorcycle in 1899. They started production for bikes such as this one in 1901, using bought-in engines from MMC.

▷ **Bayliss Thomas Excelsior 1902**

Origin UK

Engine 160 cc, single-cylinder

Top speed 25 mph (40 km/h)

Generally considered the first British motorcycle, the Excelsior was made in Coventry from 1896 with Minerva, De Dion, MMC, or Werner engines slung under a bicycle-type frame.

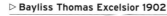

◁ **Triumph Minerva 2½ HP 1902**

Origin UK

Engine 239 cc, single-cylinder

Top speed 30 mph (48 km/h)

Siegfried Bettmann's Triumph bicycle company had built this, its first motorcycle, by 1902, using a Belgian Minerva engine, which itself originated from a Swiss design.

▷ **MMC 1903**

Origin UK

Engine 216 cc, single-cylinder

Top speed 30 mph (48 km/h)

Entrepreneur Harry Lawson's Motor Manufacturing Company of Coventry built this motorcycle powered by a close copy of the French-made De Dion engine.

◁ **Coventry-Eagle Motorized Bicycle 1903**

Origin UK

Engine 216 cc, single-cylinder

Top speed 26 mph (42 km/h)

This Victorian bicycle-maker built motorcycles from 1898. This model had an engine from MMC hung from the downtube, with a belt drive and a trailer to carry a passenger.

Early Indian model
photographed in 1910

Great Marques
The Indian Story

One of America's finest motorcycling pioneers, Indian rapidly built a reputation for quality and performance second to none. Although the company survived the Depression, strong competition in the postwar years led to production ceasing in 1953. However, a recent takeover promises to revitalize a marque that has never lost its iconic status.

GEORGE M. HENDEE originally set up The Hendee Manufacturing Company in Springfield, Massachusetts, to make pedal cycles. In 1901 he joined forces with technically minded Carl Oscar Hedstrom to build Indian motorcycles, first sold to the public in the following year.

Admired for their durability, early single-cylinder machines sold well, and the company enjoyed many successes in early American racing and endurance events, which hastened technical development. Factory riders included Canadian-born Jake de Rosier, winner of countless races on board tracks and

Indian badge
(introduced 1930)

dirt ovals, Charles B. Franklin, who covered 300 miles (438 km) in 300 minutes in 1912, and Erwin "Canonball" Baker, who rode across North America in 11 days, 12 hours, and 10 minutes in 1914. However, finishing first, second, and third in the gruelling Isle of Man Senior Tourist Trophy race of 1911 showed that Indian had arrived as a world-leading manufacturer.

In 1907 Indian developed a V-twin with the engine layout that became synonymous with American motorcycling. The 42-degree V angle became an Indian trademark, as did front suspension by a leaf spring with trailing fork links, adopted in 1913. On the 61 cu in (1,000 cc) Powerplus twin of 1915, side valves replaced the previous inlet-over-exhaust layout to create a quieter, cleaner engine. More than 40,000 twins were supplied to the US military during World War I.

In the early 1920s the 45 cu in (750 cc) Scout, the 61 cu in (1,000 cc) Chief, and the 74 cu in (1,200 cc) Big Chief were launched. Designed by Charles Franklin, they were noted for their strong performance, comfort, and reliability. Their popularity made Indian the world's largest motorcycle-maker, producing 250,000 a year.

Having bought the failing Ace company, Indian launched a version of the factory's four-cylinder bike, the Indian Ace, in 1927. Engineers then added two extra crankshaft bearings and strengthened the frame to create the first 77 cu in (1,265 cc) Four launched in 1928.

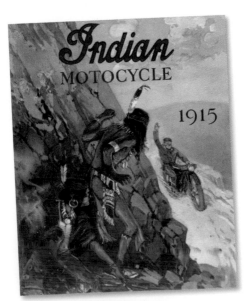

Sales brochure
As seen on this 1915 sales brochure, Native Americans featured heavily in early publicity for Indian motorcycles, stressing an image of ruggedness and adventure.

"You can't **wear out** an Indian Scout."
1920s ADVERTISING SLOGAN

Indian's achievements arguably peaked in 1928 with the 101 Scout, a sturdy and well-balanced machine still favoured for wall of death shows. However, affordable cars like the Ford Model T were beginning to erode America's motorcycle industry, and despite Indian's expertise and attempts to diversify, it made heavy losses. Fortunately the industrial giant Du Pont stepped in to buy Indian

Indian in Australia
Photographed in Australia in 1921, a uniformed driver and sidecar passenger pose on a hard-worked Indian V-twin combination with covered-in wheels.

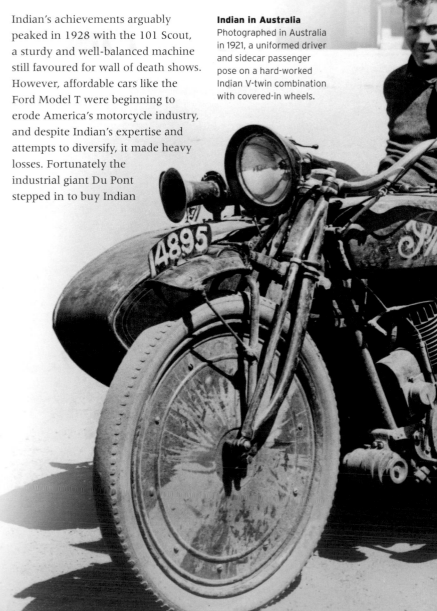

Single 1¾ HP

V-twin Roadster

Chief

Velo 500

1901 The Indian company is founded; a prototype and two production units are successfully built and tested.
1902 The first Indian motorcycles featuring innovative belt-drives and streamlined styling go on sale.
1903 Indian co-founder and chief engineer Oscar Hedstrom sets a motorcycle speed record of 56 mph (90 km/h).
1904 Indian wins the Gold Medal for Mechanical Excellence at the 1904 St Louis Exposition.

1907 Indian releases the first American production V-twin after several years of development and testing; the New York Police Department selects Indians for the first motorcycle police unit.
1909 The Indian "loop frame" positions the petrol tank on the front horizontal frame member for the first time.
1911 Indian takes a 1-2-3 finish at the Isle of Man Senior TT race.
1914 Indian sells the world's first motorcycle with electric lights and starter.

1920 The 45 cu in (750 cc) Scout is released.
1922 Launch of the 61 cu in (1,000 cc) Chief.
1928 The first all-Indian Four goes on sale.
1929 Indian is bought by Du Pont.
1937 The Indian rider Ed Kretz wins the inaugural Daytona 200 race.
1945 Ralph B. Rogers takes control of the company from Du Pont.
1947 Indian releases a new range of vertical-twin motorcycles.
1948 Floyd Emde takes Indian's last Daytona 200 win.

1949 The Brockhouse-owned Indian Sales Corp is formed.
1953 Production ends at the Springfield plant.
1955 Royal Enfield motorcycles start to be badged as Indians for the US market.
1960 British Associated Motor Cycles group acquires Indian Sales Corp.
1968 Floyd Clymer markets Indian-badged European machines.
1999 The IMC starts production in California.
2004 New owner Stellican sets up a factory.
2011 Indian is acquired by Polaris Industries.

Fleet of Indians
The Los Angeles Motor Corporation displays a new fleet of Indian motorcycles in 1922. The police used theirs to enable them to enforce relatively new speed restrictions.

shortly before the 1929 Wall Street Crash and invested heavily in motorcycle production.

The design of the Four continued to be refined, although changing from an inlet-over-exhaust valve layout to an exhaust-over-inlet layout in 1936 proved to be an error. Indian reverted to the previous format after two seasons, but sales had been lost.

In 1940 W. Briggs Weaver, a former Du Pont Motors designer, applied his talents at Indian to create the streamlined range of motorbikes with full-skirted fenders that are now icons of Americana. In the same year the Chief's and the Four's frames were equipped with plunger-type rear suspension. When the US joined World War II, Indian made the innovative 841 V-twin with transverse cylinders and shaft drive for military use.

Entrepreneur Ralph B. Rogers took over the company in 1945 with finance from the Atlas Corporation.

An all-new range of Weaver-designed overhead-valve (ohv) singles and vertical-twins was launched, eclipsing production of the V-twins. They were marketed without proper development, damaging the company's reputation. Even the revival in 1951 of the revered Chief V-twin, with an enlarged 80 cu in (1,300 cc) engine, failed to improve the company's fortunes.

Rogers accepted the blame and resigned. Financiers split the company into a manufacturing operation and the Indian Sales Corporation (ISC). The latter was owned by the British Brockhouse Engineering, maker of the Indian Papoose mini-scooter, which imported British motorcycles badged as Indians. In 1960 another British company, Associated Motor Cycles (AMC), acquired ISC.

The end of production at Springfield, in 1953, began a 20-year period when machines manufactured outside the United States were marketed as

Indian motorcycles. In 1968, after AMC's demise, automotive publisher and Indian aficionado Floyd Clymer attempted a revival. His V-twin with European cycle parts proved abortive, but Indian-badged singles and vertical-twins built by Italjet in Italy with British Velocette and Royal Enfield engines were sold. The venture ended when Clymer died in 1970.

Despite everything, the marque's iconic status endured, attracting operators seeking to make a profit from branded merchandise. In the 1990s there were rival claims to the trademark and more than one announcement that big twins would be produced again. Following a court decision, in 1999 the California-based Indian Motorcycle Company set up production using bought-in V-twin engines, but they suffered from technical problems and the venture proved unprofitable.

Five years later, British private equity companies acquired the rights to the trademark and set up Indian Motorcycle Limited (IML). A North Carolina factory made V-twins with proprietary engines from 2009 until 2011, when IML was sold to Polaris Industries of Minneapolis.

As the established manufacturer of Victory motorcycles, alongside all-terrain vehicles and snowmobiles, Polaris has the resources to put the revered Indian marque firmly back on its feet after 50 turbulent years.

Birth of an Industry

Hundreds of entrepreneurs jumped on the motorcycle-building bandwagon at the turn of the 20th century, seeing its huge growth potential. Some were motivated by cash, others by the chance to have a hand in the rapid development of new technology. All forms of suspension arrangements and early types of variable gearing were tried as engines became more refined and speed potential grew.

◁ **Laurin Klement Slavia 1½ HP Model B 1903**

Origin Bohemia (Czech Republic)

Engine 184 cc, single-cylinder

Top speed 25 mph (40 km/h)

Founded in 1895 to build bicycles in the Austro-Hungarian Empire, the company that became Skoda built motorcycles from 1899 with an underslung De Dion-type engine.

▷ **Allright 2¾ HP 1903**

Origin Germany

Engine 300 cc, single-cylinder

Top speed 40 mph (64 km/h)

Allright started making motorcycles around 1901. This model had a Belgian FN engine and front and rear contracting-band brakes; it was also sold as the Vindec Special.

◁ **Indian Single 1¾ HP 1904**

Origin USA

Engine 213 cc, single-cylinder

Top speed 25 mph (40 km/h)

George Hendee and Carl Hedström produced this, their first chain-driven motorcycle in 1901. In 1903 Hedström set the world motorcycle speed record at 56 mph (90 km/h).

▷ **Advance 2¾ HP 1904**

Origin UK

Engine 360 cc, single-cylinder

Top speed 40 mph (64 km/h)

Advance's bikes had advanced engines, which used a mechanical exhaust valve and automatic flap inlet valve. Far more engines were sold than complete motorcycles.

△ Rex 3 HP 1904

Origin	UK
Engine	372 cc, single-cylinder
Top speed	30 mph (48 km/h)

Calling itself the "King of British Motors", Rex had over 50 machines on display at the 1904 Cycle Show, including this one, with all components built in-house.

△ BAT 2½ HP 1904

Origin	UK
Engine	327 cc, single-cylinder
Top speed	35 mph (56 km/h)

Samuel R. Batson mounted De Dion and then MMC engines in this simple cycle frame with probably the first rear suspension and healthy performance.

▷ Rex 500 SV 1907

Origin	UK
Engine	500 cc, single-cylinder
Top speed	47 mph (76 km/h)

Harold and Billy Williams steered Rex to lead the British bike market, with this patented engine cradle, spring fork, sprung saddle, mechanical exhaust-valve, and more.

△ Matchless 2½ HP 1905

Origin	UK
Engine	327 cc, single-cylinder
Top speed	30 mph (48 km/h)

Matchless added leading-link front suspension to their machines in 1905, fitting a range of MMC, De Dion, or JAP engines of which this MMC was the smallest.

▷ NSU 3 HP 1906

Origin	Germany
Engine	402 cc, single-cylinder
Top speed	35 mph (56 km/h)

Originally a knitting-machine-maker NSU is named after the town of Neckarsulm. These simple and lightly built bikes benefited from the innovation learned from racing.

△ Lincoln Elk 3 HP 1908

Origin	UK
Engine	402 cc, single-cylinder
Top speed	40 mph (64 km/h)

James Kirby began making Lincoln Elk motorcycles in Lincoln in 1902 with 2¼ HP engines, later expanding the range to include 3 HP and 3½ HP variants.

△ Douglas Model D 1910

Origin	UK
Engine	339 cc, flat-twin
Top speed	45 mph (72 km/h)

From its first motorbike in 1907, Douglas built a flat-twin engine that was popular with other makers; by 1909 a two-speed gearbox was optional (though not fitted here).

Seattle Motorcycle Club, 1911
The earliest American motorcycle clubs formed soon after the machines became available. The clubs were social groups, with organized events such as picnics, hill climbs, and track races, but also great sources of information and support.

Birth of an Industry (cont.)

Many manufacturers began making their own engines, rather than buying them in or producing them under licence. As the first decades of the 20th century progressed, design stabilized around the crossbar-mounted fuel tank with the engine mounted vertically below it, and an optional gearbox behind. Foot pedals disappeared as engines became more powerful and other ways to start them were devised.

◁ **Triumph 3½HP Roadster 1908**

Origin UK

Engine 474 cc, single-cylinder

Top speed 48 mph (77 km/h)

The affordable two-stoke lightweight, nicknamed the "Baby Triumph", had a two-speed gearbox and dispensed with pedals. Uprated after WWI, it sold until 1925.

◁ **Humber 3½HP Touring 1910**

Origin UK

Engine 500 cc, single-cylinder

Top speed 57 mph (92 km/h)

Humber returned to motorcycle production in 1909 with this conventional machine featuring sprung front forks and an optional two-speed rear axle.

△ **Triumph 2¼HP Junior "Baby" 1913**

Origin UK

Engine 225 cc, single-cylinder

Top speed 35 mph (56 km/h)

Launched just before WWI, Triumph's affordable machine had a two-speed gearbox and dispensed with pedals; it could be started on its stand.

▽ **Rudge Multi 1914**

Origin UK

Engine 499 cc, single-cylinder

Top speed 65 mph (105 km/h)

A year after launching its first motorcycle, Rudge produced the Multigear, using variable groove-depth pulleys to give 21 wide-ranging forward speeds.

△ **Rudge 3½HP 1911**

Origin UK

Engine 499 cc, single-cylinder

Top speed 50 mph (80 km/h)

Long-established bicycle-maker Rudge Whitworth started selling Werner motorcycles in 1909, then in 1911 produced this inlet-over-exhaust 3½HP machine.

△ **Rover 500 TT 1913**

Origin UK

Engine 500 cc, single-cylinder

Top speed 63 mph (101 km/h)

Rover built over 10,000 motorcycles from 1902 to 1924, introducing a new 3½ HP in 1910, from which this shorter TT model was derived. It won the 1913 Isle of Man TT team prize.

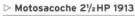

▷ **Motosacoche 2½HP 1913**

Origin Switzerland

Engine 239 cc, single-cylinder

Top speed 30 mph (48 km/h)

From 1900 Henri and Armand Dufaux sold an "engine in a bag" ("motosacoche") to attach to a bicycle such as this one; later, their MAG engines were used around the world.

△ Ariel 3½HP Roadster 1914
Origin UK

Engine 499 cc, single-cylinder

Top speed 60 mph (97 km/h)

In 1911 Ariel began building the White & Poppe engines for its own use and offered an optional three-speed gearbox (as here) on this quality low-built bike.

△ TD Cross TDC 3½HP 1914
Origin UK

Engine 300 cc, single-cylinder

Top speed 35 mph (56 km/h)

Bicycle component-maker TD Cross & Sons built engines for numerous brands, and from 1914 to 1915 made complete machines using its own make or Precision engines.

△ Sun 2½HP 1914
Origin UK

Engine 269 cc, single-cylinder

Top speed 40 mph (64 km/h)

Sun made bicycle parts in Birmingham from 1885 and its own motorcycles from 1911. In 1919 this two-stroke Villiers engine was offered, also available with two-speed gears.

△ BSA 4½HP 1914
Origin UK

Engine 556 cc, single-cylinder

Top speed 62 mph (100 km/h)

Long-established armaments-maker BSA made motorcycle components, then complete 3½HP bikes from 1910, moving up to this powerful model as WWI broke out.

△ Yale 6½HP Model 37 1914
Origin USA

Engine 1,000 cc, V-twin

Top speed 72 mph (115 km/h)

The Consolidated Manufacturing Co. added one of the first V-twins to its established 500 cc singles in 1910. The bike was given a racer frame in 1913.

▽ Sunbeam Single 1914
Origin UK

Engine 500 cc, single-cylinder

Top speed 55 mph (89 km/h)

Sunbeam made high-quality bicycles, then cars, then motorcycles, starting with this 3½HP single-cylinder in 1914 and quickly adding a twin to the range.

An Enfield Model J
from the 1930s

Great Marques
The Royal Enfield Story

The first Royal Enfield motorcycle was made in 1901, and production continues today. The story began in the Industrial Revolution in Britain and was later taken up on the Indian subcontinent. Along the way, the company has produced one of the most iconic models in the history of the motorbike in the form of the evergreen Bullet.

IN THE MID-19TH CENTURY, in the town of Redditch in the industrial heartland of England, George Townsend & Co. manufactured machine parts, including needles for sewing machines. The company expanded into bicycle production and after founder Townsend's departure in 1890 Albert Eadie and Robert Smith took over. Contracts to make rifle parts for the Royal Small Arms Factory in Enfield, Middlesex led to them becoming the Enfield Manufacturing Company in 1892, with the "Royal" prefix added the following year.

The marque's first motorized transportation was created in 1899 in the form of a 1½ hp engine that powered a vehicle available in three- or four-wheeled variants. Royal Enfield's first motorcycle was unveiled in 1909: a 2¼ hp V-twin model that would continue in a larger-capacity variant until the outbreak of World War I in 1914.

Royal Enfield badge
(introduced 1955)

Now established as a maker of solid, reliable motorcycles – reflected in the company's slogan "Made like a gun…" – Royal Enfield was tasked with providing the British Army with machines for the war effort. Its range of models included stretcher carriers and machine-gun-armed bikes. During this period Royal Enfield started to develop its first powerplants, having previously fitted engines from other companies into its frames. Innovations included a prototype featuring the world's first three-cylinder, two-stroke unit.

The postwar period saw the marque develop a range of new models and engines. A 976 cc twin engine in 1918 was followed in 1924 by Royal Enfield's debut four-stroke, single-cylinder model, which featured a JAP powerplant. By this time, the marque was capitalizing on the popularity of sidecars, producing its own examples; and a programme of expansion through the decade meant that by 1930 the company's strong line-up included smaller 225 cc side-valve motorcycles as well as big-twins.

In 1931 Royal Enfield unveiled what would become its most celebrated model, the Bullet, a single-cylinder machine that came into its own at the end of the decade with the introduction

of a 350 cc variant that was the basis for the marque's postwar models. Its innovations included telescopic front forks and an advanced rear-suspension set-up that featured the early use of a swingarm. However, before the machine could be fully taken up by the public, World War II intervened. As well as producing practical machines such as the Flying Flea, which could be parachuted down in a

cage with airborne troops, Royal Enfield was redirected to manufacture specialist items for the war effort.

In the postwar surge in the economy, Royal Enfield took up where it left off by introducing telescopic front shock absorbers and swingarm rear on the J2 model in 1947. In 1949 a 500 cc twin was released in response to the successful Speed Twin by rival Triumph. In 1949

Youth appeal
In the late 1950s Enfield diversified into lower-capacity road models such as the 250 cc Crusader, designed to appeal to young motorcyclists.

Model 182 Sports

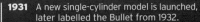

Model K

Trials Bullet

350 Bullet Machismo

1892 The Enfield Manufacturing Company is formed; "Royal" is added to the name the following year.	**1931** A new single-cylinder model is launched, later labelled the Bullet from 1932.	**1960** Enfields are now sold under their own name in the US.
1899 The first motorized models from the company include three-wheeled vehicles.	**1936** Enfield JF is released, incorporating a four-valve, single-cylinder unit.	**1962** The company is bought by the E & HP Smith Group.
1909 The 2 ¼ hp V-twin model is unveiled using an externally-made powerplant.	**1939** Bullet 350 debuts, forming the basis for postwar models.	**1965** Release of the 750 cc Interceptor twin, aimed at the US market.
1914 Enfield fits its first own engine into a V-twin model.	**1947** Telescopic forks appear on the new J2.	**1967** The Aerco Jig & Tool Co. buys the Royal Enfield name; Enfield Precision Engineers is set up.
1924 The debut four-stroke single, featuring a 350 cc JAP unit is released.	**1948** The 500 twin model is unveiled, remaining in the line-up for a decade.	**1971** The last British-made bikes are manufactured. Enfield India is now an independent concern.
	1956 Enfield India Ltd is set up as an offshoot of the parent company, making complete bikes under licence.	

1973 The Crusader model is introduced, aimed at younger Indian motorcyclists.	
1984 Enfield India begins exporting models back to the UK.	
1990 Taurus Diesel becomes the world's first diesel-powered motorcycle.	
1994 Enfield India is bought by the Eicher Group, and the company adopts the original British name of Royal Enfield Motors Ltd.	
2004 The Bullet Electra International model is launched in the UK.	

Royal Enfield was commissioned to supply Bullet models to the Indian Army, and six years later Enfield India Ltd was established. The 350 cc Bullet was originally sent over in separate parts for assembly in India, but ultimately the entire model would be constructed there.

Back in Britain, the 1950s was a fruitful decade. Enfield expanded its range to cover everything from 125 cc singles to scramblers, up to the 750 cc Meteor twin. In the US, Enfield models were sold via the Indian marque, but when the American manufacturer was bought out in 1960, the bikes were then sold under the Royal Enfield name.

When the company was acquired by the E & HP Smith engineering group in 1962, a rather stodgy image was shaken off by 250 cc sports machines aimed at young riders and even a 250 cc GP5 road racer. But they were not enough to outshine the Japanese imports and by 1967 a 750 cc Interceptor was the only model.

The Redditch plant closed and a new company, Enfield Precision Engineers, was formed in 1967 but all production ended in 1971.

Military use
Women from the Auxiliary Territorial Service ride 350 cc four-stroke Enfield motorcycles. During World War II the company also supplied the military with a 126 cc two-stroke.

At the same time, Enfield India became completely independent and grew stronger. The Bullet continued to be made, essentially to a 1954 specification but with minor improvements and some adaptation to the local environment.

Throughout the 1970s and 1980s the Enfield India marque expanded its range of models. The 175 cc Crusader two-stroke was aimed at the younger market, while new

Work and play
In addition to being used for day-to-day law enforcement duties, Royal Enfields are at the heart of the Indian police force's display team.

was being exported by 1990 and a novel but sluggish 325 cc diesel motorcycle, the Taurus, was produced from 1993 to 2002.

Although the company's fortunes dipped during the mid-1990s, they were revived by a buy-out by the Eicher Group, an Indian conglomerate, in 1996, and in 2004 the company fully secured its rights to the full Royal Enfield name.

Now producing a small range of motorbikes from its Chennai headquarters, including a selection of Bullet variants and a Classic 500 model that combines postwar styling

"Made like a gun, goes like a bullet."

THE ROYAL ENFIELD MOTTO

lightweights in the 1980s included the Silver Plus step-thru, with a semi-automatic gearchange designed to appeal to female motorcyclists. So successful was the Indian company at this time that it even began exporting its models back to the UK and Europe.

Over the next two decades the marque broadened its operations. A 500 cc version of the iconic bullet

with 21st-century features such as fuel injection, Royal Enfield has become an international success story. This originally British company has flourished under its Indian offshoot through the simple approach of pairing traditional designs with reliable, no-nonsense engines. It is a wonderful example of the empire striking back.

Multiple Cylinders

Engineers saw multiple-cylinder engines as a way of increasing power output, especially for sidecar pulling, and achieving greater flexibility along with smoother running. The V-twin seemed the ideal solution, compact and a perfect fit in a normal frame, but others tried flat-twins in various layouts, or even in-line four-cylinder engines mounted car-like, fore-and-aft in the frame.

▷ **Minerva 4½HP V-twin 1906**

Origin Belgium

Engine 577 cc, V-twin

Top speed 50 mph (80 km/h)

Sylvain de Jong's Minerva built high-quality V-twin (as here) and single-cylinder machines until 1909, but then turned production over to luxury cars.

△ **Norton 5HP V-twin 1906**

Origin UK

Engine 700 cc, V-twin

Top speed 80 mph (129 km/h)

Starting up in 1902, James Norton was soon fitting Peugot engines. His rider Rem Fowler won the twins class of the first Isle of Man TT in 1907 on a machine like this one.

△ **FN Four 1911**

Origin Belgium

Engine 498 cc, in-line four

Top speed 45 mph (72 km/h)

This revolutionary luxury four-cylinder motorbike with shaft drive started with a 362 cc capacity in 1905 and grew to 748 cc in 1914, continuing after WWI.

▽ **Wilkinson TMC 1912**

Origin UK

Engine 848 cc, in-line four

Top speed 75 mph (120 km/h)

Built by the Wilkinson Sword company from 1911 to 1916, this top-of-the-line motorcycle featured shaft drive and full suspension, with a car-type water-cooled engine.

△ **Zenith 8/10 HP Gradua 1913**

Origin UK

Engine 986 cc, V-twin

Top speed 85 mph (137 km/h)

Freddy Barnes devised the Gradua gear, combining a variable pulley with sliding the rear wheel fore and aft. It was briefly banned as an unfair advantage in competitions.

▽ **BAT Combination 1913**

Origin UK

Engine 770 cc, V-twin

Top speed 45 mph (72 km/h)

In 1905 T.H. Tessier took over BAT, which went on to build a good reputation for its sturdy and comfortable V-twins that were ideal for sidecar combinations.

◁ **NUT 3½ HP Sports 1914**

Origin UK

Engine 497 cc, V-twin

Top speed 65 mph (105 km/h)

Founded in Newcastle upon Tyne in 1912 by Hugh Mason and Jock Hall, the NUT factory made well-engineered and fast V-twins. Mason won the 1913 Junior TT on this one.

◁ **Royal Enfield 3 HP V-twin 1914**

Origin UK

Engine 425 cc, V-twin

Top speed 60 mph (97 km/h)

After concentrating for a few years on cars, Royal Enfield returned to building motorcycles in 1909. By 1913 its inlet-over-exhaust twin was enjoying race track success.

▷ **AJS Model D 1915**

Origin UK

Engine 749 cc, V-twin

Top speed 65 mph (105 km/h)

The Stevens family were building engines very early in the century and started AJS motorcycles in 1909. This big V-twin of 1913 was popular for combinations.

△ **Douglas 2¾ HP Lady's Model 1915**

Origin UK

Engine 345 cc, flat-twin

Top speed 45 mph (72 km/h)

Douglas was among the first to introduce a specific model for ladies. This bike's lower frame top tube and added guards made riding in a long skirt possible.

▷ **Wooler 2¾ HP Flat-twin 1919**

Origin UK

Engine 345 cc, flat-twin

Top speed 55 mph (89 km/h)

Boasting variable speed gearing and full suspension, the advanced Wooler, painted yellow and nicknamed the "Flying Banana", competed in the 1919 Isle of Man TT – but without success.

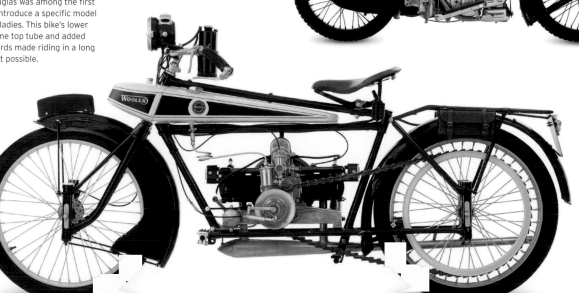

FN Four

Unveiled in 1905, the fabulous FN Four was one of the first genuinely efficient four-cylinder motorcycles on the market, sporting a shaft drive and a dedicated motorcycle frame. The original 362 cc engine was increased to the near-500 cc capacity of this 1911 model before a final 748 cc version emerged in 1914. By this stage, FN had shown that four-cylinder bikes could be just as practical and smooth-riding as singles and twins.

THE SOUTH BELGIUM-BASED FN (Fabrique Nationale d'Armes de Guerre) was an early pioneer of single-cylinder motorcycles at the start of the 20th century. By 1905 the manufacturer was breaking new ground with the development of its first four-cylinder bike. The company hired Paul Kelecom, an acclaimed engineer who had been producing highly regarded engines under his own name, as well as for other manufacturers. Kelecom used his technical know-how to construct an innovative four-cylinder motorcycle for FN,

a bike that would set the standard for other early machines with the same engine configuration. The model was progressive in other ways too, with an integrated frame, magneto ignition, and lubrication system. As the Four developed, there were further refinements: rear drum brakes from 1909; an optional two-speed gearbox from 1911; and a kick-starter from 1913. The following year saw the debut of the 700, which was produced until the early 1920s, and was the last of this classic motorcycle's line.

FRONT VIEW

REAR VIEW

Rifles to bikes
As its full name suggests, Fabrique Nationale d'Armes de Guerre (FN) originally manufactured munitions. By 1900 the company had diversified into motorcycle production, and the resulting logo – combining a rifle with cycle pedals – reflected both areas of expertise.

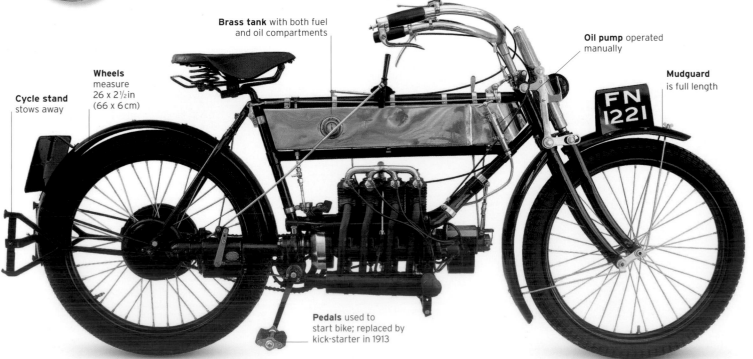

Brass tank with both fuel and oil compartments

Oil pump operated manually

Wheels measure 26 x 2½ in (66 x 6 cm)

Mudguard is full length

Cycle stand stows away

Pedals used to start bike; replaced by kick-starter in 1913

SPECIFICATIONS	
Model	FN Four (1911)
Assembly	Herstal, Belgium
Production	1904-1923
Construction	Cradle frame
Engine	498 cc, in-line four
Power output	5 hp
Transmission	Single-speed
Suspension	Bottom-link front forks, rigid rear
Brakes	Drum with contracting band, rear
Maximum speed	approx. 45 mph (72 km/h)

Transmission developments
This 1911 model offered just a single speed
through its drive shaft. FN later introduced
two-speed transmission as standard on its
Four model in 1913. When the 700 variant
was presented in 1914, a three-speed gearbox
was one of its many new features.

THE BIKE

Style and substance went hand-in-hand on the FN Four. As well as looking good, the leading link front forks helped provide a smooth riding experience, while the brass tank under the cross tube was split into fuel and oil sections. Useful features included viewing windows inside the crankcase – which made it possible to check the oil level – and auxiliary lubrication provided by a manual pump on the oil tank.

1. FN badge with rifle and pedals **2.** Carburettor air lever on handlebar **3.** Oil metering device **4.** Fuel gauge **5.** Enclosed fork springs **6.** Leather saddle **7.** Fuel tap **8.** Pivoting-link forks **9.** Final drive casing **10.** Hand-operated oil pump **11.** Chain for pedalling **12.** Back sprocket and rear brake

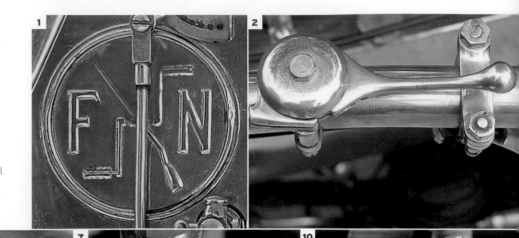

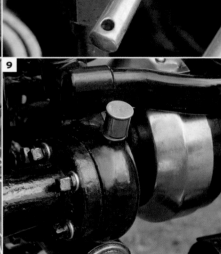

ENGINE

The FN's four-cylinder engine was enlarged a number of times over its lifetime. The engine was redesigned for 1910 and remained unchanged for the 1911 model shown. The engine size increased to 498 cc, the carburettor position was moved, and a new oiling system introduced. The final 750 cc version of the Four replaced automatic inlet valves with a mechanically operated side-valve configuration. This produced a model with sufficient power to be employed as a sidecar motorcycle, and was also used by German forces in World War I.

13. Left-side view of engine **14.** Exhaust header pipes **15.** Spark plug **16.** Single carburettor and float chamber with priming plunger **17.** Ignition distributor **18.** Oil levels

America's Golden Age

The early 20th century saw motorcycle development grow rapidly in the US, and while some bought in technology from Europe, most American makers chose to forge ahead with their own various solutions. Roads between cities were entirely unmetalled, so effective suspension was a vital development, as was rugged construction, ease of access for tyre repairs, and forms of gearing to cope with hilly terrain.

◁ Emblem 4 HP 1910
Origin USA
Engine 531 cc, single-cylinder
Top speed 48 mph (77 km/h)

Emblem's V-twins and singles had their own engines in loop frames; the smallest variety was fitted into this model. The company, whose slogan was "Class, Power, Speed, and Satisfaction", faded after WWI.

△ Pierce Four 1910
Origin USA
Engine 699 cc, in-line four
Top speed 60 mph (97 km/h)

Best-known for its cars, Pierce-Arrow began with bicycles and built the first Pierce Four motorcycle in 1909. It was innovative but expensive and bankrupted the company by 1914.

△ Pope Model L 7/8 HP 1911
Origin USA
Engine 998 cc, V-twin
Top speed 65 mph (105 km/h)

A unique rear suspension, overhead valves, and a three-speed gearbox were advanced features of the Pope Model L, which cost as much as a Ford Model T.

△ Henderson 7 HP Four 1912
Origin USA
Engine 934 cc, in-line four
Top speed 60 mph (97 km/h)

Built from 1912 to 1931, Hendersons became popular with police forces as they were faster than anything else on the roads; one was ridden around the world between 1912 and 1913.

△ Harley-Davidson Model X8 1912
Origin USA
Engine 494 cc, single-cylinder
Top speed 35 mph (56 km/h)

The original single-cylinder Harley-Davidson of 1903 had been refined into this model by 1912. The company's products of this period were known as "Silent Gray Fellows".

◁ Harley-Davidson 11 HP 1915
Origin USA
Engine 989 cc, V-twin
Top speed 60 mph (97 km/h)

With mechanical lubrication, interconnected clutch, three-speed gearchange, and an optional electric kit, this rugged machine coped well with unmetalled US roads.

△ Indian V-Twin Roadster 1912
Origin USA
Engine 633 cc, V-twin
Top speed 55 mph (89 km/h)

In addition to the touring V-twins, Indian offered these race-derived roadster models with twist-grip controls and lightweight construction – ideal for amateur competition.

▷ Indian 4 HP Single 1913
Origin USA
Engine 500 cc, single-cylinder
Top speed 40 mph (64 km/h)

Indian built 32,000 bikes in 1913, 90 per cent of them twins, but also produced this single, which benefited from advanced swinging-arm rear suspension.

▷ Sears Deluxe "Big Five" 1914
Origin USA
Engine 575 cc, single-cylinder
Top speed 50 mph (80 km/h)

The Sears Roebuck catalogue sold a range of motorcycles from 1912 to 1916, with trailing-link front suspension and engines made by Spake, as on this "magneto model".

△ Indian Two-Sixty Standard Model 1914
Origin USA
Engine 988 cc, V-twin
Top speed 55 mph (89 km/h)

This one-litre luxury twin was the first motorcycle with electric lighting fitted as standard. Some versions were made with electric starting as well.

◁ Smith Motor Wheel 1915
Origin UK
Engine 150 cc, single-cylinder
Top speed 27 mph (43 km/h)

In 1914, A.O. Smith Corporation of Milwaukee acquired US rights to the British Wall Motorwheel, which clipped onto any bicycle to provide instant power assistance.

△ Cleveland 2½ HP 1919
Origin USA
Engine 179 cc, single-cylinder
Top speed 38 mph (61 km/h)

With its small two-stroke engine turned transversely to the normal layout, this low-slung Cleveland was distinctive and, being inexpensive, sold rather well.

Racing Machines/Scooters

Organized racing burgeoned in the 1900s. Europe had city-to-city road races, while US sport favoured closed dirt tracks and wooden board Motordromes. In Britain, roads were closed for the Isle of Man Tourist Trophy (TT) races and the banked Brooklands circuit opened in 1907. At the other end of the scale, the first motor scooters were being aimed at the general public.

▽ **NLG Peugeot 1907**

Origin	UK
Engine	944 cc, V-twin
Top speed	76 mph (122 km/h)

Purpose-built by North London Garages with a highly tuned Peugeot engine, the NLG won the first motorcycle race at Brooklands in 1908, averaging 63 mph (101 km/h).

◁ **Norton 3½ HP "Old Miracle" 1912**

Origin	UK
Engine	490 cc, side-valve single
Top speed	82 mph (132 km/h)

A 1912 speed record holder, this legendary single was ridden by tuner D.R. O'Donovan at 71.54 mph (115.13 km/h) for 5 miles (8 km) in 1913 and bettered 82 mph in 1915.

△ **Indian Track Racer 1912**

Origin	USA
Engine	999 cc, ohv V-twin
Top speed	90 mph (145 km/h)

This advanced four-valves-per-cylinder twin won on US board tracks. In the UK, Charles B. Franklin covered 300 miles (483 km) in less than 300 minutes on one.

△ **Corah 6 HP 1912**

Origin	UK
Engine	746 cc, ohv V-twin
Top speed	not known

The short-lived Corah company fielded this single-speed racing machine with an overhead-valve engine made by JAP, Britain's most advanced proprietary engine-maker.

▽ Scott Two-speed TT 1913

Origin	UK
Engine	486 cc, two-stroke twin
Top speed	70 mph (113 km/h)

The unorthodox two-speed Scott two-stroke was the fastest machine in the Isle of Man TT in 1912 and 1913, winning two Senior races.

△ NSU 350TT 1912

Origin	Germany
Engine	349 cc, V-twin
Top speed	not known

NSU's 350 V-twin achieved fourth and seventh place finishes at the 1913 Isle of Man Junior TT, despite the machine's lack of suspension or gears.

◁ Flying Merkel 471 1914

Origin	USA
Engine	985 cc, V-twin
Top speed	70 mph (113 km/h)

Notable for its monoshock rear suspension, the Flying Merkel V-twin was prominent in US racing during the marque's short life from 1909 to 1915.

▽ Harley-Davidson 11KR Roadster Racer 1915

Origin	USA
Engine	988 cc, V-twin
Top speed	76 mph (122 km/h)

Successful in speed events in both the US and Europe, Harley-Davidson sold this model as the basis for a competitive privateer racer.

▽ Autoped Autoped 1915

Origin	USA
Engine	155 cc, side-valve single-cylinder
Top speed	20 mph (32 km/h)

Ridden standing up, the novel Autoped with a front-mounted engine was started and stopped by moving the handlebar column, seen here folded down for portability.

▽ Reynolds Runabout 1919

Origin	UK
Engine	269 cc, two-stroke single
Top speed	not known

The maker of this lengthy scooter took customers' comfort seriously. The seat was mounted on a combination of coil and leaf springs.

△ Stafford Mobile Pup 1919

Origin	UK
Engine	142 cc, ohv single-cylinder
Top speed	not known

The flimsy-looking Pup had a four-stroke engine driving the front wheel. It was made in Coventry by T.G. John, who later produced Alvis cars.

Scott Two-speed

One of the first examples of original British motorcycle design, the Scott Two-speed laid the foundations for the marque's success. Introduced in the first decade of the 1900s, the pioneering model incorporated several innovative features that made it stand out from the crowd. The race-going versions won the Isle of Man Senior TT in both 1912 and 1913, giving the Scott profile a boost. The standard Two-speed continued in production until the end of the 1920s.

ALFRED SCOTT'S PIONEERING approach produced the first genuinely modern-looking motorcycle that had been fully thought through. Its original design included a twin-cylinder two-stroke engine with outstanding hill-climbing ability. Fast cornering was another attribute, aided by the effective front suspension and a low centre of gravity achieved by the open, triangular frame. The two-speed mechanism, operated by a rocking pedal, switched drive between differentially-geared primary chains. As well as being technically advanced, Scotts were light and speedy. Racing versions, such as the model shown here, won the Isle of Man TT in 1912 and 1913, the first two-stroke machines to take the title. Though later Scott models – the "Squirrels" – would win wide acclaim from the 1920s, Scott's success was forged here in this fast, lightweight twin that was undeniably streets ahead of its time.

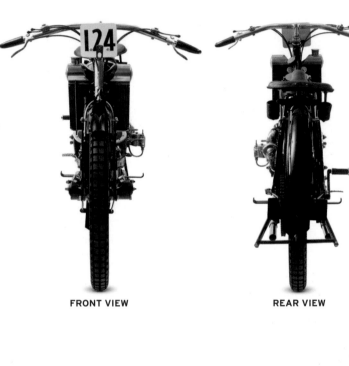

FRONT VIEW

REAR VIEW

Engineering genius
The Yorkshire-based engineer Alfred Scott first put his name to a motorcycle in 1901, when he developed a twin-cylinder, two-stroke engine to power a bicycle. Seven years later, the Scott Engineering Company was set up.

Race number of competition model (winner of 1913 Isle of Man TT)

Fuel tank mounted low with large cap for fast pit work

Radiator to provide water cooling for the engine

Fork springs are fully enclosed

Front brake with bicycle-type blocks

Kick-starter was a Scott invention

Water jacket to cool cylinder and cylinder head

Unusual profile

The open frame and low-slung fuel tank made the Scott look different from most motorcycles of the time, and the water-cooled engine was of unique design. The straight handlebars were a feature of the racing version, while road models had curved designs better suited to a traditional cycling position. Other special racing features included a rotary inlet and transfer valve behind the cylinders and twin-plug ignition. Oil for the positive lubrication system was carried in the upper frame of the motorcycle.

SPECIFICATIONS	
Model	Scott Two-speed TT (1913)
Assembly	Shipley, England
Production	Not known
Construction	Triangulated frame
Engine	486 cc, two-stroke twin
Power output	6 hp (estimated)
Transmission	Two-speed
Suspension	Slider front forks, rigid rear
Brakes	Blocks, front and rear
Maximum speed	70 mph (113 km/h) estimated

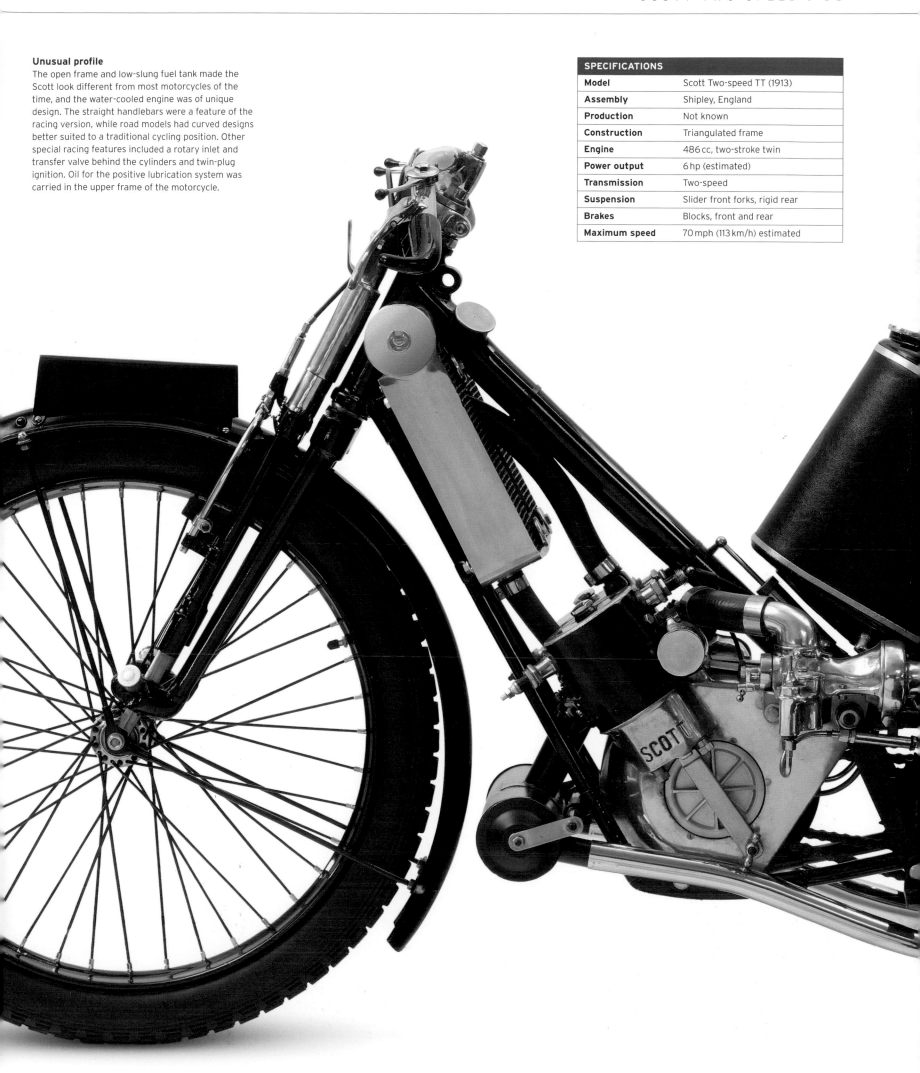

THE BIKE

Scotts of the period brimmed with original ideas. Mounting the fuel tank on the seat support tube kept weight low, and the slider-type front forks predated the telescopic forks that would be commonplace several decades later. The two-speed mechanism operated by a heel-and-toe pedal incorporated a clutch mechanism that allowed drive to switch between two primary chains, which gave different gear ratios. Scott was the first motorcycle maker to use a kick-starter, and when it was operated by racer Eric Myers at the start of the 1909 TT, the crowd cheered.

1. Scott trademark **2.** Engine oil control **3.** Cellulose handgrip **4.** Water filler **5.** Oil syringe **6.** Fork sliders **7.** Two-speed control **8.** Saddle maker's badge **9.** Front brake blocks **10.** Oil filler cap **11.** Magneto **12.** Magneto sprocket **13.** Rear sprocket

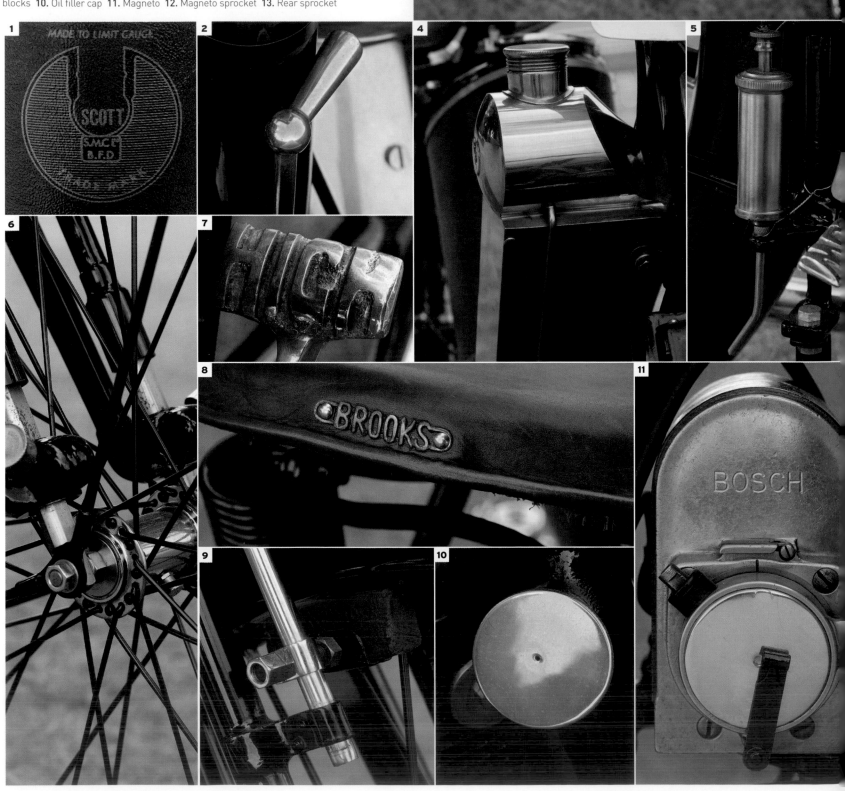

THE ENGINE

Scott's two-stroke, twin-cylinder engine was unique: like a 19th-century stationary engine it had a central flywheel with an overhung crank on each side, each of which was contained in its own low-volume crankcase. On this racing engine a rotating valve controlled inlet and transfer timings for optimum power and torque. There was no water pump the coolant was circulated through the one-piece cylinder and head by a thermosyphon effect.

14. Cylinder water jacket **15.** Rotary valve housing **16.** Carburettor **17.** Fuel float bowl primer on carburettor **18.** Rear spark plugs **19.** Silencer box

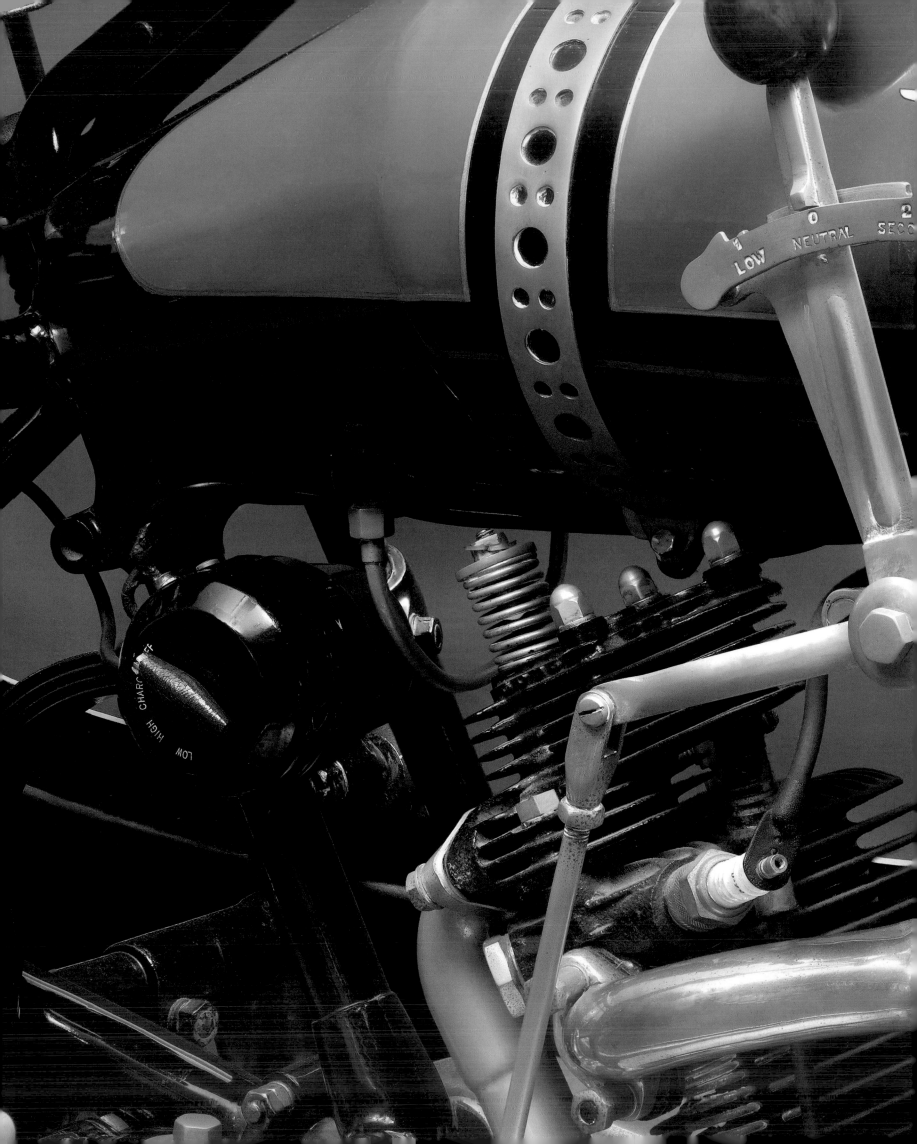

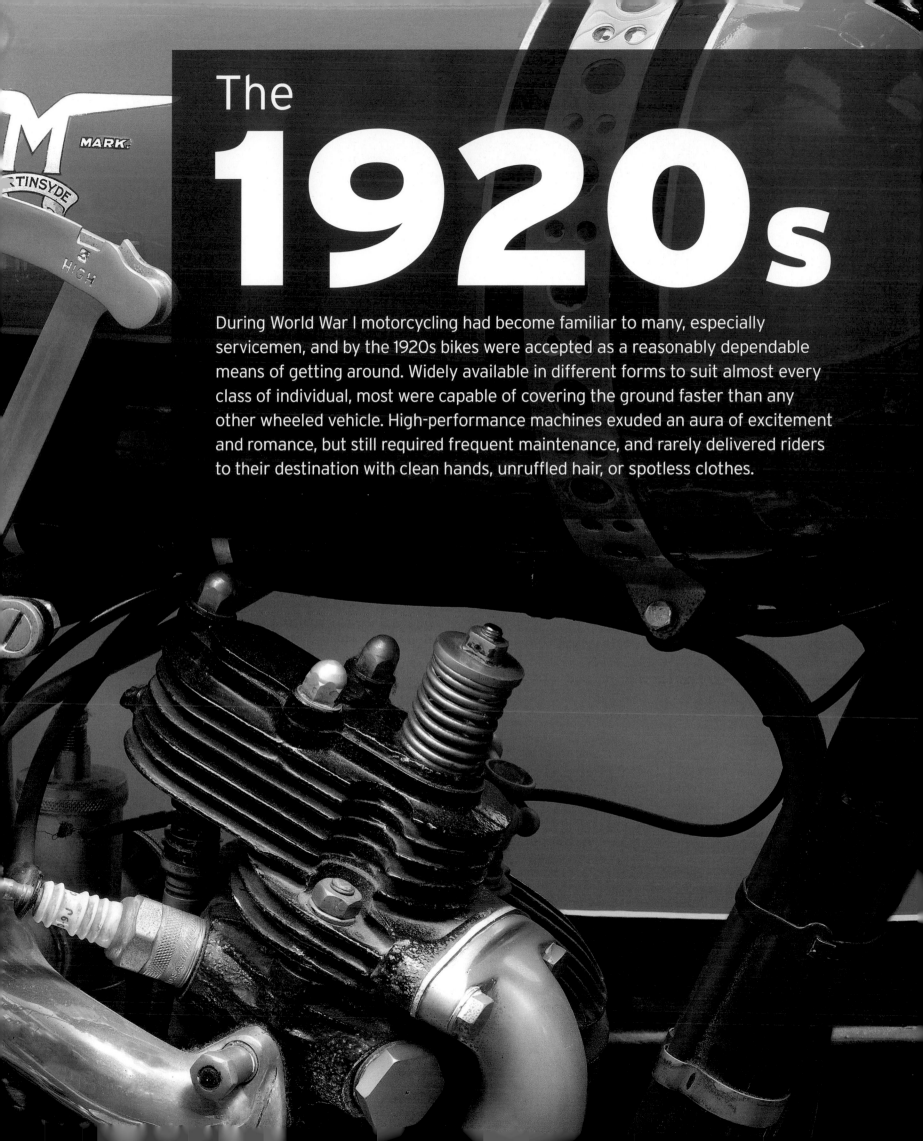

The 1920s

During World War I motorcycling had become familiar to many, especially servicemen, and by the 1920s bikes were accepted as a reasonably dependable means of getting around. Widely available in different forms to suit almost every class of individual, most were capable of covering the ground faster than any other wheeled vehicle. High-performance machines exuded an aura of excitement and romance, but still required frequent maintenance, and rarely delivered riders to their destination with clean hands, unruffled hair, or spotless clothes.

Two-wheelers for the Masses

Building the cheapest forms of motorized transport, a first step up from a bicycle, exercised the minds of numerous inventors in the 1920s, each finding their own best way to achieve it. Four-stroke engines were mostly side-valve for simplicity, while two-stroke engines with their rugged simplicity offered more power for your money. Small-wheeled scooters were still around, but in dwindling numbers.

◁ ABC Skootamota 1920
Origin UK
Engine 123 cc, single-cylinder
Top speed 15 mph (24 km/h)

The All British Cycle company's scooter was designed by Granville Bradshaw. With a rear-mounted four-stroke engine, it predated products that came decades later.

▷ DKW Hilfsmotor 1920
Origin Germany
Engine 118 cc, single-cylinder
Top speed 25 mph (40 km/h)

DKW's bicycle auxiliary engine proved very popular, being easily attachable to any lady's or gent's bicycle. Some 30,000 were sold in four years of production.

△ Triumph Knirps 2½ HP 1920
Origin Germany
Engine 276 cc, single-cylinder
Top speed 52 mph (84 km/h)

Originally an offshoot of the English Triumph company, the Nuremberg factory made typewriters as well as motorcycles. This popular two-stroke was called the Knirps, meaning "tiddler".

◁ DKW Lomos 1922
Origin Germany
Engine 143 cc, single-cylinder
Top speed 37 mph (60 km/h)

After the crude Golem scooter of 1921, DKW brought out the much neater Lomos with 143 cc and later 170 cc power. However, it failed to catch on – just 2,500 were sold.

△ Triumph Model W 1927
Origin UK
Engine 277 cc, single-cylinder
Top speed 48 mph (77 km/h)

New for 1927, this lightweight, inexpensive Triumph had a side-valve engine and just fitted within a 220 lb (98 kg) UK taxation limit, making it attractively cheap to run.

▷ Velocette D2 1921
Origin UK
Engine 220 cc, single-cylinder
Top speed 48 mph (77 km/h)

Successor to the Veloce, this Velocette two-stroke boasted throttle-controlled lubrication. Although not cheap it was practical, and variants were sold until 1946.

◁ Ardie 3PS 1922
Origin Germany
Engine 304 cc, single-cylinder
Top speed 52 mph (84 km/h)

Ardie's early motorcycles were fitted with two-stroke engines of the company's own manufacture. Modern styling and high equipment levels made them popular.

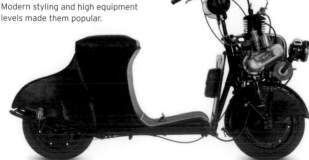

△ Autoglider Model D 1921
Origin UK
Engine 269 cc, single-cylinder
Top speed 45 mph (72 km/h)

Charles Townsend's 1919 platform machine could carry one or two people standing; a seat was added to later models, along with storage space and efficient mudguards.

◁ **Motobécane MB1 Ecclesiastique 1923**

Origin France

Engine 175 cc, single-cylinder

Top speed 42 mph (68 km/h)

Charles Benoit and Abel Bardin produced their first motorcycle in 1923. This ladies and clergy model with a lowered top tube became very successful.

△ **Royal Enfield 225L 1924**

Origin UK

Engine 225 cc, single-cylinder

Top speed 40 mph (64 km/h)

This is the ladies version of Royal Enfield successful little two-stroke runabout with two speeds. It was also available with a top-tube mounted fuel tank.

▷ **Levis Model K 1925**

Origin UK

Engine 247 cc, single-cylinder

Top speed 58 mph (93 km/h)

Built by Butterfields of Birmingham this was one of Britain's leading two-strokes. It won many races including the first 250 cc Lightweight class at the Isle of Man TT in 1922.

▽ **BSA Model B 1925**

Origin UK

Engine 249 cc, single-cylinder

Top speed 45 mph (72 km/h)

Known as the "Round Tank", this cheap and successful model was chosen by the British Post Office for its telegram service. A front brake was deemed unnecessary.

SV~6573

◁ **Puch 220 1926**

Origin Austria

Engine 223 cc, single-cylinder

Top speed 47 mph (76 km/h)

A bicycle manufacturer from 1889, Puch made cars and motorcycles from about 1900. This distinctive double-piston two-stroke machine joined the range in 1923.

◁ **Terrot FT 1927**

Origin France

Engine 247 cc, single-cylinder

Top speed 53 mph (85 km/h)

This affordable touring two-stroke bike with two or three gears came from a well-established French factory that had been making motorcycles since 1902.

▽ **Indian Prince 1928**

Origin USA

Engine 350 cc, single-cylinder

Top speed 55 mph (89 km/h)

This second attempt by Indian at a lightweight "starter" motorcycle did not catch on, even when modified from side valves to overhead valves in 1926; its sales ended in 1928.

Brough Superior SS100

Often referred to as the vintage superbike, the SS100 was guaranteed to be capable of 100 mph (160 km/h), making it the machine of choice for affluent, speed-hungry enthusiasts. One famous fan was T.E. Lawrence (Lawrence of Arabia), who owned four SS100s in succession. When the machine was launched in late 1924, its creator George Brough touted it as the "Rolls-Royce of Motorcycles". It is a testament to the Brough Superior's superb build quality and performance that the car-maker never challenged his claim.

GEORGE BROUGH was 29 when he left the established motorcycle company run by his father, William Brough, to set up on his own in 1919. George would take a very different approach to his father: rather than building his engines from scratch, George picked the best available components and assembled his machines from these. Propulsion for early Brough Superiors was provided by the smooth "90 bore" side-valve JAP V-twin engine, as well as the Swiss-built MAG V-twin

engines. The acclaimed SS80 of 1922, powered by a V-twin JAP, topped the range until 1924, when the SS100 was introduced. Powered by the overhead valve, record-breaking 1,000 cc JAP V-twin, this machine enjoyed a high profile among wealthy, sporting riders. Later SS100s incorporated Matchless V-twin engines. Ironically, the last Brough Superiors, produced until 1940, were built in Vernon Road, Nottingham – in William Brough's old works.

A superior brand
George Brough's choice of name may have rankled his father and former employer, William Brough, implying as it did that the original Brough bikes, still being built by the older man's company, were inferior machines.

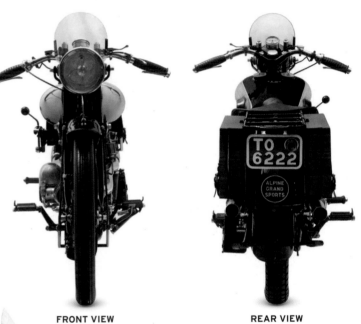

FRONT VIEW **REAR VIEW**

Hard pannier featured on the SS100 Alpine Grand Sports model

Saddle is sprung to absorb road bumps

Fuel tank is elegantly-shaped – a Brough Superior trademark

Hand-change gear lever is mounted on front petrol tank support

Lever on side of electric headlamp allows it to be dipped manually

Front forks of Harley-Davidson origin, modified and branded "Castle"

Rear brake is an 8-inch (20-cm) drum

Full cradle frame with single front down tube and box section head lug

A rare sight

Often regarded as the ultimate classic motorcycle, the SS100 is rarely seen today. Less than 400 of all variants were manufactured from 1924 to 1939, and a minority of those were in Alpine Grand Sport trim, as seen here. All surviving Brough Superiors are now highly prized by collectors.

SPECIFICATIONS	
Model	SS100 (1927)
Assembly	Nottingham, England
Production	Approximately 400
Construction	Rigid cradle frame
Engine	998 cc, V-twin
Power output	45 hp
Transmission	Three-speed
Suspension	Castle front forks, rigid rear
Brakes	Drum brake, front and rear
Maximum speed	Over 102 mph (164 km/h)

THE BIKE

Glamour and performance sold the Brough Superior. A champion rider himself, George Brough built machines to match his high standards, the cradle frame and Harley-Davidson-type front forks combining to give a very stable ride. The JAP engine was bought-in, as was the Sturmey Archer three-speed gearbox, and the Enfield hubs with drum brakes. Other features included luggage boxes equipped with inner carry cases.

1. Model logo **2.** Choke lever **3.** Petrol filler cap **4.** Friction damper with star motif **5.** Speedometer **6.** Hand-change for the gears **7.** Knee grips on either side of fuel tank **8.** Oil level sight glass **9.** Klaxon horn **10.** Gearchange linkage **11.** Fuel tap **12.** Speedo drive (in rear wheel) **13.** Front brake **14.** Front exhaust outlet with unusual tiered metal design **15.** Rear exhaust outlet **16.** Gearbox **17.** Alpine Grand Sports badge

THE ENGINE

The SS100 had JAP's overhead valve engine, which from 1927 had its ignition magneto and lighting dynamo sited alongside the crankcase and bevel drive. The single, slide-type carburettor with twin float chambers supplied both cylinders. The Alpine Grand Sports had around 45 hp, which increased to 50 hp using high-compression pistons.

18. Right side of engine **19.** Left side of engine showing magneto, dynamo, and oil pump **20.** Carburettor float bowl **21.** Oil tap **22.** Oil pump **23.** Valve rocker **24.** Combined magneto and dynamo

The Mighty V-twins

For the 1920s' rider, a V-twin represented the ultimate in performance and power. The shape of the engine fitted neatly in a motorcycle frame with no bulk at the sides and no need to make the wheelbase uncomfortably long; even a 1,000 cc V-twin could be reasonably compact. Some were built for speed, others for low-down power, hauling a heavy sidecar with all the family on board.

△ **Martinsyde 680 Combination 1921**

Origin	UK
Engine	677 cc, V-twin
Top speed	58 mph (93 km/h)

Aircraft-builders Martinsyde switched to motorcycles in 1919, using single and V-twin engine designs by Howard Newman, as in this bike. Fire destroyed the factory in 1922.

△ **Excelsior 20R 1920**

Origin	USA
Engine	1,000 cc, V-twin
Top speed	100 mph (160 km/h)

Excelsior launched its V-twin in 1911, adding a chain drive and sprung fork in 1913, three-speeds in 1915, and 1,200 cc in 1921; it was the first 100 mph (160 km/h) production bike.

▷ **BSA Model A 1922**

Origin	UK
Engine	770 cc, V-twin
Top speed	55 mph (89 km/h)

Britain's biggest motorcycle-maker produced its first V-twin immediately after WWI, with an enclosed chain drive and a three-speed gearbox.

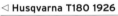

△ **James Model 12 1925**

Origin	UK
Engine	495 cc, V-twin
Top speed	53 mph (85 km/h)

Bicycle-maker turned motorcycle-builder, James made V-twins from 1913 until 1925. The Model 12 has a Burman three-speed gearbox. There was also a larger capacity model.

◁ **Husqvarna T180 1926**

Origin	Sweden
Engine	550 cc, V-twin
Top speed	60 mph (97 km/h)

Husqvarna made bicycles in the 19th century and motorcycles from 1903. This V-twin was the first to use its own engine and was modelled on US V-twins of the time.

▽ **Burney V-twin 1926**

Origin	UK
Engine	680 cc, V-twin
Top speed	70 mph (113 km/h)

Edward Alexander Burney designed the original Blackburne engine, and later made bikes in his own name. This stylish, sporty machine boasted a JAP engine and twistgrip controls.

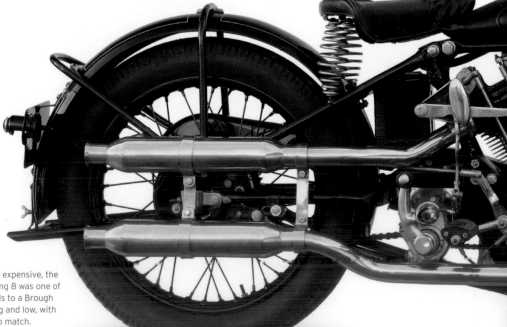

▷ **Coventry-Eagle Flying 8 1925**

Origin	UK
Engine	980 cc, V-twin
Top speed	100 mph (160 km/h)

Hand-built and very expensive, the overhead-valve Flying 8 was one of the few worthy rivals to a Brough Superior; it was long and low, with power and brakes to match.

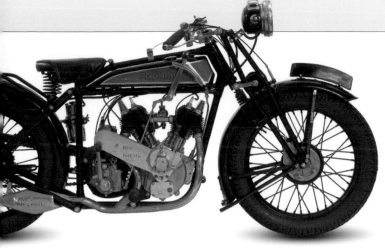

△ **Brough Superior SS100 1927**

Origin UK

Engine 998 cc, V-twin

Top speed 102 mph (164 km/h)

George Brough built the most collectable of British motorcycles, of which the SS100 is leader of the pack. Its JAP engine could power racing versions to 130 mph (209 km/h).

△ **New Imperial Model 8 1927**

Origin UK

Engine 680 cc, V-twin

Top speed 60 mph (97 km/h)

Sold principally as a sidecar combination, with coupe, tradesman's, and tandem options, New Imperial's JAP-engined V-twin was a workhorse.

△ **Harley-Davidson Model JD 1925**

Origin USA

Engine 1,213 cc, V-twin

Top speed 75 mph (120 km/h)

Harley launched its 74 cu in (1,213 cc) V-twins in 1922, and in 1925 updated its styling with a long, low, teardrop-tank. On the JD, it still offered only one colour – olive drab.

△ **Royal Enfield Model 182 Sports 1928**

Origin UK

Engine 976 cc, V-twin

Top speed 78 mph (126 km/h)

Royal Enfield produced V-twins from 1912, using both its own and proprietary engines. The saddle tank was added in 1928. Both brakes were operated by foot pedal.

△ **Indian 101 Scout 1928**

Origin USA

Engine 745 cc, V-twin

Top speed 70 mph (113 km/h)

Longer and lower than before, this front-braked Scout had a light, well-designed frame. Noted for its handling, it was popular for racing, hillclimbing, and stunt riding.

△ **BSA Cycle Cab 1928**

Origin UK

Engine 996 cc, V-twin

Top speed 50 mph (80 km/h)

BSA built around 100 sidecar taxi units from 1920 to 1925, based on the Model E/G and known as "Cycle Cabs". This big V-twin was ideal for sidecar-hauling.

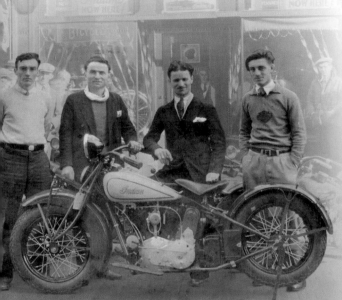

Indian Scout

"Legendary" is how the Indian Motorcycle Company likes to describe their machines. Founders George Hendee and Oscar Hedstrom had set out to lead the US market, and the Scout, unveiled in 1920, heralded a decade of domination by Indian bikes as they went on to take every speed and distance record in America. The revolutionary Scout initially boasted a 606 cc engine, which was increased to 745 cc in 1927 to challenge the growing popularity of Excelsior's rival Super X machine.

INDIAN WAS A COMPANY on the move in the early years of the 20th century, before the outbreak of WWI. Sales had soared since the birth of the company in 1901 and by the 1920s Indian was engaged in a fierce battle with Harley-Davidson for the spot of America's top motorcycle manufacturer. The Scout, designed by Irish-born Charles Bayly Franklin, was at the sharp end of Indian's drive for sales. First introduced in 1920, the bike was an instant hit. The Scout was given a thorough revamp for the 1928 season in the form of the acclaimed 101 series, with a new frame, raked-out forks, and a lower saddle height. The 101 proved especially popular with stunt riders owing to its low centre of gravity and excellent handling, making it ideal for performing feats like the "wall of death". Despite the success of the 101 model, it was discontinued in 1932. During the 1930s, Scouts became progressively heavier and handling deteriorated, although the 1934 Sport Scout redressed the problem somewhat. A favourite of the US Army, Scouts were employed extensively in World War II. The manufacture of Scouts ceased completely in 1949.

FRONT VIEW

REAR VIEW

All-American
The name Indian was chosen by the manufacturers to suggest a truly all-American product. "Scout" conjured up a certain toughness and eagerness to explore new horizons, appealing to riders who identified closely with the pioneering spirit of America.

Teardrop fuel tank forms part of the 1928 redesign for 101 Series

Hand lever controls three-speed gearbox

Electric lights are a pioneering Indian fitment

Front forks are of a leaf-sprung, trailing-link design, peculiar to Indian

V-twin engine of either 600 cc or 750 cc was fitted

Lubrication system is drip-fed from pump on crankcase

Indian Scout

If the Indian Scout was a legend, then the 101 Series was at the heart of it. If one motorcycle had to be picked to represent America's two-wheeled history then it would be the Scout; if one variant of the Scout had to be selected, it would be the 101. Performance, reliability, agility, durability, the Scout 101 had it all – the quintessential all-American motorcycle.

SPECIFICATIONS			
Model	Indian 101 Scout (1928)	Power output	18 hp
Assembly	Springfield, USA	Transmission	Three-speed
Production	17,430	Suspension	Leaf-sprung, trailing-link front forks; rigid rear
Construction	Rigid cradle frame	Brakes	Single-leading drum, front and rear
Engine	745 cc V-twin	Maximum speed	70 mph (113 km/h)

THE BIKE

The Scout 101 capitalized on what had gone before, and improved it. Wheelbase increased from 54½ in (138 cm) to 57⅛ in (145 cm), while the saddle was lowered too (to just 26¼ in/66.75 cm). Riders reckoned that the handling and stability of the Scout was near-perfect and considered the 101 Series to be the best Indian ever built. Some went further, claiming the 101 to be one of the best motorcycles ever made. It was certainly the model that sustained Indian during the period of the Great Depression. Over three times the number of the larger 750 cc model were produced than the 600 cc version.

1. Indian Scout tank script 2. Indian badge 3. Headlamp
4. Leaf spring on front wheel 5. Right handlebar with ignition
6. Fuel and oil filler caps 7. Trailing-link forks 8. Patent list
on steering head 9. Ammeter and lights switch on dashboard
panel 10. Klaxon horn 11. Oil tap 12. Kick-starter 13. Saddle
spring 14. Mudguard detail

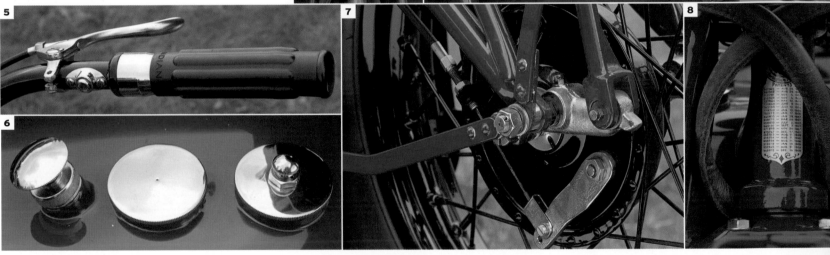

THE ENGINE

The rugged engine had two gear-driven camshafts, and the train of gears that drove them also powered the ignition magneto, which was sited ahead of the front cylinder. The oil pump was mounted on the outside of the gear casing. The three-speed gearbox was bolted onto the rear of the crankcase, with the primary drive by quiet and reliable helical gears.

15. 750 cc engine 16. Battery box 17. Side view of engine showing V-twin cylinders 18. Magneto and dynamo 19. Choke lever on carburettor 20. Fuel tap 21. External oil pump 22. Fuel priming cup

Norton rider, tuner, and later team manager, Dan O'Donovan, on an early model at Brooklands in 1920

Great Marques
The Norton Story

Great motorcycles and business brains do not always go hand in hand. Few stories illustrate the point more acutely than the mixed fortunes of Norton. But the marque that was responsible for such classics as the Dominator and the Commando has shown in recent years that it is a brand that will not die.

ONE OF THE GREAT names of British motorcycling, Norton has teetered on the brink of oblivion so many times that its successes are always in danger of being overshadowed by its failures. But the fact that Norton has been revived so often indicates just how much the marque means to many motorbike enthusiasts.

James Lansdowne Norton was only in his late twenties, when in 1898 he founded the Norton Manufacturing Company in Birmingham and began to build motorcycles. The company did not, however, emerge fully formed. For the first decade or so, engines from overseas powered motorcycles like the Engerette of 1902.

Much of the reason for Norton's assured place in British motorcycling history has been its association with the Isle of Man TT races. The connection began with a victory when the event was first staged in 1907. This was followed by many more successes over the next six decades. In 1908 a Norton bike with an actual Norton engine made its debut but the year 1913 brought another less welcome first: bankruptcy. The marque had to be bailed out, after which it traded under the name Norton Motors Ltd.

Milestone engine
Photographed in 1940, this road machine was powered by Norton's milestone overhead camshaft engine of 1928.

Norton Logo
(introduced 1914)

Just before James Norton's death in 1925, there were further TT wins, but it was the CS1 bike of 1927 that ushered in a golden period. Specializing in an overhead camshaft, these single-cylinder bikes proved popular with the public and a successful policy for the racetrack. Norton could hardly have been more dominant in the Senior TT. Eight races from 1931 to 1938 brought seven victories (with the same number in the Junior 350 cc race).

World War II interrupted the TT, but from 1947 it was business as usual, with the Norton sweeping the board in the 500 cc class for eight consecutive years. Advertisements lauded the achievement with the strapline "Unapproachable Norton".

For dealers, a major expansion to the Norton range was the twin-cylinder Model 7 Dominator of 1949.

Arguably, many of the important features of the bikes – most particularly the engine – were failing to move with the times but this was not true of the frame, especially on production machines after 1951. Irish design genius Rex McCandless, who worked with brother Cromie, had told Gilbert Smith, Norton MD, in 1949: "You are not 'Unapproachable' and you are not the world's best roadholder. I have a bicycle which is miles better." He backed these strong words with a featherbed frame that was fitted to the 500 cc Manx racing machines in 1950 and sailed through every test. It was a revolution in handling.

3½HP

500T

Dominator 88

F1 Sport

1898 James Lansdowne Norton founds the company in Birmingham.
1907 Harry Rembrandt "Rem" Fowler wins the twin-cylinder class at the first Isle of Man TT on a Norton with a Peugeot engine.
1908 Norton's own engines replace French and Swiss powerplants.
1913 R.T. Shelley & Co. rescue Norton from bankruptcy.
1922 The Model 18 production bike hits over 89 mph (143 km/h) on the track.

1924 Alec Bennett wins the Isle of Man Senior TT on a Norton, while George H. Tucker takes the Sidecar title.
1925 James Norton dies at the age of 56.
1927 The Walter Moore-designed overhead camshaft single engine has its racing debut.
1931 A decade of success starts with 350 cc and 500 cc TT wins for Tim Hunt with a redesigned overhead camshaft engine.
1937 Norton supplies over 100,000 of Britain's military motorbikes.

1949 Successful Triumph Speed Twin has a rival in Norton's Dominator Model 7.
1950 Manx Nortons become the world's best-handling racing bikes, using the featherbed frame
1952 Production bikes incorporate the featherbed frame, resulting in the Norton Dominator 88.
1954 Ray Amm gives Norton its eighth straight victory in the Isle of Man Senior TT.
1962 Norton relocates to southeast London.

1967 The 750 cc Commando, with vibration-reducing isolastic system, is viewed as the world's first production superbike.
1975 Commando Interstate MkIII is one of just two Norton machines still produced
1992 Norton receives a welcome boost when Steve Hislop wins the classic Senior TT.
2008 New owner Stuart Garner announces plans to revive the marque.
2010 The twin-cylinder Commando 961 is unveiled and small-scale production begins at the new UK factory.

Pride of Britain
An advertisement for the Norton Dominator De Luxe, which was exhibited at the 1952 Earl's Court Exhibition and promoted as "a superb example of British craftsmanship".

particular things were motorcycles and that we were supposed to be earning a living making them."

In the face of these difficulties, it was a wonder that the marque continued to produce motorcycles of quality; yet in the early 1960s the 650SS Dominator debuted with a new "slimline" featherbed frame. This proved in tests to be superior even to the Triumph Bonneville. Financial calamity, however, always

Such was the frame's popularity that Norton became a victim of its own success, unable to keep pace with demand, and in 1953, within two years of the featherbed featuring on production models, Norton was sold into the stable of Associated Motor Cycles (AMC).

The steady erosion of Norton's position in the postwar years reflected the decline of the whole British motorcycle industry. From the end of the 1950s triumphs on the track were offset by blunders in the boardroom. Inefficient and outmoded equipment and practices, policies stuck in the past, and poor industrial relations led influential designer Bert Hopwood to say of Norton's management: "Never for one moment did they seem to grasp that these

seemed close at hand. Production was moved from Birmingham to London in 1962, then AMC collapsed in 1966, resurfacing as Norton-Villiers.

Competition from Japanese imports was strong. Norton responded in forceful terms with the Commando range, taking big bikes into a new era. The smooth-riding Commando of 1968 was arguably the best British bike of the time and its 750 cc engine took Peter Williams to a popular

Senior TT win
Steve Hislop rides his 180 mph (290 km/h) rotary-engined Norton to the marque's first Isle of Man TT victory for 19 years.

> # "It's a **race-bred** bike with loads and **loads** of **torque**. It sure is a **handful**."
>
> STEVE MCQUEEN ON THE NORTON METISSE, 1966

1973 TT win on the innovative Norton Monocoque racer. Nevertheless, glorious one-offs could not stem the seemingly unstoppable flow of imports.

The marque lurched from crisis to crisis. The merger that created Norton Villiers Triumph in 1973 was followed by constant uncertainty over government subsidies. The final model in the Commando range was the Interstate MkIII 850ES of 1975 but by the end of the decade Norton was no longer a major player in Britain.

A Rotary power unit developed in the 1970s was adopted for a partially successful 1980s' relaunch under new management. But, although Steve

Hislop took an epic Senior TT win on a Norton Rotary racer in 1992, it proved to be another false dawn. Grassroots enthusiasm was always present, but the funding and organization to translate this into something more meaningful was harder to come by.

Much later, a saviour seemed to arrive in the form of an American, Kenny Dreer. Initially restoring classic Commando models, Dreer was on the cusp of launching the new-design 961 Commando, when funds ran out in 2006. The baton was then seized by British entrepreneur Stuart Garner, who oversaw the creation of several 961 variants including Special Edition and Cafe Racer models.

Norton's future now looked more promising. With the company located at Donington Park racing circuit, only around 37 miles (60 km) separated the new Norton base from where its story began. On reviewing the new model, the *Daily Telegraph* declared: "Welcome back, Norton."

Sporting Rides

In Europe, single-cylinder machines were seen as the best sporting mounts. For optimum performance, engineers looked to combustion chamber shape, overhead-valves, then overhead camshafts, and even four valves per cylinder. Engine sizes stayed small, partly for nimble handling but also because they were built to racing limits (250, 350, or 500 cc). In the US, there were no such limitations.

▷ Duzmo Sports 1920

Origin UK

Engine 496 cc, single-cylinder

Top speed 85 mph (137 km/h)

Racing enthusiasts John Wallace and Bert le Vack created the Duzmo but struggled to finance its manufacture. Its engine was built by Advance of Northampton, England.

◁ Blackburne 4 HP 1923

Origin UK

Engine 500 cc, single-cylinder

Top speed 65 mph (105 km/h)

The first Blackburne was introduced in 1913 and updated with three gears and an all-chain drive by 1919. This model, fitted with a large outside flywheel, was smooth-running.

△ Rudge Multi 1921

Origin UK

Engine 499 cc, single-cylinder

Top speed 65 mph (105 km/h)

While most other makers adopted gearboxes, the Rudge company of Coventry stuck with its variable belt system until it introduced chain drive with a three-speed gearbox on this machine in 1921.

▷ Triumph Type R Fast Roadster 1924

Origin UK

Engine 499 cc, single-cylinder

Top speed 84 mph (135 km/h)

Harry Ricardo designed this bike, with a four-valve head, which, aided by dry sump lubrication and a light aluminium crankcase, finished second in the 1922 Isle of Man TT.

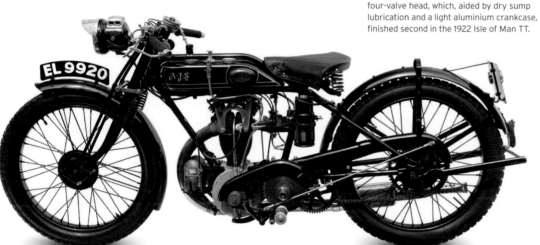

△ AJS E6 Big Port 1924

Origin UK

Engine 349 cc, single-cylinder

Top speed 75 mph (121 km/h)

These powerful machines from a 1914 design were steadily improved with overhead-valves in hemispherical combustion chambers to remain competitive in Isle of Man TT racing.

△ Monet et Goyon Tourisme 1924

Origin France

Engine 269 cc, single-cylinder

Top speed 50 mph (80 km/h)

Joseph Monet and Adrien Goyon made tricycles for disabled servicemen, then motorcycles with Villiers engines such as this one, setting world speed records with a tuned ZS model.

American Fours

In the US, bigger was always better, and the manufacturers faced fewer restrictions on engine size for their racers. Engines grew and they built in-line four-cylinder engines that were bigger than those used to power small sports cars in Europe. These engines were shoe-horned into motorcycle frames to give relaxed, long-legged performance over America's long and mostly straight roads. There was "no substitute for cubes".

△ ACE EXP-4 1923

Origin USA

Engine 1,229 cc, in-line four

Top speed 130 mph (209 km/h)

Founded by William G. Henderson in 1920, Ace set out to prove its bikes were the world's fastest, setting a world speed record of 129.61 mph (208.59 km/h) with this bike in 1923.

▷ Henderson KJ Streamline 1929

Origin USA

Engine 1,301 cc, in-line four

Top speed 102 mph (164 km/h)

Improved cooling, leading-link forks, an inlet over exhaust layout, and a five-bearing crank made this the ultimate Henderson; even the 1929 Wall Street Crash could not kill it.

△ NSU 18PS Sport 1924

Origin Germany

Engine 1,000 cc, V-twin

Top speed 76 mph (122 km/h)

NSU introduced a V-twin in 1905, enlarged it to near 1,000 cc in 1909, and set a US coast-to-coast speed record with it in 1910. It continued to develop in the 1920s, such as in the model shown.

△ Spiegler 350 1924

Origin Germany

Engine 348 cc, single-cylinder

Top speed 56 mph (90 km/h)

A beam-type frame, with sheet metal covering, gave this Speigler a distinctive look. The company made side-valve as well as overhead models from 1923 to 1932.

▷ Velocette Model K 1925

Origin UK

Engine 348 cc, single-cylinder

Top speed 75 mph (121 km/h)

Percy Goodman designed an overhead-camshaft engine for the 1925 Velocette; it was good enough to win its first Junior TT by a 10-minute margin.

△ Cleveland Tornado 1929

Origin USA

Engine 1,000 cc, in-line four

Top speed 102 mph (164 km/h)

A most unfortunately timed launch, Cleveland's guaranteed 100 mph (160 km/h) Tornado arrived weeks before the Wall Street Crash. Very few were completed before the model was dropped.

△ Indian 402 1930

Origin USA

Engine 1,265 cc, in-line four

Top speed 95 mph (153 km/h)

Indian purchased Ace in 1927 and developed the 402 with a sturdier twin-downtube frame and five-bearing crankshaft – it made for a great police pursuit machine.

Sporting Rides (cont.)

By the close of the 1920s, many makers were abandoning flat, box-shaped fuel tanks in favour of the more shapely and streamlined saddle tanks, so-called because of the way they fitted over the bike frame. Tubular frames with rigid rear ends were the norm, but there were bold attempts to break away from the "engine-in-a-bicycle" format.

△ **Schüttoff F350 RS 1926**
Origin	Germany
Engine	348 cc, single-cylinder
Top speed	70 mph (113 km/h)

Arthur Schüttoff made four-strokes and two-strokes from 1923. This four-valve 350 enjoyed racing success, but the company was absorbed by DKW in 1931.

◁ **Zündapp EM250 1927**
Origin	Germany
Engine	249 cc, single-cylinder
Top speed	60 mph (97 km/h)

Zündapp's 1921 "Motorcycle for every man" was replaced in 1925 by this improved 250 two-stroke, with a reinforced frame and fork web. It became a best-seller.

▷ **Francis-Barnett Super Sport 1927**
Origin	UK
Engine	172 cc, single-cylinder
Top speed	60 mph (97 km/h)

The F-B's bolted-up frame could be dismantled and packed in a golf bag. The Super Sport's little Villers engine boasted numerous speed records.

△ **Ardie 500 1927**
Origin	Germany
Engine	490 cc, single-cylinder
Top speed	56 mph (90 km/h)

After the death of founder Arno Dietrich, the Bendit family took over and built conventional and powerful machines like this model with British JAP engines and Hurth gearboxes.

▷ **Norton Model 18 1927**
Origin	UK
Engine	490 cc, single-cylinder
Top speed	78 mph (126 km/h)

This is a road version of Norton's first overhead-valve single, winner of both the Sidecar and Senior TT races in 1924 and holder of the world 1 km record at 89.22 mph (143.59 km/h). Road Model 18s were made until 1954.

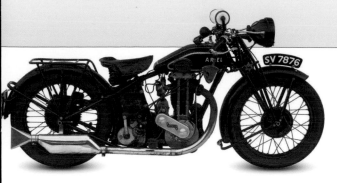

△ Ariel Model E 1928

Origin UK

Engine 499 cc, single-cylinder

Top speed 73 mph (117 km/h)

Ariel recruited Val Page to update its engines in 1925, and the new rakish-looking Ariels dramatically improved sales. Between 1927 and 1928 they were 10 times higher than in 1925.

◁ Moto Guzzi Tipo Sport 1928

Origin Italy

Engine 498 cc, single-cylinder

Top speed 76 mph (122 km/h)

Founded in 1921, the sporting Italian factory favoured a near horizontal cylinder to keep weight low. Overhead-camshaft factory racers like this one were race winners.

△ Mars A20 Sport 1928

Origin Germany

Engine 956 cc, flat-twin

Top speed 88 mph (142 km/h)

Bicycle-maker Mars started fitting engines in 1903. In 1920 Claus Franzenburger designed this legendary "White Mars", with a pressed/welded frame and Maybach engine.

△ Dot J343 1928

Origin UK

Engine 350 cc, single-cylinder

Top speed 72 mph (115 km/h)

Manchester-based Dot courted racing success in its early years; by the late 1920s it used an overhead-valve JAP engine. But the company struggled for sales.

△ Harley-Davidson Model B 1928

Origin USA

Engine 350 cc, single-cylinder

Top speed 53 mph (85 km/h)

Like Harley's other single-cylinder bikes – both side- and overhead-valve – this Model B was every inch a scaled-down V-twin. These bikes were introduced in 1926 to rival Indian's range of smaller machines.

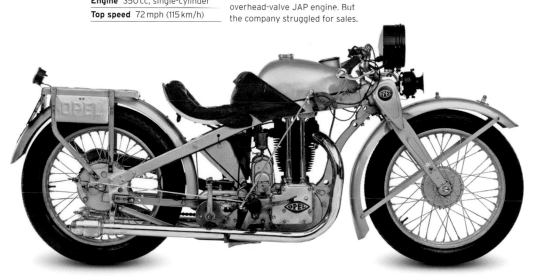

◁ Sunbeam Model 9 1929

Origin UK

Engine 493 cc, single-cylinder

Top speed 82 mph (132 km/h)

Sunbeam's high-quality range included the overhead valve long-stroke Model 9 for sports riding. It had a fully enclosed chain and this one has a picnic basket.

△ Opel Motoclub 1929

Origin Germany

Engine 496 cc, single-cylinder

Top speed 74 mph (119 km/h)

Alongside bicycles, sewing machines, and cars, Opel also made motorcycles from 1901 to 1930. Its finest bike was this overhead-valve sporting machine, with a novel pressed-steel frame.

◁ Norton CS1 1928

Origin UK

Engine 488 cc, single-cylinder

Top speed 85 mph (137 km/h)

The CS1 (Competition Senior) had Norton's landmark overhead-camshaft engine, winner of the 1927 Senior TT, which would soon be eclipsed by a redesigned engine.

◁ Norton 16H 1929

Origin UK

Engine 490 cc, single-cylinder

Top speed 68 mph (109 km/h)

The side-valve 16H was descended from Norton's earlier side-valve racer, which set many world speed records. First used in 1916, the model code survived until 1954.

TT winner Stanley
Woods on a Moto Guzzi
in the 1930s

Great Marques
The Moto Guzzi Story

With an illustrious racing pedigree and a constant emphasis on ingenuity, Moto Guzzi has been making high-quality motorcycles since the end of World War I. Its Grand Tourer and performance models have earned the marque a reputation for producing some of the finest bikes in the world.

THE SEEDS OF AN IDEA for an all-new motorcycle company were sown by three friends serving in the Italian Air Corps during World War I. However, before Carlo Guzzi, Giorgio Parodi, and Giovanni Ravelli could turn their engineering talents to bikes, tragedy ensued when Ravelli was killed in an air crash just days after the end of the war.

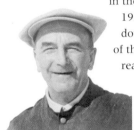

Carlo Guzzi
(1889-1964)

Undeterred, the following year Guzzi and Parodi built their first prototype in a workshop in Mandello del Lario in northern Italy, where the

Recognizing the value racing could have in promoting the new company, Carlo Guzzi entered two bikes in the Milan–Naples race of 1921. Although they finished down the field, the potential of the Moto Guzzi bikes was realized a few weeks later when Gino Finzi won the illustrious Targa Florio event for them. That the marque could take such prestigious racing laurels in its first year heralded a golden era of competition success that would see Moto Guzzi secure more than 3,000 Grand Prix wins by 1957.

"Guzzi **gadabouts** have all the fun!"

1960S' ADVERT FOR MOTO GUZZI SCRAMBLER

factory remains. Known as the GP after the two founders' initials, the 500 cc single featured elements of aircraft-engine technology and could reach 62 mph (100 km/h). Key to Carlo Guzzi's philosophy was that every component should be thoroughly considered and that the bike should be fun to ride. It was an ethos that would forever underpin the company.

The project really took shape when Parodi's father, Emanuele Vittorio, provided backing for the enterprise. By the time the first production model, the Normale, was ready, in 1921, the Società Anonima Moto Guzzi company had been formed.

The fledgling company expanded and new premises enabled annual production to shoot up from 17 bikes in 1921 to 1,200 in 1925. Innovation was always at the core of Moto Guzzi. Fitted to the Normale's frame was a centre stand – which would soon become standard on most motorcycles – and in 1928 a swingarm rear suspension was introduced on its Guzzi GT.

Wind-tunnel pioneers
In 1950 Moto Guzzi became the first motorcycle manufacturer to build a dedicated wind tunnel in which to develop its machines. This resulted in models with blistering performance.

Dondolino

V8

Le Mans MkI

Daytona 1000

1919 Friends Carlo Guzzi and Giorgio Parodi build the first prototype, a 500 cc single.	**1936** The Airone 250 debuts, featuring a pedal-operated four-speed transmission.	**1965** A 700 cc 90-degree V-twin engine is debuted; it will become the core configuration for larger models.	**1976** The 850 Le Mans is unveiled: a fast superbike that will be made until 1993.
1921 Società Anonima Moto Guzzi is established, releasing its debut Normale model; Gino Finzi wins the Targa Florio on a Moto Guzzi.	**1946** Introduction of the 65 Guzzino, a frugal two-stroke that will be developed into the Cardellino and produced into the early 1960s.	**1967** A V7 model is unveiled, which in an enlarged special version will break several speeds records at Monza in 1969; SEIMM takes over the company.	**1977** The V35 is released, featuring a V-twin unit on a smaller (350 cc) engine.
1924 Guido Mentasti wins the European Championship on a 4V model.	**1950** Moto Guzzi becomes the first manufacturer to build a dedicated wind tunnel to test its motorcycles.	**1971** The California V-twin tourer enters the US market; it is still in production.	**2000** Moto Guzzi is taken over by fellow Italian motorcycle maker Aprilia.
1928 The Guzzi GT becomes the first Grand Tourer motorcycle on the market.	**1955** Debut of the fabulous 500 cc water-cooled V8 Grand Prix racing engine.	**1973** De Tomaso Industries buys Moto Guzzi.	**2004** The Moto Piaggio Group buys the Aprilia-Moto-Guzzi concern, forming Europe's largest motorcycle manufacturer.
1935 Stanley Woods wins both the 250 cc and 500 cc TT races on a Moto Guzzi.		**1975** The Guzzi 254, featuring a four-cylinder engine, is released.	**2008** The Guzzi Stelvio adventure-touring bike is released to great acclaim.

By the mid-1930s Moto Guzzi was Italy's principal motorcycle manufacturer. A new 120-degree V-twin engine had been developed that could power the 500 cc twin to speeds in excess of 125 mph (200 km/h), while other key models included the P125 and P150, plus racing bikes such as the Condor, Albatross, and Dondolino. Notable competition wins included victory at the 1935 Isle of Man TT, the first non-English marque to achieve the feat for 24 years. The decade was rounded off with the release of the ultra-successful Airone 250 model, which would be produced until 1957.

A brief pause during World War II did nothing to halt Moto Guzzi's innovative streak. The marque met the Italian demand for lightweight, inexpensive models with offerings such as its debut twin-cylindered bike, the Guzzino 65, and in the 1950 Galletto, the world's first large-wheeled scooter. In 1955 Moto Guzzi's celebrated designer Giulio Cesara Carcano devised a landmark racing machine, the Guzzi Otto Cilindri. It was the first eight-cylinder machine seen in Grand Prix racing, capable of 177 mph (285 km/h). However, before the V8's potential was realized, commercial realities forced Guzzi to withdraw from racing at the end of 1957.

V-twin power
One of the seminal motorcycles in Moto Guzzi's history, the V7 featured the marque's first 90-degree V-twin engine.

The 1950s and early 1960s saw a dip in fortunes for Moto Guzzi, as cheap cars threatened the motorcycle market. After Carlo Guzzi's death in 1964, Giorgio Parodi's brother Enrico took over. Three years later Moto Guzzi was bought by SEIMM, and the new owner's decision to produce low-cost models was reflected in the release of mopeds such as the Trotter.

However, large-capacity bikes were not overlooked. The 1967 V7 featured the company's first transverse V-twin engine with shaft final drive, developed out of a military vehicle contract. The larger-capacity V7 Special was designed for the North American market, and served as the basis for US models, including the California.

In 1973 De Tomaso Industries bought Moto Guzzi. The new owners diversified the company's model range, and new four-cylinder bikes and small-capacity tourers were unveiled. Important high-performance models that boosted exports including the striking 850 cc Le Mans of 1977 and the 1992 Daytona 1000, with an overhead camshaft engine developed in the US by Dr John Wittner.

During the 1990s Moto Guzzi went back to producing the classically styled models for which it was renowned. However, the company went through a transitional period as profits slumped during the early part of the decade. Several changes in ownership culminated in Aprilia taking control of the Moto Guzzi marque in 2000. Moto Guzzi was again under new ownership four years later when the Piaggio Group bought the company to create Europe's largest motorcycle manufacturer. Since then, new models have been released that reflect the company's sporting (Griso 1100) and touring (Norge 1200) heritage, as well as updated versions of iconic models such as the V7 Classic of 2008.

With 90 years of uninterrupted motorcycle production under its belt, Moto Guzzi continues to personify the spirit and passion of Italy more than any other motorcycle marque.

Expanding company
In the first decade of the 21st century Moto Guzzi's output steadily increased, and it is now part of Europe's largest motorcycle manufacturing group.

Survival of the Fittest

Flexible power and easy handling were the most important requirements for the average motorcyclist in the 1920s, who simply wanted a comfortable and economical means of transport for work and play. While some machines were built more cheaply and turned out in quantity, other marques fell by the wayside as they could neither afford to update their technology nor cut their prices.

◁ Clyno 2¼HP 1920

Origin UK

Engine 269 cc, single-cylinder

Top speed 45 mph (72 km/h)

Frank and Ailwyn Smith made motorcycles from 1910, having taken over the Stevens engine factory, but moved entirely to car-making in 1923.

△ Hawker Model C 1922

Origin UK

Engine 348 cc, single-cylinder

Top speed 52 mph (84 km/h)

To occupy their aircraft mechanics in the lull after WWI, Harry Hawker and Tom Sopwith built motorcycles from 1920 to 1924, this one with a Blackburne side-valve engine.

△ Sun Vitesse 1923

Origin UK

Engine 269 cc, single-cylinder

Top speed 56 mph (90 km/h)

Sun took over production of the advanced, VTS two-stroke engine with rotary-valve induction and made this sportster. The company made no bikes from 1932 to 1948.

△ Seal Four-seater 1924

Origin UK

Engine 980 cc, V-twin

Top speed 50 mph (80 km/h)

This extraordinary Seal three-wheeler allows the driver to sit in the sidecar with the passengers, steering by remote linkage. This model was discontinued after 1924.

◁ Ivy Three 1924

Origin UK

Engine 346 cc, single-cylinder

Top speed 55 mph (89 km/h)

Ivy's two-stroke tourer has the latest type of drum front brake, footboards, and leg-shields. A 350 cc Ivy won a Brooklands 500-mile (805-km) race averaging 52 mph (84 km/h).

▷ **Quadrant 4½HP 1924**

Origin UK

Engine 624 cc, single-cylinder

Top speed 57 mph (92 km/h)

Quadrant's robust side-valve single has its inlet valve behind the cylinder, but these unexciting machines began to look dated by the mid-1920s.

◁ **Triumph Model P 1925**

Origin UK

Engine 493 cc, single-cylinder

Top speed 65 mph (105 km/h)

Britain's cheapest 500 ever, this was Triumph's first mass-produced motorcycle; 1,000 were turned out every week. Early quality problems were sorted out by 1926.

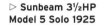

△ **Henley Blackburne Tourer 1925**

Origin UK

Engine 545 cc, single-cylinder

Top speed 57 mph (92 km/h)

Henley made motorcycles in Birmingham from 1920, soon settling on a range of side-valve Blackburne engines. This largest one was also sold with a sidecar.

▷ **Sunbeam 3½HP Model 5 Solo 1925**

Origin UK

Engine 499 cc, single-cylinder

Top speed 80 mph (129 km/h)

The Model 5, with its low-revving, long-stroke, side-valve engine, was built to go long distances. Sunbeam's 1922 Senior TT win was the last by a side-valver.

◁ **Wanderer K500 1928**

Origin Germany

Engine 499 cc, single-cylinder

Top speed 59 mph (95 km/h)

This is a sophisticated shaft-drive machine with leaf spring forks. Wanderer, who had built motorcycles since 1902, stopped production in 1929 and then sold this design to Jawa.

△ **BSA S28 1928**

Origin UK

Engine 493 cc, single-cylinder

Top speed 60 mph (97 km/h)

Harold Briggs joined BSA from Daimler in the 1920s to design new engines, including this flexible side-valve 500 that was ideal for touring and combinations.

La Jumella ("The Twin"), 1922
Captured at the Champ-de-Mars, Paris, this unusual motorcycle is possibly an extended version of an early Ner-a-Car model. Similar in concept to a forecar, but with just two wheels, it may have been used as a commercial taxi.

Out of the Mainstream

Innovative engineers experimented with many new ideas for two-wheeled transport in the 1920s, some brilliantly practical, others technological dead ends. Air, water, and oil were used as coolants, horizontally opposed cylinders were laid transversely across the frame, and radical ideas were tried in attempts to boost power from two-stroke engines. Chassis technology was slower to change, although there were some bold attempts to break the mould.

◁ **Humber 4¹/₂HP 1921**

Origin UK

Engine 601cc, flat-twin

Top speed 60mph (97 km/h)

After a most unusual flat-three in 1913, Humber made flat-twins from 1915, including this quality "Silent Humber" with a three-speed gearbox and chain transmission.

△ **ABC 400 1921**

Origin UK

Engine 398cc, flat-twin

Top speed 70mph (113 km/h)

Innovative designer Granville Bradshaw's ABC pioneered the transverse flat-twin engine and rear frame springing. It was built by Sopwith Aviation.

△ **Sheffield Simplex Ner-a-Car 1921**

Origin UK

Engine 285cc, single-cylinder

Top speed 35mph (56 km/h)

Designed by American Carl Neracher and built both in the US and UK, this was a very stable bike with constantly variable transmission, a low build, and hub-centre steering.

△ **OK Bradshaw 1922**

Origin UK

Engine 349cc, single-cylinder

Top speed 60mph (97 km/h)

Fred Dawes and Ernie Humphries made motorcycles from 1911. The Bradshaw engine relied on oil cooling for its cylinder barrel, but was known as the "oil boiler".

△ **BMW R32 1923**

Origin Germany

Engine 486cc, flat-twin

Top speed 59mph (95 km/h)

The first motorcycle from BMW had the now-traditional flat-twin layout with wet sump lubrication and aluminium alloy cylinders and heads, plus a shaft drive.

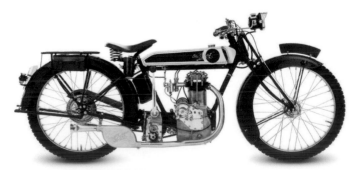

△ **DOT Bradshaw 1922**

Origin UK

Engine 349cc, single-cylinder

Top speed 60mph (97 km/h)

Harry Reed of Manchester built successful sporting bikes; this one had an oil-cooled Bradshaw engine, internal expanding brakes, three gears, and a chain drive.

△ **Smart Celle du Salon 1923**

Origin France

Engine 150cc, single-cylinder

Top speed 50mph (80 km/h)

This simple two-stroke model with a two-speed gearbox and enclosed primary drive, was the product of a short-lived marque that only lasted from 1923 to 1927.

△ Dunelt Model K 1925

Origin	UK
Engine	249 cc, single-cylinder
Top speed	65 mph (105 km/h)

Reliable Dunelt Model K engines used double-diameter pistons to boost cylinder filling from the crankcase. An earlier 500 cc version was replaced by this 250 cc single.

△ Böhmerland Three-seater 1927

Origin	Czech Republic
Engine	603 cc, single-cylinder
Top speed	70 mph (113 km/h)

This extraordinary bike has cast-alloy wheels, rear-mounted fuel tanks, and a very long tubular frame with tension spring front forks. The engine has open valve gear.

▽ Scott Super Squirrel 1927

Origin	UK
Engine	498 cc, in-line twin
Top speed	80 mph (129 km/h)

Alfred Scott's innovative two-stroke engine design lasted well after his death in 1923. The popular three-speed Super Squirrel sports bike was sold in 500 cc, as here, or in 600 cc form.

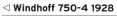

◁ Windhoff 750-4 1928

Origin	Germany
Engine	748 cc, in-line four
Top speed	74 mph (119 km/h)

An unorthodox machine with an oil-cooled overhead-camshaft, in-line four-cylinder engine. A subframe fixed to the power unit carried the shaft-driven rear wheel.

△ Levis Six-port 1929

Origin	UK
Engine	247 cc, single-cylinder
Top speed	66 mph (106 km/h)

Levis won an Isle of Man TT with its sporty two-strokes and this was their fastest. The Six-port had extra cylinder ports that cooled the piston with incoming unburnt fuel.

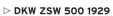

▷ DKW ZSW 500 1929

Origin	Germany
Engine	494 cc, in-line twin
Top speed	62 mph (100 km/h)

DKW was the world's largest motorcycle-maker at the time, so could afford to experiment with unconventional machines like this water-cooled, two-stroke twin.

Track Contenders

Many motorcycle-makers subscribed to the view that racing improved the breed, and there was plenty of evidence to support that contention. Overhead camshafts and four-valve cylinder heads became more common on racing machines in the 1920s, while minimizing weight led to the construction of clean, simple, and effective frames, and the use of lightweight alloys for engine and transmission casings.

△ Norton Model 9 1920

Origin UK

Engine 490 cc, single-cylinder

Top speed 70 mph (113 km/h)

The Model 9's side-valve engine dated back to James Lansdowne Norton's first engine of 1908. It was flexible and powerful but outdated, with no clutch or gears.

▷ Indian Model H 1920

Origin USA

Engine 1,000 cc, V-twin

Top speed 120 mph (193 km/h)

Indian's powerful V-twins were top contenders in board track racing from the start. This machine uses a side-valve engine based on the Powerplus model.

△ Harley-Davidson Eight-valve Racer 1920

Origin USA

Engine 1,000 cc, V-twin

Top speed 120 mph (193 km/h)

Also known as the Model 12 racer, this bike was built in very small numbers up to 1928. It was a highly specialized machine with four valve heads, no exhaust pipes, just one speed, and no brakes.

△ Harley-Davidson Model 28S Board Racer 1926

Origin USA

Engine 345 cc, single-cylinder

Top speed 85 mph (137 km/h)

Called "peashooters" because of the noise they made, Harley's ultra-light 216-lb (98-kg) board racers with overhead-valve engines cleaned up on the flat tracks in the 1930s.

◁ Megola 1921 1923

Origin Germany

Engine 640 cc, rotary five-cylinder

Top speed 88 mph (142 km/h)

A Monosoupape aero engine driving the front wheel (and rotating with it) was the method of propulsion for the Megola. The bike won a German Championship race in 1924.

◁ OEC Claude
Temple 1923

Origin UK

Engine 996 cc, V-twin

Top speed 121 mph (195 km/h)

Lincoln motorcycle-maker OEC built frames for Brooklands champion Claude Temple, who fitted this bike with a British Anzani aero engine to set world speed records from 1923 to 1926.

△ Sunbeam Sprinter 1923

Origin UK

Engine 499 cc, single-cylinder

Top speed 95 mph (153 km/h)

After WWI and throughout the 1920s, stripped-down Sunbeams like the Sprinter were hugely successful in sprints and racing, winning all over Europe.

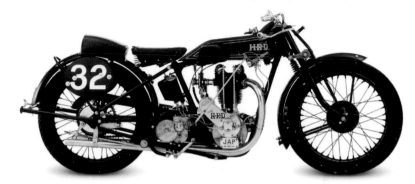

△ HRD HD90 1924

Origin UK

Engine 488 cc, single-cylinder

Top speed 100 mph (160 km/h)

One of his early motorcycles, Howard Raymond Davies (HRD) built bikes from 1924 to 1928 to race in the Isle of Man TT and for road use. He won the TT on his own machine in 1925.

▽ Indian Scout
Hillclimber 1927

Origin USA

Engine 740 cc, V-twin

Top speed 75 mph (120 km/h)

With a low build, small front wheel, negligible brakes, and a big rear cog, this Indian was built for hill climbing – a sport developed to encourage sales of smaller bikes.

◁ Scott TT Super
Squirrel 1927

Origin UK

Engine 498 cc, in-line twin

Top speed 95 mph (153 km/h)

The water-cooled Scotts won the Isle of Man Senior TT race before WWI. The bikes were competitive in the 1920s too, but did not win. This Super Squirrel is British rider Harry Langman's 1927 TT bike.

▷ Moto Guzzi SS 1928

Origin Italy

Engine 247 cc, single-cylinder

Top speed 78 mph (126 km/h)

After WWI, the aircraft mechanic Carlo Guzzi designed an overhead-camshaft, horizontal engine that continued to be manufactured for the next for 45 years; in a rigid, light frame, it gave a low centre of gravity.

▷ Chater-Lea Special
"Copperknob" 1929

Origin UK

Engine 348 cc, single-cylinder

Top speed 110 mph (177 km/h)

Ben Joe Bickell built Copperknob with a damaged Chater-Lea frame and an overhead-camshaft Chater-Lea engine, then won races at Brooklands.

The
1930s

The Great Depression that followed the 1929 collapse of the New York Stock Exchange shifted the emphasis of motorcycle production from speed to economy. Some manufacturers came through the crisis as buyers looked for the best-value transport, but many were unable to compete and disappeared. In the later 1930s international markets opened up, spreading innovative ideas around the world. European racing saw a flowering of engine technology; by contrast, US racing moved to special editions only available to a few,

THE BIKE

The Square Four was not really about brisk performance, but aimed to achieve exceptional smoothness and flexibility. These qualities were combined with reliability in the more sedate post-1936 overhead-valve models. The 1,000 cc version was considered the ultimate civilized touring machine and ideal for pulling sidecars. The ride-on post-war version was improved by telescopic front forks and the option of plunger rear suspension, while the MkII, manufactured from 1953, was the first version capable of hitting 100 mph (160 km/h).

1. Ariel badge **2.** Choke lever on handlebar **3.** Lights switch **4.** Six-volt headlamp **5.** Comfortable saddle **6.** Four-speed hand-change gearbox **7.** Fuel cap and dashboard panel **8.** Drive sprocket **9.** Front suspension damper **10.** Horn **11.** Rear brake pedal **12.** Kick-starter **13.** Silencer

THE ENGINE

Turner's original four-cylinder engine was created by using two parallel twin units within a single crankcase. Engine capacity increased to a final 995 cc unit on the 1937 4G model, with an ohv configuration. Later key changes included replacing the MkI's iron cylinder head and barrel with lighter, alloy components from 1949, and a redesigned head on the MkII in 1953.

14. Compact engine unit **15.** Ignition magneto under six-volt dynamo **16.** Camshaft chain casing **17.** Main and reserve fuel taps **18.** Ignition distributor **19.** Air intake

Speed Club (cont.)

By the 1930s the motorcycle market had become relatively sophisticated, with a variety of buyers seeking different styles of bikes. For many, performance was a major factor and the manufacturers responded by offering sporting versions of their basic models, or by creating special high-performance machines with highly tuned engines that were, in some cases, directly related to racing models. And obviously it was important to advertise the bike's potential by making sure that it looked good too.

△ **Indian Sport Scout 1936**

Origin USA

Engine 737 cc, side-valve V-twin

Top speed 85 mph (137 km/h)

The Scout formed the basis for many racing machines; owners removed the headlight and other extras, tuned the engine, and took to the track.

◁ **AJS R10 1936**

Origin UK

Engine 495 cc, ohc single-cylinder

Top speed 90 mph (145 km/h)

Matchless took over AJS and continued production. The super sporting R10 boasted a race-proven engine with chain drive to the overhead camshaft.

▷ **BMW R51 RS 1938**

Origin Germany

Engine 494 cc, flat-twin

Top speed 95 mph (153 km/h)

Developed from BMWs landmark R5 overhead-valve twin engine, the R51 featured plunger rear suspension. This is an RS in racing trim.

△ **Royal Enfield JF 1936**

Origin UK

Engine 499 cc, ohv single-cylinder

Top speed 85 mph (137 km/h)

The JF was one of the few machines built in the 1930s fitted with a four-valve cylinder head. Enfield also tried three-valve heads before reverting to two.

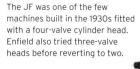

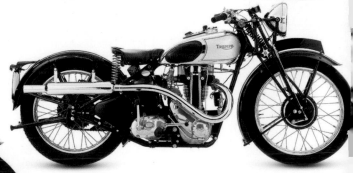

◁ **Triumph Speed Twin 1937**

Origin UK

Engine 498 cc, ohv parallel-twin

Top speed 94 mph (151 km/h)

The Speed Twin, with its parallel twin-cylinder engine, set the pattern for British motorcycles for the next 40 years. It was compact, stylish, and fast.

△ **Triumph Tiger 80 1937**

Origin UK

Engine 349 cc, single-cylinder

Top speed 78 mph (126 km/h)

When Edward Turner was appointed to head Triumph, he revamped this 350 with a chrome tank, polished cases, high exhaust, new paint, and a racy new name.

◁ **Vincent HRD Rapide Series A 1938**

Origin UK

Engine 998 cc, ohv V-twin

Top speed 110 mph (177 km/h)

By doubling up their single-cylinder engine, Vincent created a superfast V-twin. A war-time design would create the most iconic Vincent twin.

◁ **Vincent HRD Comet 1938**

Origin UK

Engine 498 cc, single-cylinder

Top speed 92 mph (148 km/h)

Philip Vincent, who bought HRD in 1928, adopted a high-camshaft engine designed by Australian Phil Irving from 1935. The engine powered racers as well as this Comet.

▽ **Crocker 1938 1938**

Origin USA

Engine 1,000 cc, ohv V-twin

Top speed 110 mph (177 km/h)

Only made from 1936 to 1942, Crocker V-twins were fast, of high quality, and very expensive. This is the later type with vertical overhead valves.

△ **BSA Empire Star 1936**

Origin UK

Engine 496 cc, ohv single-cylinder

Top speed 80 mph (129 km/h)

BSA shed its stodgy image with the dashing Star series series of sports singles. Forerunner to BSA's famous Gold Star, the Empire Star was redesigned in 1937.

▽ **BSA M24 Gold Star 500 1938**

Origin UK

Engine 496 cc, ohv single-cylinder

Top speed 95 mph (153 km/h)

This all-alloy engined bike named after the badge awarded for lapping Brooklands at 100 mph (160 km/h), which a tuned BSA single did in 1937.

◁ **Matchless G80 1939**

Origin UK

Engine 498 cc, ohv single-cylinder

Top speed 85 mph (137 km/h)

The chrome tank and high-level exhaust of the London-built G80 made it a good-looking machine; it delivered good performance too.

Sunbeam Model 9, c.1930
A handsome motorcyclist riding a Sunbeam clearly impresses a group of sunbathing beauties in this 1930s' advert. The Sunbeam's distinctive black tank with gold-leaf pinstriping was a match for its excellent build quality.

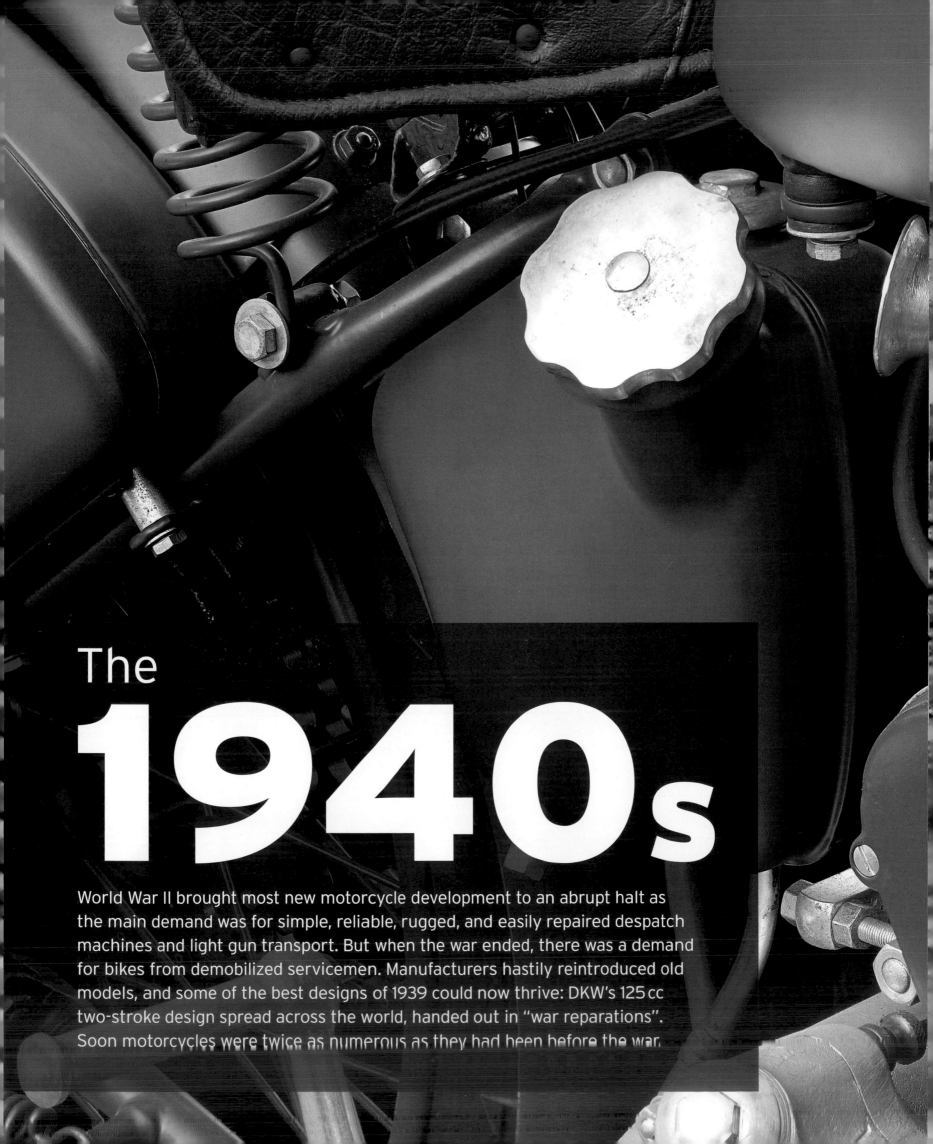

The
1940s

World War II brought most new motorcycle development to an abrupt halt as the main demand was for simple, reliable, rugged, and easily repaired despatch machines and light gun transport. But when the war ended, there was a demand for bikes from demobilized servicemen. Manufacturers hastily reintroduced old models, and some of the best designs of 1939 could now thrive: DKW's 125 cc two-stroke design spread across the world, handed out in "war reparations". Soon motorcycles were twice as numerous as they had been before the war.

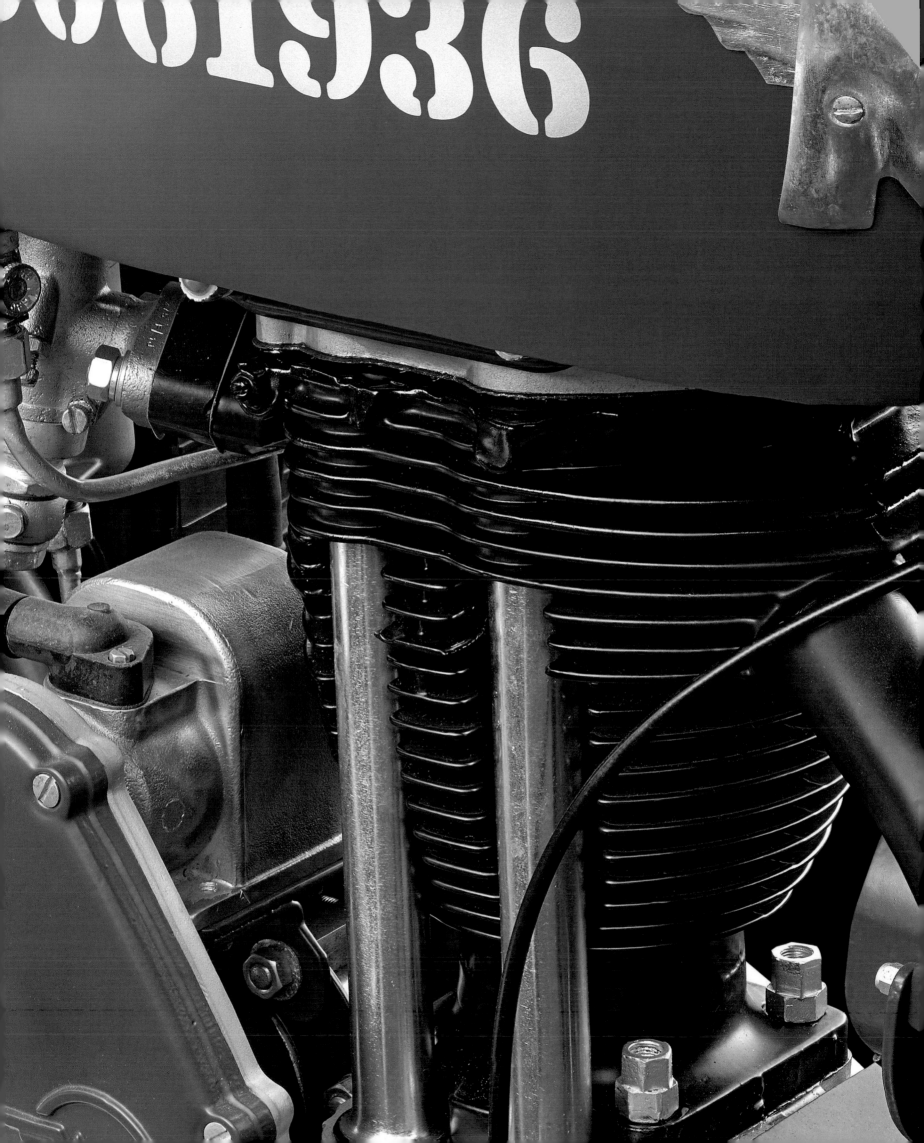

Canadian despatch riders, 1943
Fast and reliable motorbikes were essential for delivering urgent messages between military units. A wing of despatch riders from the Canadian Army is briefed by a senior officer before going on duty during World War II.

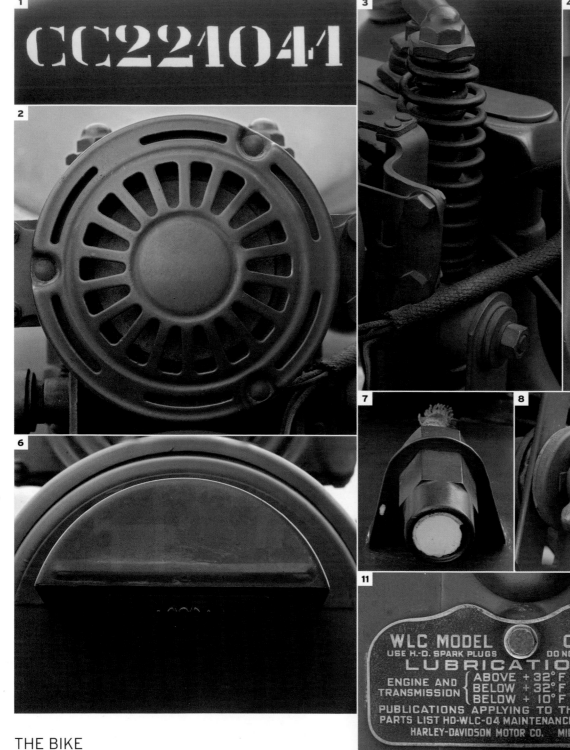

CC221044

THE BIKE

The military WLs were based on the W Series "baby flathead" twins already in production. Special equipment included a revision to Harley-Davidson's traditional leading-link forks to allow increased ground clearance, as well as footboards and protective crash bars. The WLC saw action in several theatres of war from 1941 to 1945, including the Normandy landings and many other major conflict zones across Europe.

1. Identification number 2. Horn 3. Fork spring 4. Speedometer 5. Gear change 6. Headlamp mask revealing only a small rectangle of light 7. Front marker lamp 8. Front fork ride adjuster knob 9. Fuel filler 10. Rear sprocket 11. Data plate attached to top of tank 12. Kick-starter 13. Canadian emblem displayed on either side of tank 14. Clutch control 15. Rear lights

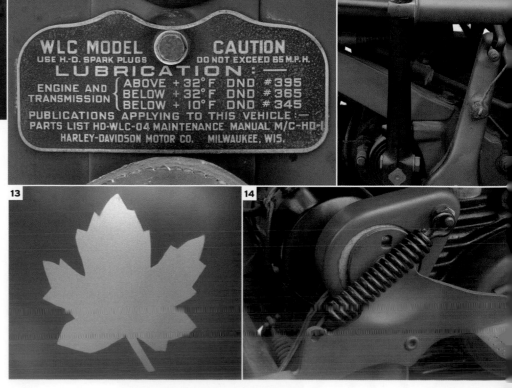

THE ENGINE

Key to the success of Harley's side-valve (or "Flathead") V-twin was the absence of any moving parts in its cylinder head, which simplified maintenance in battlefield conditions. The bike's reliability was further enhanced by an upgraded lubrication system and an oil-bath air filter to keep out dust, grit, or sand.

16. Air intake hose 17. Rugged side-valve engine
18. Ignition timing unit 19. Carburettor floatbowl
20. Inlet manifold

The 1950s

The decade began with the British motorcycle industry at the fore, thanks to an aggressive export policy that would support it for years to come. In most of Europe, motorcycles served as essential everyday transport and as cars were still too expensive for many, simple, cheap, economical two-strokes were the obvious choice. The Italian scooter and French moped spread throughout the world, selling in millions. Prosperity in the US saw the shrinking home industry battling for sales against a mounting tide of European imports.

Lambretta LD 150

The Lambretta LD was a stylish runabout that epitomized Italian manufacturer Ferdinando Innocenti's initial inspiration for a motor scooter. The fully enclosed model was technically superior to earlier Lambrettas, combining the simplicity and reliability that people came to expect from the Innocenti stable with extra power and flair. First entering the market as a 125 cc model late in 1951, a 150 cc version (featured here) was presented In 1954, which successfully combined classy design with low running costs.

INNOCENTI'S 1950 ADVERTISING CAMPAIGN encouraged long-distance scooter journeys with the slogan "More than 100,000 kilometres on a Lambretta", setting the tone for the decade. Scooter clubs, rallies, and newsletters created an exciting atmosphere of youthful freedom, and longer trips were now possible on scooters with increased power and reliability. The Lambretta LD 150, with its single-cylinder, two-stroke engine generating 6 bhp and a top speed of 50 mph (80 km/h), helped to demonstrate that scooters could be used for more adventurous outings, as well as for short hops. Comfort for the driver and passenger was increased by the addition of a hydraulic damper to the torsion bar in the new rear suspension, while a forced-draught cooling system using a fan positioned on the flywheel prevented the engine from overheating, even on long journeys. The Lambretta LD was the first of Innocenti's models to be manufactured outside Italy. A great commercial success, it had a production run lasting more than six years. The end of its construction also signalled the end of the company's shaft-driven vehicles.

FRONT VIEW

REAR VIEW

Made in Milan
Production of the first Lambretta scooters began in 1947 at the Innocenti factory in Milan. The name Lambretta derives from the Lambro, a small river near the manufacturing works.

Spare wheel
mounted with fuel/oil container and carrier

Handle for passenger

Steel panels
enclose engine and transmission

Storage compartment
also serves as base for speedometer and clock

Legshields
protect against wind, rain, and dirt

Pressed-steel
wheels are interchangeable and shod with low-inflation-pressure tyres

Silencer box
is a pressed steel chamber with outlet to rear

Luxury features
An array of smart catalogued and aftermarket accessories embellish this Lambretta LD 150 MkIII. Most obvious are the front windshield, a rear carrier with spare wheel and extra fuel tank, heel plates, and footboard extensions.

SPECIFICATIONS	
Model	Lambretta LD 150 MkIII (1957)
Assembly	Milan, Italy
Production	110,186
Construction	High-tensile steel tube frame
Engine	148 cc, single-cylinder
Power output	6 hp at 4,600 rpm
Transmission	Three-speed
Suspension	Trailing-arm front, torsion bar/hydraulic damper rear
Brakes	Drums, front and rear
Maximum speed	50 mph (80 km/h)

THE BIKE

Advertised as "the ideal personal transport machine", the Lambretta LD 150 boasted a winning combination of balance, comfort, and simplicity. Its controls were easy to master, allowing those who had never driven a motorized vehicle before to quickly acquire confidence on the road. The high-tensile steel tube frame ensured rigidity and minimized vibration, the interchangeable wheels were easily removed, and changing gear with the handlebar twistgrip was a breeze. Novices found it approachable, while experienced drivers relished its reliability and extra power.

1. Maker's badge **2.** Key locks steering **3.** Lights switch **4.** Handlebar gear change **5.** Clock **6.** Rear brake pedal **7.** Horn **8.** Spare fuel and oil tank **9.** Filler for petrol/oil mix **10.** Footboard **11.** Panel release for engine access **12.** Air outlet **13.** Chromed guard accessory **14.** Kick-starter **15.** Air intake **16.** Front wheel and braking system **17.** Rear lamp and indicators **18.** Twin exhaust outlet

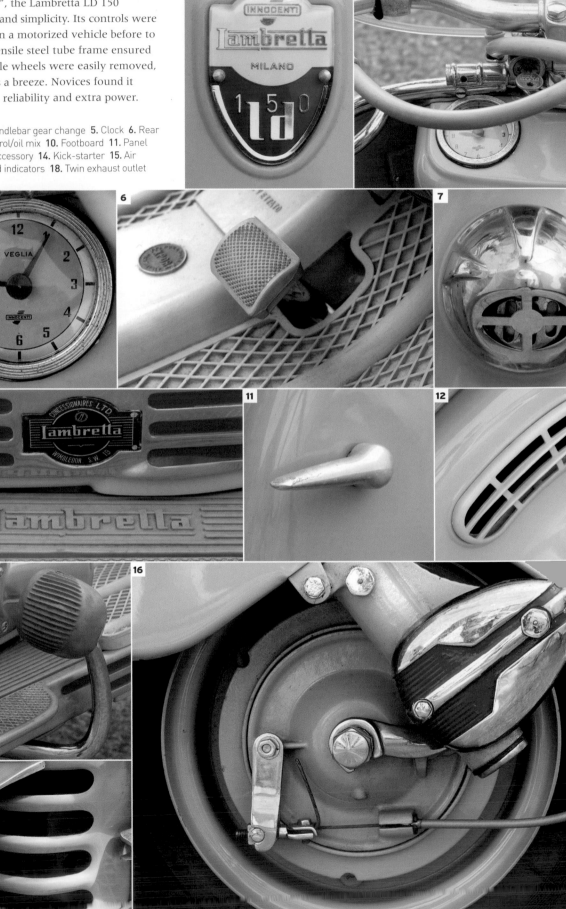

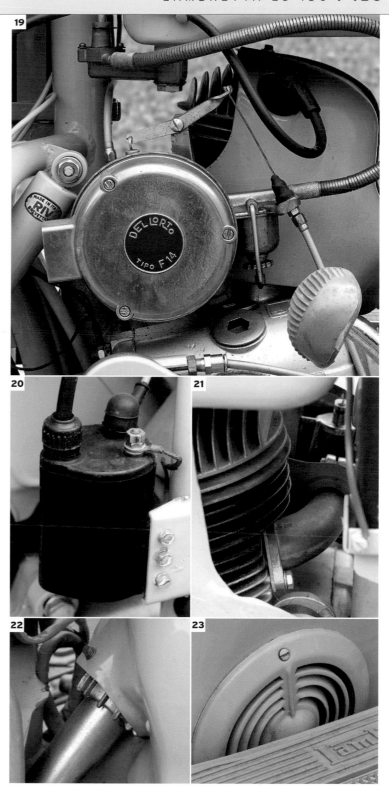

ENGINE

The single-cylinder, two-stroke engine and transmission of the Lambretta LD 150 were completely enclosed, leading distributors to advertise that "no protective clothing is necessary" to ride the bike – a campaign aimed at stylish dressers and women riders. The fan-cooled engine had a flywheel ignition magneto, an inclined cast-iron cylinder with an alloy cylinder head, a high-tensile steel connecting rod, built-up crankshaft, multi-plate clutch, and three-speed gearbox with constant mesh gears. Designed to keep the peace in built-up areas, noise was diminished by fitting an expansion chamber to the exhaust pipe and adding an air cleaner to prevent dust particles entering the carburettor.

19. Casing removed to show engine **20.** Ignition coil **21.** Intake manifold
22. Exhaust down pipe **23.** Fan intake

Lively Lightweights

Machines of 250 cc and under were popular in Europe. Their benefits included low taxation, economy, easy handling, and suitability for commuting. Lightweights were also ideal for young novice riders, so manufacturers offered sports versions, often with two-stroke engines offering a favourable power-to-weight ratio. The end of the decade saw early Japanese arrivals, a foretaste of the future.

◁ **Indian 250 Warrior 1951**

Origin USA

Engine 500 cc, in-line twin

Top speed 85 mph (137 km/h)

Indian struggled after the war: the vertical twin Warrior was a brave try but was poorly developed and no match for cheaper and more reliable imports from Europe.

△ **Excelsior Talisman Sports 1952**

Origin UK

Engine 244 cc, in-line twin

Top speed 65 mph (105 km/h)

This long-established company outshone UK rivals with this zesty twin-carburettor two-stroke twin, although it had basic undamped suspension and weak electrics.

△ **MV Agusta 175CSS Supersport 1953**

Origin Italy

Engine 172 cc, single-cylinder

Top speed 62 mph (100 km/h)

A shapely fuel tank earned MV's overhead-camshaft sport bike the nickname Disco Volante ("Flying Saucer"). The leading link front forks are a British Earles design.

△ **Moto Morini Turismo 2T 1953**

Origin Italy

Engine 123 cc, single-cylinder

Top speed 55 mph (89 km/h)

Alfonso Morini judged the postwar market well, introducing this lively two-stroke bike with three-speed gearbox just after the war, even winning races with one.

◁ **Victoria V35 Bergmeister 1953**

Origin Germany

Engine 345 cc, V-twin

Top speed 80 mph (129 km/h)

This sophisticated, shaft-drive, four-stroke motorcycle was a perfect mid-range machine for the German market, though a delayed release hampered sales.

△ Triumph Tiger Cub 1954
Origin UK
Engine 199 cc, single-cylinder
Top speed 68 mph (109 km/h)

A neat and effective four-stroke single with a reasonable turn of speed for its time, the Tiger Cub was considered rather noisy – a bike for young riders with pretensions.

△ Adler MB200 1954
Origin Germany
Engine 195 cc, in-line two
Top speed 65 mph (105 km/h)

The beautifully engineered Adler two-strokes featured clockspring front suspension and other ingenious details. Production dried up as Adler turned to making typewriters.

◁ NSU Supermax 1957
Origin Germany
Engine 247 cc, single-cylinder
Top speed 78 mph (126 km/h)

NSU steadily improved its 250 singles throughout the decade, adopting a monocoque pressed-steel frame in 1953. By 1955 it was the world's biggest motorcycle builder.

△ FB Mondial 175 Turismo Veloce 1956
Origin Italy
Engine 181 cc, single-cylinder
Top speed 65 mph (105 km/h)

Founded by Count Giuseppe Boselli in 1948, FB was soon making small top-quality motorcycles such as this one, as well as winning world championships with its racers.

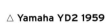

△ Ambassador Super S 1958
Origin UK
Engine 249 cc, in-line twin
Top speed 70 mph (113 km/h)

Heavy mudguarding was added to this conventional lightweight bike with a Villiers engine in 1958. Ambassador was founded after World War II by racing driver Kaye Don.

△ Yamaha YD2 1959
Origin Japan
Engine 247 cc, in-line twin
Top speed 68 mph (109 km/h)

The first Yamaha sold in Europe (from 1960), the YD2 had a super-reliable two-stroke twin engine based on the Adler design, but with oil injection, and very chunky styling.

◁ Ariel Leader 1959
Origin UK
Engine 249 cc, in-line twin
Top speed 70 mph (113 km/h)

A brave attempt to build a motorcycle that would keep its rider as clean as on a scooter, the Ariel Leader was a good but expensive effort with a new Adler-like two-stroke engine.

Soichiro Honda at the Asama Kazan race, in 1955

Great Marques
The Honda Story

For the past 50 years the Honda Motor Company has been the world's largest motorcycle manufacturer. However, the Japanese company's birth in the mid-1940s was a very low-key affair, which belied its multi-billion dollar future. That dream outcome was down to the initiative, determination, and vision of one man – Soichiro Honda.

POST-WORLD WAR II Japan was a nation stricken by overcrowded public transport and fuel restrictions. It was against this backdrop that self-taught engineer Soichiro Honda came up with an idea that would eventually allow for his company to bring motorcycles to the masses.

Honda acquired 500 war-surplus two-stroke electric motors designed for portable electric generators used in military radios, and adapted them for attaching to push-bikes. The makeshift motorbikes were so successful that when they sold out Honda designed and built his own 50 cc unit. The Honda Motor

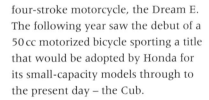

Honda badge
(introduced 1988)

Company was formed in 1948, and the next year the first Honda motorcycle to feature a Honda-designed motor and frame was produced. The two-stroke 98 cc machine was called the Model D, with the D standing for "Dream" – a name that would regularly be used over the next few decades.

Keen to expand its range, in 1951 Honda introduced its first four-stroke motorcycle, the Dream E. The following year saw the debut of a 50 cc motorized bicycle sporting a title that would be adopted by Honda for its small-capacity models through to the present day – the Cub.

As a racing fan, the company's founder was soon developing models that could be pushed to their limits

The 1960s saw Honda flourish as it capitalized on its competition success and expanded overseas. A foothold was established in the US through the establishment of a dedicated sales division in Los Angeles. Despite a slow start, the marque grew at a phenomenal rate, and by the end of 1962 Honda was selling 40,000 bikes a year in America.

Key to this expansion was the creation of a dealership network and a promotional drive that focused on the fun aspect of its different-looking new "clean" motorcycles – principally the 50 cc Super Cub model. An example was a 1962 advertising campaign that ran with the slogan, "You meet the nicest people on a Honda". For consumers used to the traditional oil-stained image of the motorcycling world, this was a breath of fresh air.

company's inaugural long-distance tourer, the 1974 Goldwing, and the successful 250 cc Elsinore motocross model. In 1979, the Elsinore rolled off the production line at a new plant in Ohio, making Honda the first Japanese manufacturer to build bikes in the US.

Grand Prix racing continued to prove fruitful for Honda. Freddie Spencer's 1983 and 1985 wins in the 500 cc World Championship were highlights among several achievements in this and other race series. Key road models such as the VF750F and a new

"It was a **devastating win** for the Orient."

THE *ISLE OF MAN EXAMINER*, ON HONDA'S 1961 TT VICTORY

Honda Benly poster
A 1950s poster advertises the first-generation Honda Benly. Appearing with a four-stroke engine and a new frame with a pressed steel backbone, the Benly had a shaky start but eventually became a highly popular model.

on the racetrack. Soichiro Honda found inspiration from the European bikes he witnessed at the Isle of Man TT races in the mid-1950s. The marque was first represented at the famed race series in 1959, when several 125 cc machines secured Honda the manufacturers' title in the ultra-lightweight class. Two years later, the company announced its arrival on the world racing scene when British rider Mike Hailwood became 250 cc World Champion.

By the end of the 1960s, Honda's model development programme had produced a wide variety of bikes, ranging from small mopeds to large road bikes. Arguably the most important of its bikes was the CB750, which set new standards for what could be achieved on a production model in terms of equipment levels and performance capabilities.

Over the following two decades Honda broadened its line-up further, with classic offerings such as the

Model D

CB750

Goldwing GL1500 SE

CBR1000RR Fireblade

1948 The Honda Motor Company is formed.
1949 The 98 cc Model D becomes the company's first motorcycle.
1951 Honda's first four-stroke bike, the Dream E, makes its debut.
1958 The Super Cub 50 cc model is released; in this and later variants it will become the world's best-selling vehicle, with 60 million built by 2008.
1959 The company makes its first appearance at the Isle of Man TT races.
1961 Honda wins the 125 cc and 250 cc TTs.

1963 Honda sets up its first overseas plant, in Belgium; it becomes the first foreign sponsor of the Oscars, providing huge publicity in the US.
1966 Honda becomes the first manufacturer to win the motorcycle World Championship in all solo classes: 50 cc, 125 cc, 250 cc, 350 cc, and 500 cc.
1968 The 10-millionth Honda motorcycle rolls off the production line.
1969 The CB750 makes its debut as Honda's first four-cylinder model.

1974 Honda enters the touring market with the Goldwing, a model that finds favour with North American buyers.
1978 The NR500 model is introduced; developed for grand prix racing, it has 32 valves and oval pistons.
1982 French rider Cyril Neveu wins the motorcycle class of the Paris-Dakar Rally on a Honda XR500R.
1986 Motorcycle production starts in Spain.
1991 The founder of Honda, Soichiro Honda dies, aged 84.

1996 Honda's CBR1100 Blackbird becomes the fastest production motorcycle on the planet, at 177 mph (285 km/h).
2001 The marque records its 500th motorcycle grand prix victory.
2007 Spanish rider Toni Bou wins the Trials World Championship on a Spanish-built Montessa-Honda.
2008 Honda builds its 200-millionth bike.
2010 The cutting-edge VFR1200F, featuring a push-button gear-change system is unveiled.

US-made Goldwing tourer featuring a huge six-cylinder, 1,520 cc engine ensured that Honda remained one of the world's leading manufacturers.

In 1991 the company mourned the passing of its founder, Soichiro Honda. Nevertheless, the expansion plans continued with initiatives to make inroads into the Chinese market and the introduction of class-leading products that included the RC45 superbike and the CBR900RR Fireblade, which redefined the sports bike through its exceptional power-to-weight ratio. Notable milestones were reached when the 20-millionth Super Cub model was manufactured, in 1992, and an impressive total of 100 million bikes had been produced by Honda by 1997.

The new millennium brought with it an exciting new racing V-twin, the SP-1, which secured the World Superbike Championship in its debut year of 2000, while Valentino Rossi took MotoGP titles in

Honda engine
This cutaway illustration of a Honda 750 cc K2 motorcycle engine shows its gearbox (bottom left) and clutch (bottom right). The four-cylinder, four-stroke engine is a single overhead camshaft type.

2002 and 2003. A continued dedication to overseas markets led to the opening of new plants in China and the expansion of operations in other parts of the world. With a raft of innovations, such as the world's first motorcycle airbag and investment in fuel-cell technology, the pioneering spirit of Soichiro Honda remains very much alive within the company.

MotoGP testing
Italian MotoGP rider Max Biaggi takes a curve on his Repsol-Honda motorbike during the official test session at Catalunya's racetrack, near Barcelona, Spain, in 2005.

Tourers

In the 1950s mature riders who were unconcerned by racer performance had a wide selection of comfortable, powerful, and practical machines to choose from. Built to provide smooth, quiet cruising, these bikes were used for weekend recreation as well as daily transport. Machines of 500 cc or more were often used to pull a sidecar for a partner or child.

▷ Watsonian JAP Combo 1950

Origin UK

Engine 996 cc, V-twin

Top speed 80 mph (129 km/h)

Ron Watson built Watsonian sidecars, and had this prototype motorcycle with a sturdy JAP engine made to haul them; but JAP declined production so this was the only example ever built.

△ Royal Enfield 500 Twin 1951

Origin UK

Engine 496 cc, in-line twin

Top speed 78 mph (126 km/h)

Built for comfort with excellent suspension for its time, the Enfield twin was a great touring bike that continued in production for 10 years.

▽ Royal Enfield Constellation Airflow 1959

Origin UK

Engine 692 cc, in-line twin

Top speed 100 mph (160 km/h)

At 700 cc the Constellation was the biggest parallel-twin in the market. This innovative "Airflow" version had an aerodynamic moulded fairing as well as a touring screen.

△ Ariel KH Hunter 1954

Origin UK

Engine 498 cc, in-line twin

Top speed 80 mph (129 km/h)

Ariel's first parallel twin engine was launched in 1948 and their updated KH Hunter with swinging arm suspension and an alloy cylinder head followed in 1954.

△ BSA A10 Golden Flash 1953

Origin UK

Engine 646 cc, in-line twin

Top speed 95 mph (153 km/h)

BSA followed rivals by enlarging its 500 to a 650 in 1950, targeting the US market. Flexible and strong, the Golden Flash was well able to haul a sidecar if required.

▽ Ariel Square Four MkII 1955

Origin UK

Engine 995 cc, Square Four

Top speed 100 mph (161 km/h)

This Ariel features the improved and final 1954 to 1959 version of their 1,000 cc Square Four. Its flexible engine pulled from 10 mph to 100 mph (16 km/h to 160 km/h) in top gear.

△ Hoffmann Gouverneur 1954

Origin Germany

Engine 248 cc, flat-twin

Top speed 70 mph (113 km/h)

Established in 1948, Hoffmann developed its own flat-twin, four-stroke engine for the Gouverneur, but it had problems with overheating. The company failed in 1954.

△ **Harley-Davidson FL Panhead 1955**

Origin USA

Engine 1,200 cc, V-twin

Top speed 95 mph (153 km/h)

Harley-Davidson's overhead-valve "Panhead" V-twin was introduced in 1948 and used until 1965. This FL tourer is in US police trim, carrying special equipment.

△ **Douglas Dragonfly 1955**

Origin UK

Engine 348 cc, flat-twin

Top speed 70 mph (113 km/h)

This last Douglas motorcycle to be made had a BMW-like flat-twin engine layout and shaft drive. It was smooth and comfortable but lacked power.

▷ **Vincent D Black Prince 1956**

Origin UK

Engine 998 cc, V-twin

Top speed 120 mph (193 km/h)

Last of the legendary Vincent V-twin motorcycles, the Black Prince boasted fully enveloping glassfibre bodywork. However, sales were poor and production ended after 1955.

△ **IFA BK350 1956**

Origin Germany

Engine 343 cc, flat-twin

Top speed 68 mph (109 km/h)

East German IFA's flat-twin, two-stroke had a low centre of gravity combined with a shaft drive and full suspension, which made this a comfortable touring machine.

△ **BMW R50 Combo 1957**

Origin Germany

Engine 494 cc, flat-twin

Top speed 72 mph (115 km/h)

The torque and flexibility of the R50's flat-twin made it a natural choice for pulling a sidecar. Germany's Steib unit shown here, matches the BMW's superior quality.

△ **Triumph Twenty-one 3TA 1958**

Origin UK

Engine 349 cc, in-line twin

Top speed 80 mph (129 km/h)

Perhaps with an eye on the success of scooters, Triumph introduced this middleweight bike with a rear enclosure that was nicknamed the "bathtub". It had relatively small 17-in (43-cm) wheels.

Flyweights

For the vast majority of people at the beginning of the 1950s, the only personal transport option was the bicycle. Many leapt at the option to motorize it for a relatively small outlay: adding a motorized rear wheel cost around £25. As the decade progressed, manufacturers – led by Italy and Japan – offered ever more integrated packages, and the moped was born.

△ **Triumph BDG 125 1950**

Origin Germany

Engine 123 cc, split-single-cylinder

Top speed 56 mph (90 km/h)

Made by Triumph Werke Nürnburg (TWN), this ultra lightweight featured a split single two-stroke engine with two pistons and one combustion chamber, as pioneered by DKW.

△ **Cyclemaster 1951**

Origin UK

Engine 32 cc, single-cylinder

Top speed 23 mph (37 km/h)

This pre-war German DKW design was built by EMI and sold as Cyclemaster in the UK from 1950; popular and easy to fit to any bicycle, it grew from 26 cc to 32 cc in 1951.

△ **Trojan Mini-Motor 1951**

Origin UK

Engine 50 cc, single-cylinder

Top speed 20 mph (32 km/h)

Designed in Italy in 1946 and made under licence in the UK by Trojan, the engine powered a bicycle via a roller onto the rear tyre.

▽ **Whizzer Pacemaker 1951**

Origin USA

Engine 199 cc, single-cylinder

Top speed 35 mph (56 km/h)

From the late 1930s, Whizzer built motorized bicycle kits for the US, with more power than those of its European counterparts. The Pacemaker was its first complete machine.

◁ **BSA Winged Wheel 1952**

Origin UK

Engine 35 cc, single-cylinder

Top speed 23 mph (37 km/h)

Attachable to any standard cycle frame (though BSA did make some frames of their own, with front suspension), the bicycle motor was soon superseded by the moped.

△ **Honda Cub Type F 1952**

Origin Japan

Engine 49 cc, single-cylinder

Top speed 22 mph (35 km/h)

Honda's first products were bicycle motors providing basic powered transport in postwar Japan. The company made 6,500 Cub kits per month in the early 1950s.

△ NSU Quickly N 1954

Origin Germany

Engine 49 cc, single-cylinder

Top speed 28 mph (45 km/h)

Half a million Quicklys were built from 1954 to 1958. It was one of the best mopeds with a pressed-steel backbone frame and forks, two gears, and a front suspension.

△ Honda Super Cub C100 1958

Origin Japan

Engine 49 cc, single-cylinder

Top speed 30 mph (48 km/h)

This brilliant design propelled Honda to success – the rider-friendly Cub four-stroke with an automatic clutch and plastic leg-shields was a massive seller in South East Asia.

△ Moto Guzzi Galletto 200 1958

Origin Italy

Engine 192 cc, single-cylinder

Top speed 55 mph (89 km/h)

The Galletto (cockerel) four-stroke scooter made from 1950 to 1958 had motorcycle-like stability, thanks to large wheels. A spare was mounted across the leg-shields.

△ New Hudson Autocycle 1957

Origin UK

Engine 98 cc, single-cylinder

Top speed 32 mph (51 km/h)

BSA acquired New Hudson during WWII and reintroduced the inexpensive Autocycle, updating it through the 1950s. A forerunner of the later mopeds, it survived until 1958.

UXG 567

△ Kreidler Florett K53M 1959

Origin Germany

Engine 49 cc, single-cylinder

Top speed 35 mph (56 km/h)

Kreidler began making small bikes in 1951 and by 1959 had cornered a third of the German motorcycle market with its powerful and well-built, full-suspension mopeds.

◁ Motom Super Sport 1958

Origin Italy

Engine 48 cc, single-cylinder

Top speed 50 mph (80 km/h)

Motom fitted a small yet powerful four-stroke engine in a pressed-steel frame with integral fuel tank to create one of the earliest sports mopeds.

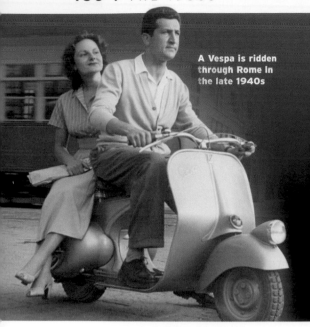

A Vespa is ridden through Rome in the late 1940s

Great Marques
The Vespa Story

Although it was born out of a need to provide a means of cheap travel in the impoverished post-war years, the Vespa became a style icon for the free-spirited, carefree, and fashion-conscious around the world. The scooter whose name means "wasp" in Italian created a buzz that none of its rivals could equal.

AFTER WORLD WAR II, with Italy crippled financially and physically in disarray, Enrico Piaggio needed to find a new purpose for his factory in the Tuscan town of Pontedera. The company he had inherited with his brother had produced boats, railway carriages, and, most notably, aircraft. Now they had to satisfy a consumer need for cut-price goods. Extensive bomb damage had left the country's roads pockmarked with craters, so Piaggio saw a gap in the market for a form of transport that would be able to negotiate the pitted road surfaces swiftly and safely. The new motorcycle was to be

Enrico Piaggio (1905-1965)

manoeuvrable, streamlined, and good value. But these considerations were not to be at the expense of style.

Piaggio did not like the first prototype, called the MP5, so he turned to Corradino D'Ascanio, an aeronautical engineer. D'Ascanio's initial standpoint for the design was his dislike of motorcycles; seeing them as cumbersome and ugly, D'Ascanio steered well clear of traditional production templates. In his design, he was "trying to build the machine as simply as possible".

Scooters had been made before, but not like this. The concealed engine was mounted above the rear wheel and the gear lever was incorporated into the handlebar. Influenced by his aeronautical background, D'Ascanio shaped the body from sheet metal. There was no drive chain because the rear wheel was powered from the transmission. Helped by the front splash guard, this made dirt-free riding a possibility. The famous step-though feature left the centre area of the bike free, which increased its appeal to women. The fact that the front and rear were linked by this slim middle section led Piaggio to compare the machine to a wasp, immediately renaming the MP6 prototype "Vespa".

However, acceptance was by no means immediate. In early 1946 journalists and the public alike were

intrigued but confused by the Vespa 98. Sales of the first 50 models were sluggish. With a top speed of 37 mph (60 km/h), it was slow to fire the imagination. But its combination of being relatively inexpensive (payment could be settled in instalments) but very stylish soon turned its fortunes round.

Sense of freedom
By the mid-1960s Vespa had established a strong identity as a manufacturer of stylish and fun scooters that were attractive to the youth market.

As early as 1947 a black-market trade to avoid waiting lists had built up. Between 1947 and 1950 Vespa sales rose dramatically – from 2,500 to 60,000. The money-can't-buy publicity through Vespas many appearances in films helped

Vespa GS

paradiso per due

Scooters for all
As this advertisement from the early 1960s highlights, Vespa was keen to promote the idea that its scooters were an object of desire for women as well as men.

125

VBB Sportique

ET3

LX 50

1946 On 23 April a patent is submitted for what would become the Vespa.
1948 The Vespa 125 is the first model to come with rear suspension.
1950 The Vespa 125 Corsa takes first and second at the Bologna Grand Prix.
1951 The Vespa Torpedo sets a record for the flying kilometre, covering the distance in just over 21 seconds at an average speed of 106.3 mph (171.1 km/h).
1952 Worldwide membership of the Vespa Club reaches 50,000.

1953 The brand is given a huge boost through exposure in the hit film *Roman Holiday*.
1954 The release of the Vespa 150 is a landmark for Piaggio and for scooters in general.
1956 The 1-millionth Vespa is sold, just a decade after the first model appeared.
1962 Surrealist artist Salvador Dalí customizes a Vespa belonging to two students in his own inimitable way.
1965 Enrico Piaggio dies.

1970 Regulations in France oblige the Vespa 50 to be fitted with pedals; the feature makes the model highly collectable.
1972 A first for Vespa: a 200 cc model, with electronic ignition to boot.
1977 The Vespa P125 X features a reworked front suspension and re-designed handlebars.
1985 The PX series is given a sporty makeover with the T5 Pole Position, which also has a revised rear end and a small windscreen at the front.

1991 The Vespa 50 Special Revival is released.
1996 The ET4 is fitted with a four-stroke engine; with the Vespa celebrating its half-century, total estimated sales now stand at 15 million.
2001 The ET2 and ET4 signal the reintroduction of the Vespa to North America after a gap of 20 years.
2003 The Granturismo (GTS) 125 and 200 come with 12-inch wheels.
2008 Piaggio releases the Vespa GTS 300 Super, the most powerful Vespa ever.

"It looks like a **wasp**!"

ENRICO PIAGGIO, ON SEEING THE VESPA PROTOTYPE

Cult exposure
Quadrophenia, the 1979 movie about British mods and rockers, reflected how the Vespa had become an emblem of the mod subculture in the 1960s.

to transform the brand into an international phenomenon. Defined by Gregory Peck and Audrey Hepburn zipping through the streets of the Eternal City in the 1953 film *Roman Holiday*, the Vespa became cinematic shorthand for cool. When ridden by a movie character, it conveyed youth and liberation. As Hollywood stars rode them both on and off screen, sales skyrocketed, and markets opened up across Europe and further afield, from South America to East Asia.

Although one-off models such as 1950's Montlhéry and the following year's Torpedo both set world speed records, power was never really the point of the single-cylinder, two-stroke Vespa. However, Enrico Piaggio took the step of discontinuing the 98 cc models at the close of 1947; the focus was now on 125 cc machines. In turn, these were followed in the mid-1950s by the Vespa 150 – the model regarded as perhaps the most striking production scooter ever. The GS version even broke the 60 mph (97 km/h) barrier.

The markets certainly responded, as seen in the early 1960s when the Vespa 50 proved irresistibly seductive to cost-conscious young riders. As the last Vespa designed by D'Ascanio, it marked the end of an era.

With total sales of the model having reached 3 million, it was a fitting way to bow out. However, that did not signal the end of Vespa innovation. For a time in the 1960s more Vespas were sold in the UK than in any other country. The swinging 60s would have been missing one of its major icons without this scooter. Into the 1970s the marque released the Vespa 200 Rally, which offered riders increased speed and electronic ignition.

In an era when the full-throated motorbikes coming out of Japan were presenting formidable challenges, Vespa countered with a more aggressive body design allied to greater engine performance figures. The T5 Pole Position of 1985 was a feisty and sporty addition, while in 1996 the traditionally two-stroke Vespa engine became a four-stroke operation with the ET4 125.

There was a damaging two-decade absence from the North American market from the early 1980s, but encouraging inroads first made by the ET series were followed by the GTS and LX. An updated and improved 2011 version of the PX, originally released three decades earlier, still maintained the importance of the Vespa tradition. As the British *Independent* newspaper stated in its review: "What you are getting is the classic scooter experience". As well as the marque re-establishing a US presence, financial concerns closer to home were taken care of by Roberto Colaninno, who assumed presidency of the Piaggio Group.

With a firm direction for the 21st century, Vespa remains beloved and, what is more, relevant, with urban parking an increasing problem and the Vespa's low running costs making more sense than ever. Not that enjoyment has been diminished in any way. Listen to Vespa owners and certain words crop up repeatedly: fun, lifestyle, and liberation. For this timeless scooter, trends are temporary, but class is permanent.

Useful Lightweights

Those who could afford a "proper" motorcycle in the 1950s expected something that was a definite cut above the basic bicycle-based transport of the past. Manufacturers responded with ever more comfort and sophistication, wrapped around small, mostly two-stroke engines of neater appearance. Unit construction arrived for engine and gearbox, full suspension became commonplace, and even electric gear selection was tried.

▷ **James Comet 1950**

Origin UK

Engine 98 cc, single-cylinder

Top speed 40 mph (64 km/h)

James's postwar bikes were two-stroke, Villiers-powered until AMC took over in 1951, substituting its own engines on all bikes except the Comet, which was made up to 1964.

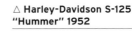

△ **NSU 251 OSL 1951**

Origin Germany

Engine 242 cc, single-cylinder

Top speed 65 mph (105 km/h)

Descended from a 1933 design used by wartime despatch riders, the lively, overhead-valve single would be superseded in 1953 by the more modern NSU Max.

▷ **Excelsior Skutabyk 1954**

Origin UK

Engine 98 cc, single-cylinder

Top speed 38 mph (61 km/h)

Looking like a half-hearted attempt to cash in on the scooter boom, this 100 cc motorcycle, clad with leg-shields and ungainly steel enclosures, did not sell.

△ **Harley-Davidson S-125 "Hummer" 1952**

Origin USA

Engine 123 cc, single-cylinder

Top speed 53 mph (85 km/h)

Harley-Davidson acquired the 125 cc DKW two-stroke engine design as part of war reparations, and used it in this novice bike, known as the Hummer from 1955.

▽ **Express Radex 200 1954**

Origin Germany

Engine 197 cc, single-cylinder

Top speed 67 mph (108 km/h)

This handy runabout was powered by a JLO engine. Along with a number of other German marques, Express was absorbed into the Zweirad Union motorcycle combine in 1957.

◁ **Victoria KR21 Swing 1956**

Origin Germany

Engine 199 cc, single-cylinder

Top speed 59 mph (95 km/h)

The technically advanced Swing's engine and transmission pivoted inside the frame, moving with the rear suspension. Electric gear changing was added from 1956.

▷ **MZ RT 125 1956**

Origin East Germany

Engine 123 cc, single-cylinder

Top speed 50 mph (80 km/h)

The original 1939 DKW 125 continued in production after WWII in the original factory in East Germany, where it became known as an MZ. This model was built up to 1965.

△ **DKW RT 175 VS 1957**

Origin Germany

Engine 174 cc, single-cylinder

Top speed 65 mph (105 km/h)

The company that made two-stroke motorcycles popular continued to build them after WWII. Upgraded front and rear suspension was added to the VS model in 1956.

◁ **BMW R26 1957**

Origin Germany

Engine 247 cc, single-cylinder

Top speed 80 mph (129 km/h)

BMW's luxury single was steadily updated from its introduction in 1948. By 1956 it had an enclosed driveshaft, swinging-arm rear suspension, and Earles forks.

△ **Simplex Servi-cycle 1957**

Origin USA

Engine 125 cc, single-cylinder

Top speed 40 mph (64 km/h)

Simplex improved its original 1935 direct-drive single with an automatic clutch and variable transmission. The two-stroke engine's rotary-valve helped it return 100 mpg (35 km/l).

△ **Velocette LE MkII 1958**

Origin UK

Engine 192 cc, flat-twin

Top speed 52 mph (84 km/h)

Conceived as transport for everyman, the LE had a silent, water-cooled engine, with a hand-starter in a sheet-steel frame. A large number were used as police patrol bikes.

▷ **BSA C15 1958**

Origin UK

Engine 249 cc, single-cylinder

Top speed 68 mph (109 km/h)

The C15's unit-construction engine was a cousin of the Triumph Tiger Cub. Stolid rather than exciting, it was extremely popular with learner motorcyclists in Britain.

Singles

The four-stroke single was the ideal machine for postwar Europe. It was economical and robust and suitable for touring, commuting, and, with minor modification, for racing, scrambles, or trials competition. In the 1950s most machines were based on successful pre-war designs, but were gradually re-styled and upgraded, with the addition of an improved suspension as the decade progressed. However, the arrival of faster and more luxurious twin-cylinder machines gradually overshadowed them.

◁ BSA Gold Star 1950
Origin UK
Engine 349 cc, ohv single-cylinder
Top speed 90 mph (145 km/h)

A tuned version of the standard BSA single, the Gold Star was a versatile, amateur competition bike or a road-going hot rod for tearaways.

▽ Gilera Saturno 1951
Origin Italy
Engine 498 cc, ohv single-cylinder
Top speed 85 mph (137 km/h)

The Saturno was a high-quality machine with the engine and gearbox in a unitary construction, and fitted with a unique rear-suspension system.

◁ Vincent Comet 1952
Origin UK
Engine 499 cc, ohv single-cylinder
Top speed 90 mph (145 km/h)

Vincent's single-cylinder models were as well engineered as the company's big twins, but lacked the impressive performance of the bigger machines.

▷ Moto Guzzi Falcone 1952
Origin Italy
Engine 498 cc, ohv single-cylinder
Top speed 84 mph (135 km/h)

The horizontal single-cylinder engine with an exposed flywheel used on the Falcone had been a feature on Guzzis since the first model in 1921.

△ Norton 30M International 1953
Origin UK
Engine 490 cc, ohc single-cylinder
Top speed 95 mph (153 km/h)

The final version of the International, now with the Featherbed frame, won the 1953 Isle of Man Senior Clubman's TT. It sold until 1957.

◁ **BSA B31 1956**

Origin	UK
Engine	348 cc, ohv single-cylinder
Top speed	70 mph (113 km/h)

BSA added a spring frame to its worthy ohv single in 1954; it made the bike more comfortable but increased weight and dulled performance.

△ **Ariel NH 350 Red Hunter 1955**

Origin	UK
Engine	346 cc, ohv single-cylinder
Top speed	70 mph (113 km/h)

Based on an engine introduced in 1925, the NH 350 evolved from a rigid-framed sportster to a trusty plodder over a long production run.

▽ **Horex Regina 1955**

Origin	Germany
Engine	342 cc, ohv single-cylinder
Top speed	75 mph (120 km/h)

The Regina was a popular machine in postwar Germany, featuring an enclosed final drive chain and a plunger rear suspension.

△ **Ariel HS Mk3 1957**

Origin	UK
Engine	499 cc, ohv single-cylinder
Top speed	85 mph (137 km/h)

A scrambler version of Ariel's 500 single, the HS had an alloy cylinder and other upgrades, but was still eclipsed by the BSA Gold Star.

◁ **Matchless G3LS 1955**

Origin	UK
Engine	348 cc, ohv single-cylinder
Top speed	70 mph (113 km/h)

The Matchless 350 was given a spring frame in 1949, and the distinctive shape of the suspension units gave it its "jam pot" nickname.

▽ **Velocette MAC 1958**

Origin	UK
Engine	349 cc, ohv single-cylinder
Top speed	80 mph (129 km/h)

Velocette did not rush to embrace change. The long-running MAC model got a sprung frame in 1953, but there were few other changes before production ended in 1960.

△ **Velocette Venom 1959**

Origin	Italy
Engine	499 cc, ohv single-cylinder
Top speed	100 mph (160 km/h)

The sporting version of the Velocette single had a mix of engineering quality and eccentricity that encouraged owners with similar values.

Vespa line-up, c.1955
Following its starring role in the Hollywood film *Roman Holiday*, the Vespa scooter became synonymous with style. As Vespas became increasingly popular with women, they began to figure prominently in Vespa advertisements.

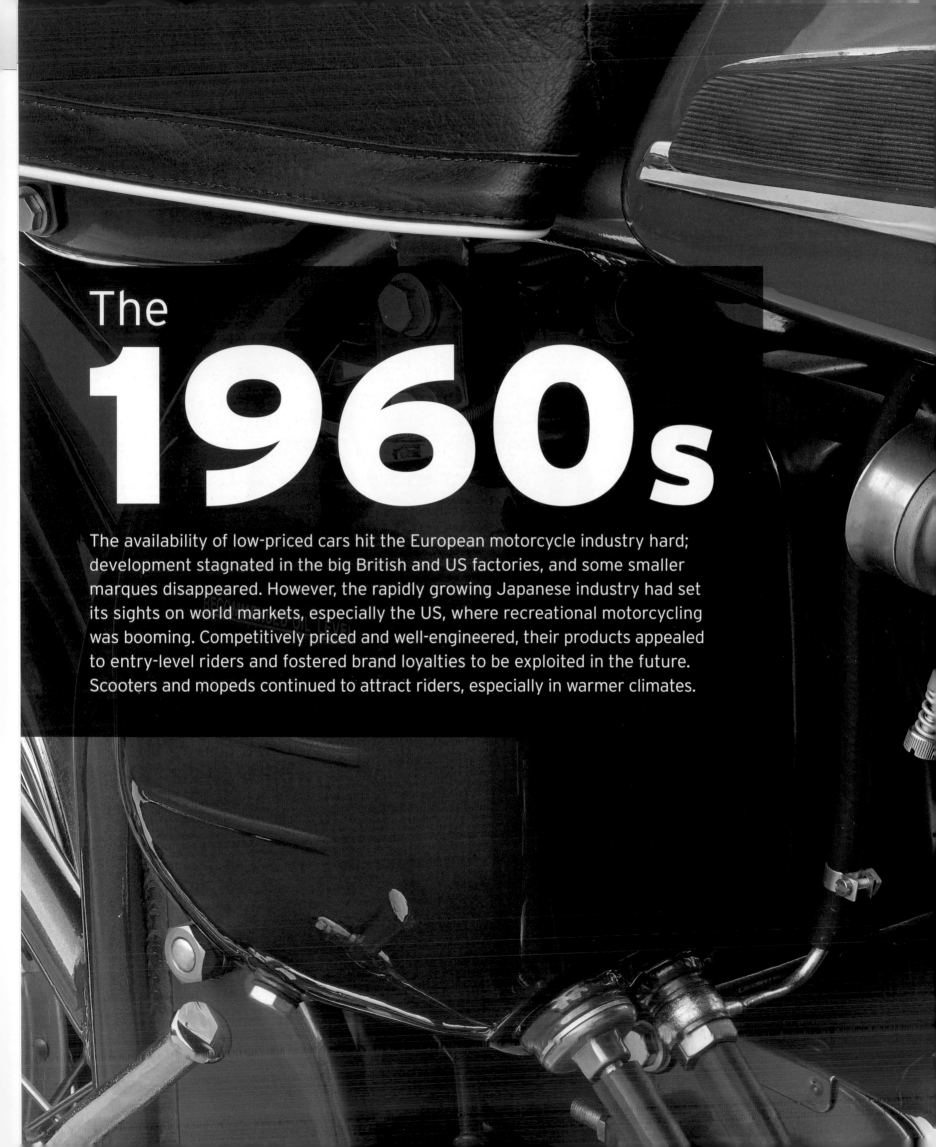

The 1960s

The availability of low-priced cars hit the European motorcycle industry hard; development stagnated in the big British and US factories, and some smaller marques disappeared. However, the rapidly growing Japanese industry had set its sights on world markets, especially the US, where recreational motorcycling was booming. Competitively priced and well-engineered, their products appealed to entry-level riders and fostered brand loyalties to be exploited in the future. Scooters and mopeds continued to attract riders, especially in warmer climates.

Roadburners

As cars became affordable and the world more prosperous in the 1960s, the motorcycle's role changed from essential transport to leisure and fun. America's post-war baby boomers wanted fast and stylish machinery, while Britain was in the grip of the speed-obsessed Café Racer craze. The arrival of Honda's sensational CB750 Four in 1969 signalled the end of the dominance of British marques.

◁ BSA Gold Star DBD34 1960

Origin UK

Engine 499 cc, single-cylinder

Top speed 110 mph (177 km/h)

Winner of 11 Clubman's TTs, the Gold Star single was a raw and aggressive, street-legal racer with its big Amal carburettor and alloy engine. Its passing in 1963 was mourned by many.

▷ Matchless G15 CSR 1965

Origin UK

Engine 745 cc, in-line two

Top speed 115 mph (185 km/h)

The ultimate sporting Matchless, with a twin carburettor Norton Atlas engine, swept-back exhausts, slim alloy mudguards, and dropped handlebars, was built up to 1968.

▷ BSA A65L Spitfire MkII 1966

Origin UK

Engine 654 cc, in-line two

Top speed 110 mph (177 km/h)

The super-sports version of BSA's biggest twin featured Amal GP track carburettors and a glassfibre fuel tank. A top speed of 120 mph (193 km/h) was claimed.

◁ BSA Rocket 3 A75 1970

Origin UK

Engine 740 cc, in-line three

Top speed 125 mph (200 km/h)

With its Triumph-derived aluminium triple engine, three Amal carburettors, and great handling, the showroom sales of Rocket 3 did not reflect its success on the track.

△ Indian Velocette 1969

Origin USA

Engine 499 cc, single-cylinder

Top speed 107 mph (172 km/h)

Floyd Clymer briefly revived the Indian brand in 1969. His 500 cc machine sported a single-cylinder British Velocette engine and an Italian frame. Just 200 were built.

▷ Royal Enfield Interceptor Series 1 1965

Origin UK

Engine 736 cc, in-line two

Top speed 115 mph (185 km/h)

The first British 750 cc twin – from one of the oldest makers – the beefy Interceptor was made in Series 1 form in 1962, and in final Series 2 guise from 1969 to 1970.

▷ Velocette Thruxton Venom 1967

Origin UK

Engine 499 cc, single-cylinder

Top speed 105 mph (169 km/h)

Velocette, another old British marque soon to be wiped away by Japanese innovation, built this powerful bike to win production races. It won an Isle of Man TT in 1967.

Grand Tourers

Affluent riders, preferred sophisticated high-status machines that were built for travelling at speed over long distances, rather than mere street-cruising or blasting from one café to the next. top choices included the stately 1.2-litre Harley Electra Glide V-twin, the exclusive and charismatic MV Agusta Four, and Germany's colossal and costly, high-velocity autobahn cruiser, the Münch Mammoth.

△ Harley-Davidson FLHB Electra Glide 1966

Origin USA

Engine 1,208 cc, V-twin

Top speed 80 mph (129 km/h)

The last of the legendary "Panhead" engined Harleys was the first to boast electric starting. Its large high-output battery is situated on the right side of the frame. In 1966 Harley-Davidson introduced the revised "shovelhead" engine, produced until 1984.

◁ **Norton Atlas
750SS 1962**

Origin UK

Engine 745 cc, in-line two

Top speed 119 mph (192 km/h)

Built for export, principally to the US, the Atlas suffered from vibration that was characteristic of a large two-cylinder engine. Yet it offered great performance and high-speed cruising.

△ **Triumph Bonneville T120R 1966**

Origin UK

Engine 649 cc, in-line twin

Top speed 110 mph (177 km/h)

Continuously improved, the Bonneville was reaching the peak of its form, and was in great demand worldwide. Versions produced from 1966 to 1970 are considered to be the best.

◁ **Norton Commando
Fastback 1969**

Origin UK

Engine 745 cc, in-line two

Top speed 120 mph (193 km/h)

With an ingenious new frame isolating the rider from the engine's inherent vibrations, the Commando was a great success despite its now aged engine design.

△ **Triumph Trident T150 1969**

Origin UK

Engine 740 cc, in-line three

Top speed 125 mph (200 km/h)

Triumph chose three-cylinders for its 750 cc flagship, to avoid twin-cylinder vibration. Although fast, Trident could not match the superior specification of the Honda CB750.

△ **Honda CB750 1969**

Origin Japan

Engine 736 cc, in-line four

Top speed 125 mph (200 km/h)

On this pioneering machine, Honda popularized the transverse in-line, overhead-cam, four-cylinder layout, together with the front disc brake, for the ultimate sports bike.

◁ **Münch Mammoth
4TTS 1967**

Origin Germany

Engine 1,177 cc, in-line four

Top speed 130 mph (209 km/h)

Friedl Münch built a gargantuan motorcycle with an NSU car engine (tuned to 88 bhp in TTS form) and many innovative details, such as the steel V-spoke rear wheel.

△ **MV Agusta 600 1968**

Origin Italy

Engine 592 cc, in-line four

Top speed 106 mph (170 km/h)

The first roadster four from the top 500 cc Grand Prix marque MV, the Agusta featured twin camshafts and disc front brakes. It had shaft final drive.

Triumph Bonneville

Marketed as "The Ultimate in Power", the Bonneville T120 was a landmark model from the golden era of British motorcycles. Unveiled in late 1958, the "Bonnie" featured an iconic 649 cc vertical-twin engine that made it the envy of rival manufacturers and one of the fastest production bikes in the world. Models such as the T120R were exported around the world, and by the time the original Bonneville ceased production in 1983, it had become a legend – the coolest sports motorcycle to come out of Britain.

IN 1956, A MOTORCYCLE powered by a Triumph engine broke the land speed record at the Bonneville Salt Flats, Utah, with Johnny Allen reaching a scorching 214 mph (345 km/h). The 650 cc twin-carb engine, designed by Edward Turner, Triumph's acclaimed design chief, would provide the basis for Britain's most celebrated motorcycle, while the site of the achievement would inspire its name: the Bonneville T120. First presented in 1958, the twin-carb T120 had strong acceleration and a top speed of around 115 mph (185 km/h). By the time the 1966 T120R model (shown) was released, the Bonnie was in huge demand in the UK and worldwide, particularly the US. During the 1960s, engine performance was sharpened and handling greatly improved. Into the '70s, the Bonneville held its own by rivalling Japanese products on roadholding, economy, and ease of maintenance. The old Triumph factory closed in 1983, but the marque was reborn with an all-new Bonneville in production since 2000.

FRONT VIEW

REAR VIEW

Germanic roots
The Triumph name was first used to sell motorbikes in 1902. An apparently thoroughbred English company, Triumph was actually founded in the 1880s by two Germans.

Rear mudguard in stainless steel

Rear suspension system is adjustable with Girling dampers

Dual seat with ample space for rider and pillion passenger

Chromed headlight accentuates sporty look

Fork protected by rubber gaiters

Front drum brake is 8 in (20 cm) in diameter

Engine and gearbox combined in one single unit

Ribbed tyre with dimensions of 3.25 x 19 in (8 x 48 cm)

SPECIFICATIONS

Model	Triumph Bonneville T120R (1966)	**Power output**	47 hp at 6,700 rpm
Assembly	Meriden, England	**Transmission**	Four-speed
Production	Not known	**Suspension**	Telescopic front forks, swingarm rear
Construction	Tubular steel cradle frame	**Brakes**	Drums, front and rear
Engine	649 cc, in-line twin-cylinder	**Maximum speed**	110 mph (177 km/h)

Original "Cool Brittania"

This US export version of the Bonneville had clean lines, a sleek fuel tank, and judicious use of chrome and polished stainless steel, all of which went towards making the Bonneville T120R a style icon that reflected Britain's position at the centre of the Swinging Sixties. Despite being basically a 1930s design, the engine had the gutsy performance needed to make the T120 the most sensational ride of its time.

THE BIKE

"Think of a superlative, double it… but no, don't even try. Words alone cannot describe the Bonneville T120", ran a gushing review in *The Motor Cycle* magazine in 1964. A fine handler by 1966, the T120R's frame and suspension were much improved over the original and just as handy for city jaunts as for reaching breathtaking speeds on the open road. A redesign for 1970 misfired, but after the "Bonnie" grew to 750cc it recovered to survive into the 1980s as a versatile sports tourer.

1. New badge design for 1966 **2.** Engine cut-out button **3.** Fuel filler cap **4.** Chrome headlamp **5.** Rear brake light mechanism **6.** Girling rear shock **7.** Rev-counter and speedometer **8.** Hinged seat release **9.** Front brake drum **10.** Decal guide on oil tank **11.** Ammeter **12.** Rod-operated rear brake **13.** Lights switch and ignition **14.** Air filter **15.** Kick-starter **16.** Rear lamp **17.** Exhaust with silencer

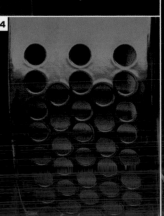

THE ENGINE

The Bonneville's twin-carburettor, overhead-valve power plant was constantly refined during the model's lifetime. Featuring a cast-iron barrel, high-compression pistons, and dry-sump lubrication, the engine was adapted to a combined engine-gearbox unit construction in 1963, with better engine performance on the 1966 T120R.

18. Engine and gearbox are single unit 19. Rocker box oil feed 20. Finned exhaust clamps 21. Rev-counter drive 22. Amal Monobloc carburettor with integral floatbowl

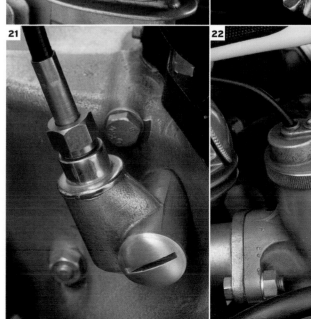

Youth Appeal

The light and lively end of the market saw the greatest change in the 1960s. The decade started with easy-to-handle but unsophisticated, mostly British bikes, and ended with the market awash with highly developed Japanese bikes with features like gearboxes with up to six gears and push-button starting. They outshone offerings from British and US marques, which failed to keep pace.

△ Honda C77 Dream 300 1961
Origin Japan
Engine 305 cc, in-line two
Top speed 88 mph (142 km/h)

First released in 1956 but redesigned for 1960, the Dream was a high-specification, well-equipped bike that looked rather expensive alongside more basic machines.

△ FB Mondial 48 Sport 1960
Origin Italy
Engine 48 cc, single-cylinder
Top speed 45 mph (72 km/h)

Mondial's racy 50 cc model was aimed at enthusiastic young riders. This type of machine's popularity was reflected by the 1962 launch of a 50 cc Grand Prix class.

△ Honda CB92 Benly Super Sports 1961
Origin Japan
Engine 124 cc, in-line two
Top speed 70 mph (113 km/h)

The fastest 125 of its day, this model was a great standard bearer for Japan's motorcycling industry. The little CB92's ruggedly made overhead-camshaft engine revved to more than 10,000 rpm.

△ Honda CB72 Dream 1961
Origin Japan
Engine 247 cc, in-line two
Top speed 80 mph (129 km/h)

Honda favoured pressed-steel frames that used the power unit as a stressed member, leading link front forks, and styling that looked slightly odd to Western eyes. Noted for its quality engineering, this model sold well.

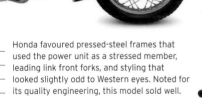

△ Harley-Davidson Sprint H 1962
Origin USA/Italy
Engine 246 cc, single-cylinder
Top speed 76 mph (122 km/h)

Made in Italy by Aermacchi, the Sprint singles filled the gap in Harley's model line that was being exploited by Japanese imports. A 350 cc bike was introduced for 1969.

◁ Harley-Davidson BTH Bobcat 1966
Origin USA
Engine 175 cc, single-cylinder
Top speed 60 mph (97 km/h)

The Bobcat was descended from the earlier Hummer two-stroke and this final version was unusually styled with an ABS moulded fuel tank and tailpiece.

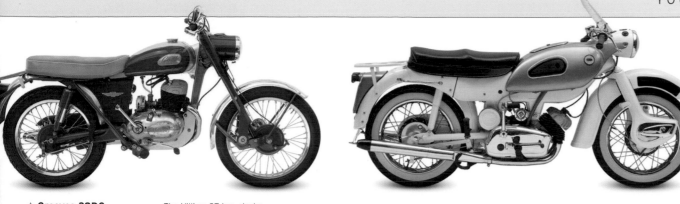

◁ **Ariel Arrow Super Sports 1963**

Origin UK

Engine 249 cc, in-line two

Top speed 78 mph (126 km/h)

Sales resistance to their all-enclosed "Leader" model led Ariel to market the Arrow. A fine handler, this bike was also speedy in its "Golden Arrow" Super Sport form.

△ **Greeves 32DC Sports Twin 1961**

Origin UK

Engine 322 cc, in-line two

Top speed 70 mph (113 km/h)

The Villiers 3T two-stroke engine powered the biggest roadster made by Greeves, a small factory with a great reputation for trials and motocross machinery.

△ **Ducati 250 Mach I 1964**

Origin Italy

Engine 249 cc, single-cylinder

Top speed 100 mph (160 km/h)

A milestone in Ducati history, this was the first roadgoing 250 to top 100 mph (160 km/h), given the right gearing. In race form, it gave Mike Rogers victory in the 1969 Isle of Man Production 250 cc TT.

▷ **Bridgestone Hurricane 1968**

Origin Japan

Engine 177 cc, in-line two

Top speed 70 mph (113 km/h)

A high-quality two-stroke with rotary inlet valves and hard-plated cylinder bores, the Hurricane is seen here in the street scrambler guise. After 1968 Bridgestone only made tyres.

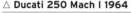

△ **Suzuki TC250 1968**

Origin Japan

Engine 247 cc, in-line two

Top speed 90 mph (145 km/h)

Suzuki's X6 Hustler (or T20 Super Six) of 1966 was the world's first production six-speed motorcycle. This voguish TC250 street scrambler version has upswept exhausts.

Suzuki TC250

Suzuki had already set pulses racing in late 1965 with the launch of the T20 Super Six - the machine that was to form the basis of the TC250. From their first appearance in 1952, Suzuki motorcycles were known for their dependable, solid build, rather than for their blistering performance. The T20 and the stylish TC250 "street scrambler" version, available from 1967 to 1969, changed all that. Featuring technology straight from world-class-winning Grand Prix racers, these machines were a total sensation.

IN THE DAYS WHEN a five-speed gearbox was a rarity and something to shout about, the six-speeder featured on the T20 Super Six, and then on the TC250 series, was almost beyond imagination. The 250 cc Suzukis offered riders such a range of new experiences that they catapulted a reliable, but previously rather unexciting, firm into the consciousness of biking enthusiasts everywhere. With UK learners restricted to 250 cc bikes, a sporty T20 Suzuki was at the top of the wish list of every bike-mad 16 year old.

The TC250 version of the bike was aimed squarely at the US market. Europeans tended to equate performance with low handlebars and swept-back exhausts, but in the US high handlebars and upswept exhausts denoted power and the TC250's amended design reflected this preference. Its street scrambler styling had wide appeal among American teens, and also the power and drive to impress a wider audience because of its 30 hp engine – one hp more than the machine that spawned it.

FRONT VIEW

REAR VIEW

Making a name
Founder Michio Suzuki gave his name to the company. The stylized "S" graced the products from Hamamatsu from 1952 and continues to do so to this day.

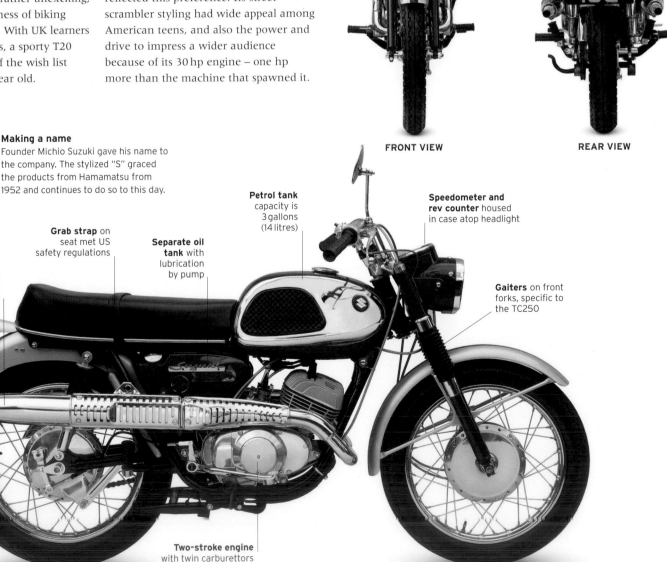

Petrol tank capacity is 3 gallons (14 litres)

Speedometer and rev counter housed in case atop headlight

Grab strap on seat met US safety regulations

Separate oil tank with lubrication by pump

Exhaust system is high rise on the TC250

Gaiters on front forks, specific to the TC250

Two-stroke engine with twin carburettors

SPECIFICATIONS

Model	TC250 (1968)
Assembly	Hamamatsu, Japan
Production	Not known
Construction	Twin-shock cradle frame
Engine	247 cc, two-stroke twin
Power output	29 hp at 7,500 rpm
Transmission	In-unit six-speed
Suspension	Telescopic forks front, twin-shock rear
Brakes	Drums, front and rear
Maximum speed	90 mph (145 km/h)

Japan on the rise
In many ways the TC250 epitomizes the extraordinary progress Japanese companies were making in the 1960s. With a ridiculously high specification and performance for its time, it signalled that the Japanese were not just serious contenders, but were also on their way to domination of the motorcycle industry.

THE BIKE

The TC250, or Scrambler as it was known in the US, used the more powerful engine from the Japanese market "super sports" T21. It came fitted with a raised exhaust, gaitered forks, and deep-treaded tyres, making it appear suitable for light off-road use. In truth, these extra features were little more than a styling exercise and certainly not a serious tool for keen fans of the rough stuff. A so-called GT kit, which consisted of a different petrol tank and seat, fitted by dealers on request, was also available.

1. Tank badge 2. Side panel script 3. Steering damper knob 4. Ignition key slot on headlamp 5. Combined instruments 6. Horseshoe headlamp 7. Fork gaiter 8. Oil tank cap 9. Gearbox oil filler 10. Fuel level indicator 11. Front brake operation 12. Kick-starter 13. Rear sprocket 14. Rear lamp 15. Tyre inflator 16. Silencer outlet

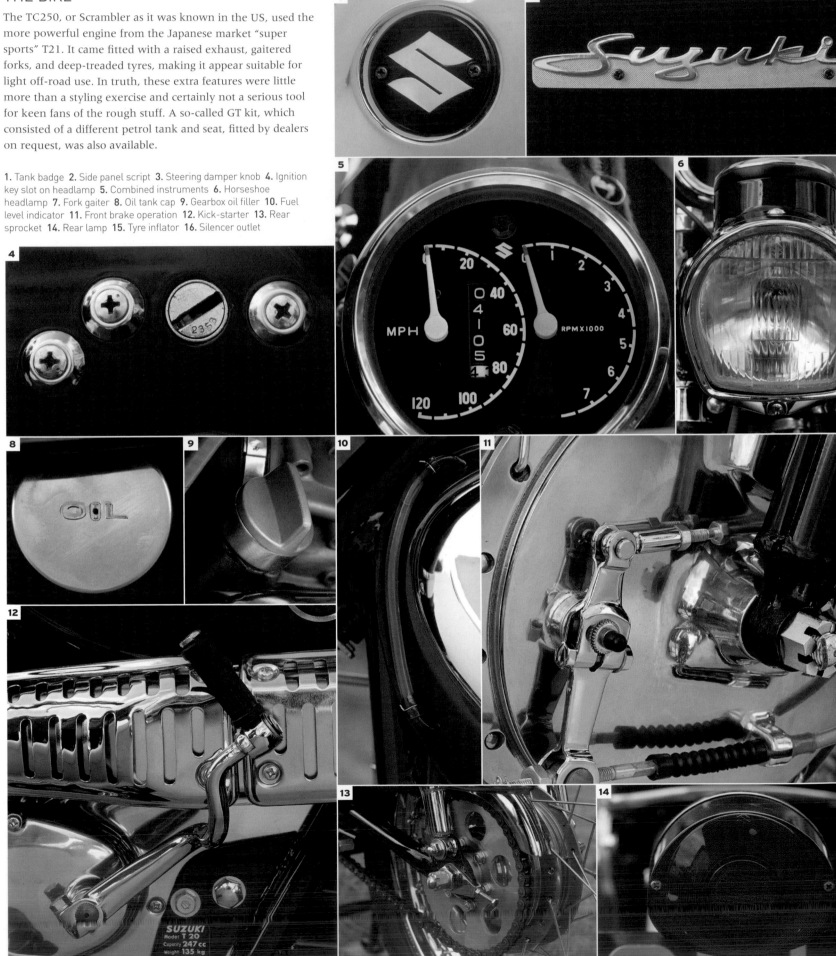

THE ENGINE

The TC250 used the T20's twin-cylinder, two-stroke, 250 cc engine. At first glance, the engine appeared to be simply a development of its forerunner, the T10; however, all that remained from the earlier version was the horizontally split crankcases, inclined cylinders (the heads and barrels remained separate), and the outer covers for the primary drive and generator. Of square dimensions (54 mm bore and stroke, which gave a capacity of 247 cc), the engine was reckoned to make 29 hp at 7,500 rpm. These were outstanding figures for the time and meant that the TC250 was able to comfortably outperform most machines twice its size – and some that were three times its capacity.

17. View of engine showing deep cylinder fins **18.** Upswept exhaust
19. Fuel tap **20.** Carburettor with cold-start lever

Scooters and Mopeds

In the 1960s scooters became lighter and more sophisticated, as riders – often women – sought machines that demanded less physical effort to lift, start, and ride. Increasingly, two-wheelers were used instead of cars for short journeys, shopping, or just for fun, especially in countries and regions with a warm, dry climate. Mopeds were ideal for teenagers seeking freedom through mobility.

△ Lambretta Li 125 1960

Origin Italy

Engine 123 cc, single-cylinder

Top speed 43 mph (69 km/h)

Stylish and excellent value for money, the Series 2 Li 125 and 150 had a faired-in headlight and larger carburettor to help maintain Lambretta's worldwide sales supremacy.

△ Honda Juno M85 1962

Origin Japan

Engine 169 cc, flat-twin

Top speed 62 mph (100 km/h)

Only made for one year the Juno was an innovative steel monocoque scooter with an exposed flat-twin engine and variable hydraulic mechanical transmission.

▽ Mustang Thoroughbred 1962

Origin USA

Engine 320 cc, single-cylinder

Top speed 60 mph (97 km/h)

Built by a war-time aircraft manufacturer in California, the Mustang had a basic side-valve engine but, on this model, a swingarm rear suspension and four-speed transmission.

△ Lambretta Li 150 Series III 1963

Origin Italy

Engine 148 cc, single-cylinder

Top speed 58 mph (93 km/h)

Innocenti updated a proven product by re-shaping the bodywork for 1963. The Series III Lambretta, known as the "Slimstyle" because it was sleeker and narrower than before, enjoyed strong sales worldwide.

△ Honda 50 Super Cub 1963

Origin Japan

Engine 49 cc, single-cylinder

Top speed 45 mph (72 km/h)

Still going strong, the sturdy Honda 50 step-thru was well on its way to becoming the world's best-selling vehicle, with more than 60 million built.

◁ Vespa VBB Sportique 1963

Origin Italy

Engine 150 cc, single-cylinder

Top speed 50 mph (80 km/h)

The VBB brought four gears to Vespa's smaller scooters for the first time to create one of the most usable classic scooters, with extremely durable running gear.

▷ Vespa GS160 1963

Origin Italy

Engine 159 cc, single-cylinder

Top speed 62 mph (100 km/h)

The Vespa, with its pressed-steel unitary construction (no frame) was designed to get Italy mobile again after WWII. This Gran Sport (GS) was the luxury sporting model.

△ **Triumph Tina 1964**

Origin UK

Engine 99 cc, single-cylinder

Top speed 45 mph (72 km/h)

BSA Triumph expected big sales for this belt-drive, automatic transmission scooter, promoted by British singer Cliff Richard, but its dated appearance meant sales were poor.

△ **NSU Quickly S2/23 1964**

Origin Germany

Engine 49 cc, single-cylinder

Top speed 27 mph (43 km/h)

Built from 1953 to 1963, the NSU Quickly was a simple yet attractive moped with a distinctive pressed-steel frame and two gears (three on this updated model); nearly a million were sold.

△ **Harley-Davidson AH Topper Scooter 1964**

Origin USA

Engine 164 cc, single-cylinder

Top speed 40 mph (64 km/h)

Harley's Topper had little in common with other scooters; the horizontal two-stroke engine drove through an advanced, continuously variable transmission.

◁ **Raleigh RM5 Supermatic 1964**

Origin UK

Engine 50 cc, single-cylinder

Top speed 30 mph (48 km/h)

Cycle-maker Raleigh began selling mopeds in 1958 and had a range of 10 mopeds by the mid-1960s; the RM5 was a Motobécane built under licence.

▷ **Agrati Capri Scooter 1966**

Origin Italy

Engine 78 cc, single-cylinder

Top speed 45 mph (72 km/h)

The Agrati cycle group owned Garelli, which produced the engine for this attractive but very conventional scooter, sold with 50 cc, 70 cc, 80 cc, or 98 cc two-stroke engines.

▽ **Vespa Allstate Cruisaire 1964**

Origin Italy

Engine 123 cc, single-cylinder

Top speed 47 mph (76 km/h)

The mail-order catalogue shop Sears sold Vespas badged "Allstate" in huge numbers in the US. These had a lower specification (for example, no front dampers) than the normal Vespas.

△ **Clark Scamp 1968**

Origin UK

Engine 50 cc, single-cylinder

Top speed 30 mph (48 km/h)

A clever adaptation of a small-wheeled bicycle, this was made by a mast-maker on the Isle of Wight. Production was halted by a court case with the engine designer.

▽ **Motobécane Mobylette 1968**

Origin France

Engine 50 cc, single-cylinder

Top speed 40 mph (64 km/h)

France's largest motorcycle-maker sold 14 million Mobylettes over 48 years, starting from 1948. "La Bleue" was a simple, reliable, motorized yet sophisticated model for the 1960s.

Count Domenico Agusta in 1949 with a rider on one of the marque's 125cc racers

Great Marques
The MV Agusta Story

The Italian MV Agusta company initially made its name as a manufacturer of innovative, low-capacity motorcycles in the years following World War II. After diversifying into larger models, the marque achieved legendary status in Grand Prix racing. Production ceased in the 1970s, but MV Agusta was resurrected in the 1990s.

MV AGUSTA'S ORIGINS date back to 1910, when Count Giovanni Agusta first set up his aircraft manufacturing company in the Lombardy region of northern Italy. The count's death in 1927 forced his wife, Giuseppina, and son, Domenico, to take up the reins during a decline in the aeronautical industry. Their decision to venture into motorcycle manufacture would lead to the formation of one of the world's most respected marques.

Development of the first model, a 98cc two-stroke, was halted by the outbreak of war, but resumed in 1945 when Count Domenico Agusta set up Meccanica Verghera (MV) – named for the region of Lombardy where the bikes were made. His plan to market the debut bike as the Vespa 98 failed when rival Piaggio used the name first, so in the autumn of 1945 it was unveiled as simply the 98. The next year MV Agusta entered the racing arena with almost instant success on the track and the first of many wins on the hallowed Monza circuit.

By the end of the decade, the 98 had been supplemented, and then replaced, by 125cc and

MV Agusta badge
(introduced late 1940s)

250cc models. In the 1950s MV Agusta achieved memorable racing success through the use of advanced components on bikes such as the 175 CSS. The knock-on effect was increased demand for the marque's road models, with standout machines such as the 125 Motore Lundo – then considered one of the finest sports motorcycles on the market – boosting the company's growing reputation both at home and abroad.

The company ethos of applying creative solutions at every level was reflected in the

two-seater 83 model from 1956. The marque also showed a willingness to experiment with new technology, such as fuel injection and hydraulic gears on a series of prototypes. In 1959 this pioneering approach resulted in an advanced new lubrication system, which was later adopted on MV Agusta's whole range of bikes. By increasing engine reliability to a level never previously seen, it

enabled the company to offer impressive 100,000km warranties on its powerplants.

The 1960s and early 1970s saw MV Agusta in its prime on the Grand Prix motorcycle circuit. Count Agusta's

Race legend
Among the many iconic riders for MV Agusta was John Surtees, who became world champion. The Englishman is pictured in 1956 breaking the lap record at Crystal Palace on a 250cc MV Agusta.

125 Turismo

600

Ipotesi Sport

910S Brutale

1945 The MV Agusta company is formed by Count Domenico Agusta.

1947 The Luxury 98cc and 250cc 4T models are presented at the Milan Salon.

1950 The 125 Motor Lungo model is unveiled, and goes on to become a class-leading sports bike.

1953 MV Agusta builds a new plant in Spain specifically for the assembly of export models; the 175 CSS model debuts.

1956 MV Agusta wins the 125cc, 250cc, and 500cc world championships.

1958 The marque's racing team wins 63 out of 76 races between now and 1960.

1966 The three-cylinder 500cc model is unveiled, ridden to Grand Prix victory for several years by Giacomo Agostini.

1967 The four-stroke, four-cylinder 600 bike debuts with front disc brakes.

1969 The 250B model is introduced.

1969 The 350B Sport machine is unveiled.

1971 Count Domenico Agusta passes away.

1975 The 750 Sport America is unveiled, a powerful bike aimed at the US market.

1976 This is the last year that MV Agusta competes in Grand Prix racing. Giacomo Agostini takes the team's final 500cc win at the Nürburgring.

1980 A slump in the late 1970s means that by this time the production of motorcycles has ceased.

1986 MV Agusta Grand Prix machinery is dispersed among American and Italian collectors.

1992 Claudio Castiglioni's Cagiva Group buys the MV Agusta trademark.

1997 The F4 is the first new model from the new MV Agusta company.

2008 The MV Agusta wins the Italian Superbike Championship.

2010 Having bought the MV Agusta company two years previously, Harley-Davidson now sells the company back to Claudio Castiglioni again.

2011 MV Agusta announces the release of the F4 RR Coscacorta superbike, featuring ultra-lightweight materials and 200+hp performance.

Model swansong
The 125 Sport from 1975 was one of MV Agusta's final new models before the company went out of business at the end of the decade.

obsession with securing competition success led him to hire the world's finest engineers and riders. With rivals Gilera and Moto Guzzi out of Grand Prix racing, the marque's silver and red bikes won the World Championship in the 500cc class for 17 consecutive years from

strong by broadening its line-up. Competition triumphs continued into the 1970s, but MV Agusta now faced dark times, with competition from Japanese imports flooding the market,

but also around the world. However, in 1992, after sinking into obscurity, the MV Agusta name was revived when the Italian Cagiva Group bought the company trademark. Cagiva's finest engineers were tasked with building a new model that would incorporate innovative features in the tradition of the original company.

Unveiled in 1997, the resulting 750cc F4 model immediately won over fans and journalists with its classic MV Agusta silver and red livery, plus futuristic technological components such as removable transmission. Sporting a carbon frame and achieving astonishing performance figures of

close to 186mph (300km/h), it was a worthy machine to resurrect the iconic racing marque. Originally available in a limited edition of 300 Gold Series bikes, this was a model for wealthy motorcycle aficionados.

The F4 was received so positively that Cagiva went on to create the more affordable F45 variant. Over the next few years the company introduced an expanded line-up of sports bikes under the MV Agusta name, including the Brutale. In 2005 the Tamburini 1000 model was released in recognition of motorcycle designer Massimo Tamburini, and it was regarded by many critics as the finest sports bike in the world.

A series of changes in the ownership of MV Agusta through the 2000s have not prevented the marque's resurgence, and a return to competition has delighted fans who remember when MV Agusta's unbeatable Grand Prix bikes were the finest racing machines for a generation.

"MV Agusta offered me the chance to ride some beautiful machines, some of the best I ever rode."

GIACOMO AGOSTINI, ITALIAN RIDER FOR MV AGUSTA FROM 1966 TO 1972

1958 to 1974. The winning riders included legends such as John Surtees, Mike Hailwood, and Giacomo Agostini (who alone won seven titles in a row).

The wide range of road models on offer from MV Agusta during the 1960s included several that benefited from racing technology; in particular the four-cylinder 600, from which the blisteringly fast 750S America developed, as well as smaller offerings like the long-running 50cc Liberty. In a period when sales were generally in decline in the face of competition from cheaper cars, the marque skilfully found a way of remaining

and the death of Count Agusta in 1971. The result was a change in direction, with new owners EFIM phasing out the marque's racing programme to save costs. But this wasn't enough to prevent the motorcycle side of Agusta from falling into rapid decline, and production ceased by 1980. The loss of such a prestigious marque was felt by motorcycle enthusiasts not just in Italy,

Powerful new machines
Unveiled in 1997 the 750cc F4 was the first new model from the rejuvenated MV Agusta marque. Initially released in limited edition, it was expanded to a full range into the 2000s.

Willing Workers

For some workers and businesses in the 1960s, motorcycles still represented the most practical and cost-effective means of transport, either for getting to and from work or for police duties or transporting tools for the breakdown services. Machines ranged from simple commuter or learner bikes to heavy-duty, powerful-engined bikes that could haul sidecars.

▷ **James L25 Commodore 1960**

Origin UK

Engine 249 cc, single-cylinder

Top speed 65 mph (105 km/h)

An attractive economy ride, the Commodore was unfortunately let down by the poor design of its two-stroke engine, made by AMC the company that had owned James since 1951.

▽ **BSA M21 1960**

Origin UK

Engine 591 cc, single-cylinder

Top speed 63 mph (101 km/h)

Developed from BSA's WWII military bike, the M21 with its big, lazy, side-valve engine was used by the UK's Automobile Association to haul a sidecar full of tools and spares.

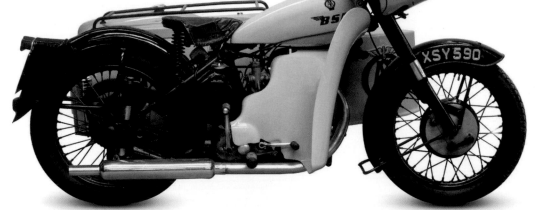

△ **BSA Bantam D10 1967**

Origin UK

Engine 173 cc, single-cylinder

Top speed 65 mph (105 km/h)

By the 1960s, Bantams sported a two-stroke 175cc engine and a four-speed gearbox. They remained a firm favourite with UK novices and commuters.

▷ **Allstate Compact 1961**

Origin Austria

Engine 60 cc, single-cylinder

Top speed 44 mph (71 km/h)

"More sizzle than a schnitzel" ran the US advertising for the Allstate Compact, an Austrian Puch D60 sold under its own name by the US retail giant Sears from 1961 to 1963.

◁ **Norton Model 50 1963**

Origin UK

Engine 348 cc, single-cylinder

Top speed 75 mph (120 km/h)

Introduced in 1956, the Model 50 was based on a prewar design, used Norton's "Featherbed" frame from 1959 but it was a gentle, traditional British bike.

△ **Royal Enfield Bullet 1962**

Origin UK

Engine 499 cc, single-cylinder

Top speed 90 mph (145 km/h)

Virtually unaltered since 1948, this 500 cc version of the long-running Bullet slogger, in its final British form, boasted coil ignition and a big long-haul fuel tank.

▷ **Velocette Vogue 1964**

Origin UK

Engine 192 cc, flat-two

Top speed 55 mph (89 km/h)

With a water-cooled engine and an all-enveloping glassfibre bodywork, the Vogue was aimed at the scooter market, but was expensive and slow. Fewer than 400 were sold.

△ **Triumph 6TP "Saint" 1966**

Origin UK

Engine 649 cc, in-line two

Top speed 100 mph (160 km/h)

Triumph's machine, supplied to British police fleets for pursuit duties, was based on the 650 cc Thunderbird tourer. Said to "Stop Anything In No Time", it became known as the "Saint".

◁ Honda CL90 Scrambler 1967

Origin Japan

Engine 90 cc, single-cylinder

Top speed 59 mph (95 km/h)

A rugged little bike with a punchy, overhead-camshaft engine and full road equipment, the CL90 was a fashionable street scrambler, rather than a serious off-roader.

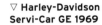

◁ Honda CD175 1967

Origin Japan

Engine 174 cc, in-line two

Top speed 78 mph (126 km/h)

Quieter and more comfortable than most of the competition, the "touring" CD175 offered an attractive combination of a lively, overhead-camshaft engine and effective silencing.

△ Suzuki M15 1969

Origin Japan

Engine 49 cc, single-cylinder

Top speed 35 mph (56 km/h)

Suzuki's practical and comfortable baby motorcycle with a two-stroke 49 cc engine, twin seat, and full mudguards introduced many young riders to motorcycling.

▷ MZ ETS/2 Trophy 1969

Origin East Germany

Engine 243 cc, single-cylinder

Top speed 78 mph (126 km/h)

Simple, soundly built, and cheaper than any other 250 when new, the ES250 found a ready market among those not concerned with its looks.

▽ Harley-Davidson Servi-Car GE 1969

Origin USA

Engine 740 cc, V-twin

Top speed 63 mph (101 km/h)

Made from 1932 to 1973, the three-wheeler utilitarian Servi-Car, with its side-valve engine and a reverse gear, had many uses, including police work.

Easy Rider, 1969
The customized choppers ridden by Peter Fonda and Dennis Hopper in the film *Easy Rider* were based on Harley-Davidson Hydra-Glides. The sense of wanderlust inspired by this film made the chopper style extremely popular.

Tourers

When speed was not a priority, there were plenty of luxurious touring bikes on offer, with BMW's horizontally opposed, twin-cylinder machines pre-eminent for reliability, smooth-running, and comfort. While British marques mostly offered dressed-up 1950s or even 1940s designs, Japanese motorcycles showed their hand in the touring market too – their reliability and low maintenance were a big plus for long-distance riders.

▽ **Harley-Davidson FLH Duo-Glide 1960**

Origin USA

Engine 1,213 cc, V-twin

Top speed 100 mph (160 km/h)

Harley's big tourer finally received swinging-arm rear suspension in 1958, and a new name to advertise this: Duo-Glide. Many were fitted with touring accessories.

▽ **Triumph Thunderbird 1960**

Origin UK

Engine 649 cc, in-line twin

Top speed 98 mph (158 km/h)

The successful 1946 Thunderbird entered the 1960s with a new duplex tube frame and stylish rear skirt. It was now regarded as a touring, not performance, machine.

▽ **Norton Dominator 99 De Luxe 1960**

Origin UK

Engine 597 cc, in-line twin

Top speed 100 mph (160 km/h)

For 1960 Norton updated the Dominator range with narrower top frame tubes for improved comfort, and offered semi-enclosed bodywork on De Luxe models.

◁ **Norton Navigator 1963**

Origin UK

Engine 349 cc, in-line twin

Top speed 82 mph (132 km/h)

Norton's Jubilee grew up in 1960, with a completely revised and enlarged engine, heavier forks, and a bigger front brake; with minor changes it could reach 100 mph (160 km/h).

△ **Allstate 250 "Twingle" 1965**

Origin Austria/USA

Engine 248 cc, split single-cylinder

Top speed 69 mph (111 km/h)

The Puch SGS250, sold under licence by Sears, was nicknamed the "Twingle" due to its unusual double-piston, two-stroke system. It was made up to 1970.

△ **BMW R60/2 1965**

Origin Germany

Engine 594 cc, flat-twin

Top speed 80 mph (129 km/h)

Designed principally for sidecar hauling, over 20,000 R60s were built from 1956 to 1969. Smooth and sturdily built, they proved ideal long-distance touring machines.

◁ **Honda CB450 1965**

Origin Japan

Engine 444 cc, in-line twin

Top speed 110 mph (177 km/h)

With double overhead camshafts, torsion bar valve springs, and electric starting, this Honda showed the quality of engineering that would make Japanese bikes pre-eminent.

△ **BMW R75/5 1969**

Origin Germany

Engine 749 cc, flat-twin

Top speed 110 mph (177 km/h)

BMW reinvented its R Series, adding 12-volt electrics, electric starting, telescopic forks, and better brakes to make a versatile touring bike, not just a sidecar hauler.

◁ **Kawasaki W1 1965**

Origin Japan

Engine 624 cc, in-line twin

Top speed 108 mph (174 km/h)

Developed from a 1950s BSA design that Kawasaki acquired with the Meguro company, the W1 was aimed at export markets, especially the US, but it was outdated.

▽ **Gilera 124 Speciale Strada 1966**

Origin Italy

Engine 124 cc, single-cylinder

Top speed 70 mph (113 km/h)

Gilera built small-engined motorcycles with big performance and its 124 cc single was sold in the US by Sears, as well as in Europe. Piaggio bought Gilera in 1969.

△ **Moto Guzzi V7 Special 1969**

Origin Italy

Engine 757 cc, V-twin

Top speed 115 mph (185 km/h)

Designed by Giulio Carcano to win a contest to be the new Italian police bike, the sturdy, shaft-drive V-twin would become Moto Guzzi's staple into the 2000s.

The first Suzuki Isle of Man TT team, in 1960

Great Marques
The Suzuki Story

Suzuki began production almost 50 years after other manufacturers, but quickly became one of the world's leading motorcycle makers. A consistent technological flair has kept it ahead of its competitors, and the marque's production models have benefitted from many notable competition successes in several racing disciplines.

NOW A GLOBAL CORPORATION

producing everything from motorcycles to cars and outboard motors to quad bikes, Suzuki had its origins in textiles. In 1909 Michio Suzuki set up the Suzuki Loom Works in the Japanese town of Hamamatsu. The Suzuki Loom Manufacturing Company, established in 1920, built first an apparatus for weaving cotton, and later, silk. Over the next few decades the venture became a major success.

After a break from production during World War II, the immediate postwar period saw the company suffer financially, which led to the decision to diversify. Seeing an opening in the market for cheap personal transportation in a country whose infrastructure had largely been destroyed, in 1947 Suzuki began testing out motors attached to bicycles.

In 1952 the 36 cc Power Free became the debut offering from what was still Suzuki Loom Manufacturing.

Suzuki logo
(introduced 1958)

Featuring an intuitive motor drive system, the two-stroke, air-cooled motorized bicycle attracted numerous plaudits, and the following year was joined by the larger-capacity Diamond Free. Demand for the new model rocketed after its class success in the Mount Fuji Hill Climb event, and the firm was soon manufacturing 6,000 units a month.

The company's name was changed to Suzuki Motor Company in 1954, but it would be a few years until models carried the Suzuki name. From 1954 the business introduced a series of genuine motorcycles – rather than bicycles with engines – using the name Colleda (meaning "This is it!"). The first was the CO, a steel-framed four-stroke of 125 cc. By the time an electric starter was introduced on the Colleda Twin at the end of the decade, the Suzuki "S" logo had been adopted and the marque was forging an identity as a two-stroke specialist.

Grand tourers
First presented in the early 1970s, Suzuki's GT range featured two-strokes from 125 cc to 750 cc, with one, two, and three cylinders.

Early in the 1960s Suzuki gained international recognition after winning the 50 cc class at the 1961 Isle of Man TT races, and reigned as 50 cc World Champions from 1962 until 1967. Meanwhile, an expansion in overseas operations led to the US Suzuki Corporation being set up in Los Angeles in 1963 to sell machines directly to the North American market. Among these was the X6 Hustler (T20 Super Six in Europe) from 1965, billed as the world's fastest 250 cc motorcycle. Its innovative features included a tubular-steel cradle frame and six-speed transmission. Exceptionally popular around the world, it was joined three years later by the T500, which was the largest-capacity two-stroke bike on the market and capable of 112 mph (180 km/h) performance.

By the 1970s export markets were at the fore of Suzuki's business, and the company's first overseas manufacturing plant had been built in Thailand. This was also a decade of notable

Factory gates
Rows of Suzuki models are lined up outside the company's headquarters in Hamamatsu City, Japan, in 1967. Today, the city is home to six plants.

TC250

GS750

RG500

Hayabusa GSX 1300R

1909 Michio Suzuki founds the Suzuki Loom Works in Hamamatsu, Japan.	**1965** The T-20 model is unveiled as the world's fastest 250 cc production bike.	**1976** The four-stroke GS Series is introduced, first with the 250 cc, 400 cc, and 750 cc.	**1999** The Hayabusa 1300, the world's fastest production bike, is launched; the total

1909 Michio Suzuki founds the Suzuki Loom Works in Hamamatsu, Japan.
1920 The Suzuki Loom Manufacturing Company is formed; this date is seen as the birth of the motor company.
1952 Suzuki enters the motorcycle market with the 36 cc Power Free model.
1954 Formation of the Suzuki Motor Company.
1958 The "S" logo is used for the first time on Suzuki's motorcycles.
1962 Suzuki wins its first TT race and the inaugural 50 cc World Championship.

1965 The T-20 model is unveiled as the world's fastest 250 cc production bike.
1966 The Suzuki company flag and official song are introduced.
1967 The first Suzuki motorcycles to be made outside Japan are built at a plant in Thailand.
1971 The GT750 two-stroke model, featuring a novel three-cylinder engine, is introduced.
1974 The RE-5 becomes the first Japanese motorcycle with a rotary engine.

1976 The four-stroke GS Series is introduced, first with the 250 cc, 400 cc, and 750 cc.
1980 GSX models are released, sporting a range of engines from 250 cc to 750 cc.
1982 The Love model is unveiled, the first of several 50 cc scooters in the 1980s.
1993 Suzuki makes a landmark deal to produce motorcycles in China; Kevin Schwantz wins the 500 cc World Championship for Suzuki.
1996 The first Suzuki motorcycles are built in Vietnam.

1999 The Hayabusa 1300, the world's fastest production bike, is launched; the total number of Suzuki motorcycle sales reaches 40 million.
2002 The Burgman 650 debuts as the largest-capacity scooter on the market.
2006 The M109R model is released, with a 1,783 cc engine that features the largest pistons in any production motorcycle or car.
2007 The B-King is unveiled as the marque's flagship "naked" (non-faired) bike.

racing success as Suzuki took World Championship titles in top categories, including the 250 cc Road title and the 125 cc and 500 cc Motocross titles. Arguably the greatest wins were in the 500 cc category, in which British rider Barry Sheene became World Champion in 1976 and 1977.

New road models in the 1970s included the marque's first four-stroke, four-cylinder bikes in the GS series, which was launched in a range of capacities, including up to 1,000 cc. Experimentation led Suzuki to develop a rotary-engined machine – the RE-5 – in the mid-1970s, though ultimately it was a commercial failure.

The 1980s and '90s were a period of Grand Prix glory for Suzuki as it won the 500 cc World Championship once more. New machines were introduced, among them several scooters, class-leading motocross bikes, and the pioneering GSX Series, which included the top-spec 1,100 cc Katana designed for overseas markets.

The company also agreed deals with China to initially export bikes and then to set up manufacturing plants in the country. This was another example of Suzuki's successful ongoing overseas expansion; by 1995 20 million motorcycles had sold outside Japan.

In 1999 Suzuki introduced the Hayabusa 1300 – a lean, aerodynamic sports bike for riders keen to push the limits; its top speed of just over 186 mph (300 km/h) made it the world's fastest road bike at the time.

Into the first decade of 2000 Suzuki strengthened its position further through tie-ins with General Motors and a deal with fellow Japanese motorcycle manufacturer Kawasaki.

"... I felt tremendous pressure as well as pride, in the unified Suzuki spirit... "

MITSUO ITO, ONLY JAPANESE RIDER TO WIN THE ISLE OF MAN TT

In the 2000s novel products set new standards across various market sectors. The GSX-R1000 of 2001 combined fine handling, light weight, and great fuel-injected performance in a world-beating track bike, while the Burgman 650 redefined the scooter, with its massive 650 cc engine and pioneering transmission system with one manual and two automatic modes.

With strong worldwide sales, Suzuki maintains its reputation for solid growth. With a futuristic fuel-cell scooter released in 2011, a raft of futuristic prototypes, and dedication to investing in alternative technologies, this famous marque with its forward-thinking ethos remains at the fore.

Superbike winners
Suzukis pictured in action during a superbike event in 2005, the year when the manufacturer won both the Riders' (with Troy Corser) and Constructors' Superbike World Championships.

Built for Speed

An explosion of advanced technology occurred in racing as the main Japanese contenders vied with each other in the World Championships. Honda, the four-stroke maker who had led the way in 1960, was under attack from Suzuki and Yamaha's ever-more-powerful two-strokes. Some European factories were in contention, however, while the US stuck with its own multi-disciplinary championships.

▽ Harley-Davidson KR 750 1961

Origin USA

Engine 744 cc, V-twin

Top speed 110 mph (177 km/h)

Despite an archaic side-valve engine, the KR was the one to beat on the US flat-track ovals. Tarmac versions with brakes like this could hit 150 mph (241 km/h) with fairings fitted.

▷ Norton Manx Norton 30M 1962

Origin UK

Engine 499 cc, single-cylinder

Top speed 135 mph (217 km/h)

While no match for multi-cylinder machines, the Manx was still a strong grid presence in 1960s racing, the final most refined edition being sold in 1962.

▽ Honda RC163 1962

Origin Japan

Engine 249 cc, in-line four

Top speed 136 mph (219 km/h)

With four cylinders, twin camshafts, and 16 tiny valves, the Honda won all nine 250 cc Grands Prix in 1962. Jim Redman, winner of six, became champion.

◁ Kreidler Renn-Florett 1963

Origin Germany

Engine 50 cc, single-cylinder

Top speed 100 mph (160 km/h)

Moped-maker Kreidler contested early 50 cc World Championships with tiny 12-speed two-strokes developed to a high pitch. They won seven Grands Prix in 1962 and 1963.

DIY Winners

Even though well-funded, factory-run works teams now dominated mainstream motorcycle racing, there was still scope for individuals to show their engineering prowess in sidecar road racing, record attempts, and drag racing. This produced some of the most dramatic-looking and wildly engineered machines of the decade, such as the supercharged Sprint winning Vincent "Methamon", drag racer "Mighty Mouse", and Tom Kirby's BSA sidecar.

▷ Vincent Sprinter Methamon 1962

Origin UK

Engine 1,148 cc, V-twin

Top speed 150 mph (241 km/h)

Maurice Brierley's supercharged sidecar unit set world records two-up in 1964 and averaged 100 mph (161 km/h) on the standing start km; its name meant "methanol burning monster".

△ Yamaha RD05 1965
Origin Japan
Engine 249 cc, V4
Top speed 135 mph (217 km/h)

Giving a phenomenal 200 hp per litre, Yamaha's water-cooled, twin crankshaft, disc-valve, two-stroke V4 engine took Phil Read to World Championship victory in 1968.

△ MZ RE125 1965
Origin East Germany
Engine 123 cc, single-cylinder
Top speed 120 mph (193 km/h)

Despite small budgets, MZ had pioneered disc valves in the 1950s and remained competitive in the smaller classes through the 1960s.

△ Harley-Davidson CRTT 1967
Origin USA
Engine 250 cc, single-cylinder
Top speed 100 mph (161 km/h)

The Italian-designed single was a leading privateer machine in Europe's 250 cc and 350 cc classes. Part ownership of Aermacchi meant it was also raced in the US.

△ Suzuki GP RT63 1963
Origin Japan
Engine 124 cc, in-line two
Top speed 115 mph (185 km/h)

Suzuki's early successes were in the 50 cc and 125 cc classes. The little RT63 twin took Hugh Anderson to a world title in 1963.

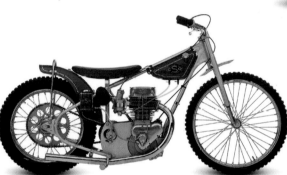

△ ESO Speedway DT-5 1966
Origin Czechoslovakia
Engine 497 cc, single-cylinder
Top speed 90 mph (145 km/h)

Top choice for hectic methanol-fuelled Speedway racing on cinder ovals in the 1960s. By 1966 Eso had been absorbed by the bigger Jawa company.

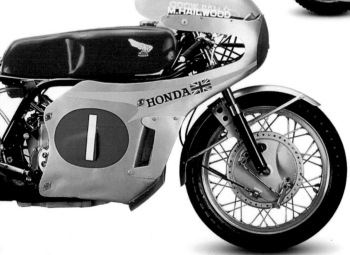

◁ Honda RC166 1966
Origin Japan
Engine 249 cc, in-line six
Top speed 150 mph (241 km/h)

Honda's deafening 18,000 rpm six-cylinder engines represented the ultimate in 1960s racing development. They took Mike Hailwood to two 250 cc and one 350 cc world titles.

△ Suzuki XR05 TR500 1969
Origin Japan
Engine 493 cc, in-line two
Top speed 147 mph (237 km/h)

Suzuki's first 500 had an air-cooled engine based on the T500 roadster. Its first victory was at Sears Point, USA, in 1969 with Art Baumann aboard.

▷ Vincent Mighty Mouse 1966
Origin UK
Engine 498 cc, single-cylinder
Top speed 160 mph (257 km/h)

Drag raced by builder Brian Chapman with a supercharged 500 cc Vincent engine, "Mighty Mouse" ran the world's first 500 cc sub-nine second ¼-mile (400m) at Santa Pod, UK in 1977.

◁ Kirby BSA sidecar outfit 1968
Origin UK
Engine 750 cc, in-line twin
Top speed 150 mph (241 km/h)

Ridden by Terry Vinicombe and John Flaxman, this machine won the 1968 Isle of Man 750 cc Sidecar TT. Sponsored by Tom Kirby, it was the last British outfit to win a TT for 18 years.

Rough Riders

Several factors stimulated the development of off-road motorcycles during the 1960s. Motocross circuit racing was booming at both international and grass-roots level. Cross-country scrambles held in the deserts of Western US were attracting huge entries and there was a demand for more refined machinery to ride in observed trials. Non-competitive trail riding was also becoming very popular.

△ **Greeves Hawkstone 1961**

Origin	UK
Engine	249 cc, in-line two
Top speed	70 mph (113 km/h)

Villiers single- or twin-engined scrambling bikes from the small British manufacturer Greeves had many wins including Dave Bickers' 1960 and 1961 250 cc Motocross World Championships.

△ **Husqvarna 250 1963**

Origin	Sweden
Engine	250 cc, single-cylinder
Top speed	75 mph (120 km/h)

Better known for chainsaws, Husqvarna has made motorcycles since 1903. Their custom-built 250 cc and 500 cc competition bikes won many scramble titles in the 1960s.

△ **Rokon Trail-breaker 1963**

Origin	USA
Engine	134 cc, single-cylinder
Top speed	20 mph (32 km/h)

The only all-wheel drive motorcycle to enter production – invented by Charlie Fehn of California in 1958 – is the Rokon. It was designed for low-speed use on rough terrain.

△ **Honda CL72 Scrambler 1964**

Origin	Japan
Engine	247 cc, in-line two
Top speed	75 mph (120 km/h)

Honda entered the scrambling market with a variant of the CB72 roadster. The bike had lower gearing, a cradle frame, and high exhausts, but no starter motor.

◁ **Velocette MSS Scrambler 1963**

Origin	UK
Engine	499 cc, single-cylinder
Top speed	82 mph (132 km/h)

Heavy despite a purpose-built and all-alloy engine, The MSS Scrambler was a solid, dependable, cross-country competition machine, but seldom a winner.

△ **Bultaco Sherpa T 1964**

Origin	Spain
Engine	244 cc, single-cylinder
Top speed	75 mph (120 km/h)

Bultaco worked with Irish Trials supremo Sammy Miller to develop an agile two-stroke that changed the face of trials overnight, giving Bultaco many wins from 1965.

◁ **Dot Demon 1965**

Origin UK

Engine 250 cc, single-cylinder

Top speed 75 mph (121 km/h)

Dot of Manchester increasingly specialized in scramble/motocross bikes during the 1950s and often won UK under 250 cc classes with the Demon.

◁ **Rickman Metisse MK3 Scrambler 1965**

Origin UK

Engine Triumph 490 cc, in-line two

Top speed 85 mph (137 km/h)

Derek and Ron Rickman made scramble bikes from 1960, supplying them as kits for buyers to fit their own engines. They proved to be very successful motocross machines.

▽ **Triumph Bonneville TT Special 1966**

Origin UK

Engine 649 cc, in-line two

Top speed 120 mph (193 km/h)

The Bonneville TT Special was sold in the US with a tuned engine and minus road equipment such as lights, ready for scrambles and dirt-track racing.

△ **BSA Victor Enduro 1967**

Origin UK

Engine 441 cc, single-cylinder

Top speed 85 mph (137 km/h)

The 1964–65 motocross world championship winners inspired BSA to market the Victor in full-race Grand Prix form and as this road-legal Enduro model.

◁ **Yamaha DT-1 1968**

Origin Japan

Engine 246 cc, single-cylinder

Top speed 80 mph (129 km/h)

Yamaha spotted an untapped market for a mass-production dual-purpose on/off road bike in the US. Selling well, it resulted in a line of Yamaha DT models.

△ **Yamaha YR2-C Grand Prix 1968**

Origin Japan

Engine 348 cc, in-line two

Top speed 100 mph (160 km/h)

The YR1 of 1967 was Yamaha's first 350, closely followed by the 110 mph (177 km/h) YR2. This YR2-C is the dual-purpose scrambler version, which offered moderate off-road capability.

△ **Norton P11A Ranger 1968**

Origin UK

Engine 745 cc, in-line twin

Top speed 115 mph (185 km/h)

Using the powerful Atlas engine in a light Matchless frame, the P11 was built for the growing US sport of desert racing. This P11A is the road-legal model.

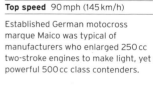

◁ **Maico MC30 1969**

Origin Germany

Engine 352 cc

Top speed 90 mph (145 km/h)

Established German motocross marque Maico was typical of manufacturers who enlarged 250 cc two-stroke engines to make light, yet powerful 500 cc class contenders.

▷ **AJS Stormer 1969**

Origin UK

Engine 247 cc, single-cylinder

Top speed 75 mph (120 km/h)

First sold in kit form, the successful Stormer resulted from AJS and Villiers coming under joint ownership from 1966. It later spawned a 410cc version.

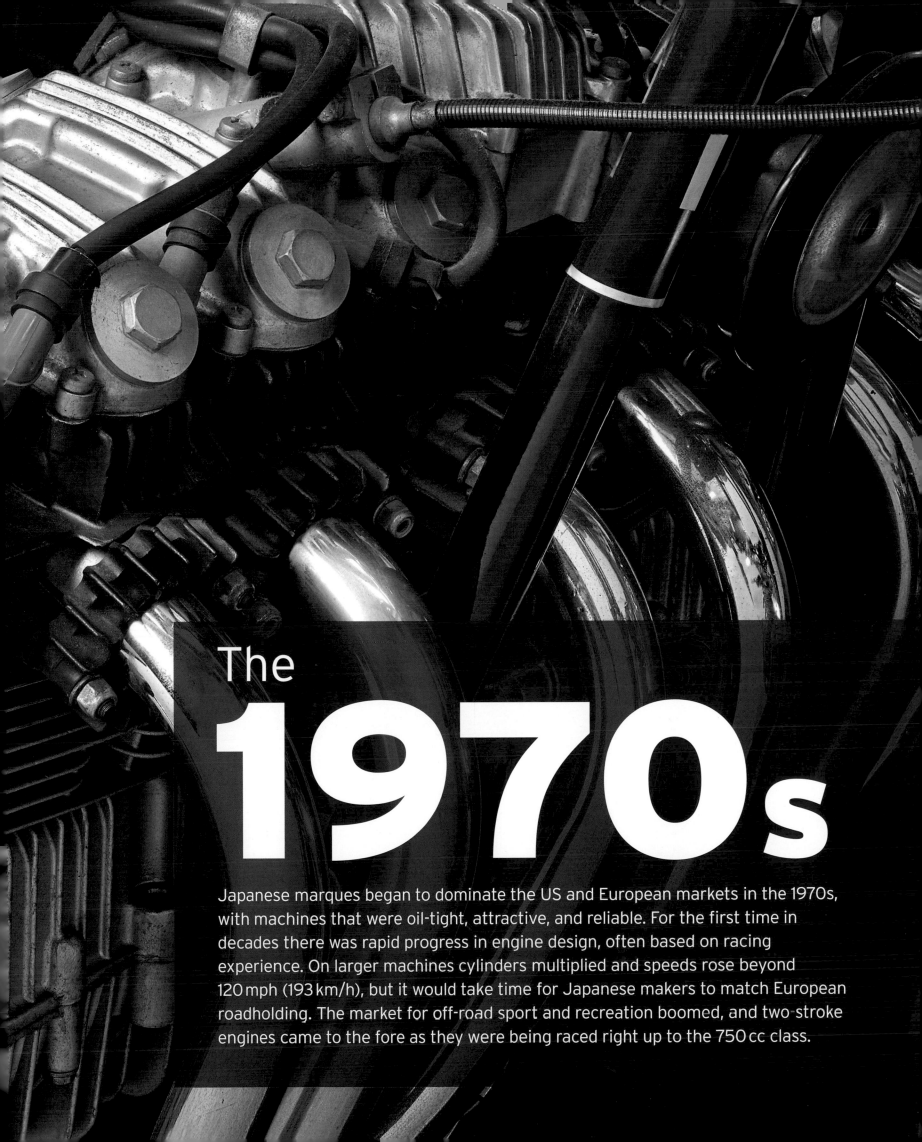

The 1970s

Japanese marques began to dominate the US and European markets in the 1970s, with machines that were oil-tight, attractive, and reliable. For the first time in decades there was rapid progress in engine design, often based on racing experience. On larger machines cylinders multiplied and speeds rose beyond 120 mph (193 km/h), but it would take time for Japanese makers to match European roadholding. The market for off-road sport and recreation boomed, and two-stroke engines came to the fore as they were being raced right up to the 750 cc class.

Superbikes

Led by Honda's launch of the 125 mph (201 km/h) four-cylinder CB750, a new generation of glamorous high-performance machines transformed the motorcycling scene in the 1970s. The term "superbike" was coined to describe these exciting new motorcycles that mostly came from Japan and Italy. Having set the pace for so long, the antiquated the British industry was being eclipsed.

△ Honda Goldwing GL1000 1975

Origin Japan

Engine 999 cc, flat-four

Top speed 125 mph (201 km/h)

Advanced automotive technology made the Goldwing a sophisticated, powerful, and heavy machine that became the definitive touring motorcycle.

△ Honda CB750 1970

Origin Japan

Engine 736 cc, in-line four

Top speed 125 mph (201 km/h)

This was the first superbike: Honda changed the face of sports bikes in 1969 with its overhead-camshaft four-cylinder engine, disc brake, and refined details.

△ Laverda 750SF2 1974

Origin Italy

Engine 744 cc, ohc parallel-twin

Top speed 118 mph (190 km/h)

Laverda's first large-capacity bikes were sturdily built overhead-camshaft twins with inclined cylinders. The SF sport versions handled well and were successful in Endurance races.

△ Kawasaki Z1 1973

Origin Japan

Engine 903 cc, in-line four

Top speed 135 mph (217 km/h)

The double overhead-camshaft Z1 was immensely powerful, good looking, and affordable. Handling was not first-rate but the engine was raced successfully.

◁ Ducati 750 Sport 1973

Origin Italy

Engine 747 cc, ohc V-twin

Top speed 122 mph (196 km/h)

Based on Ducati's proven singles, this sleek bike was an elemental sporting mount built for speed, not comfort. It revived interest in V-twin engines.

△ **MV Agusta Sport America 1975**
Origin Italy
Engine 789 cc, in-line four
Top speed 120 mph (193 km/h)

MV's uprated shaft-drive 750S four had a bigger engine and had twin disc brakes in the front. As its name implies, this machine was aimed directly at the US market .

△ **MV Agusta 750S 1972**
Origin Italy
Engine 743 cc, dohc in-line
Top speed 115 mph (185 km/h)

This famous Grand Prix marque based its four-cylinder road bikes on racer technology, but fitted shaft drive. The machines were expensive and consequently very rare.

◁ **Kawasaki H2C 1975**
Origin Japan
Engine 748 cc, three-cylinder
Top speed 126 mph (203 km/h)

This Mach IV was the most powerful of Kawasaki's charismatic, high-performance two-strokes, which were killed off by increasingly stringent emissions controls.

△ **Rickman Enfield Metisse 1974**
Origin UK
Engine 736 cc, ohv parallel-twin
Top speed 110 mph (177 km/h)

Using 750 cc Royal Enfield engines in a chassis of their own construction, the Rickman brothers built a limited number of the Metisse bikes.

△ **Moto Guzzi V7 Sport 1972**
Origin Italy
Engine 748 cc, ohv V-twin
Top speed 120 mph (193 km/h)

Guzzi's rugged V-twin engine and shaft drive were ideal for touring bikes, but they were also used successfully in sports machines like this V7 Sport.

△ **Moto Guzzi Le Mans MkI 1976**
Origin Italy
Engine 844 cc, ohv V-twin
Top speed 132 mph (212 km/h)

Developed from the earlier V7 Sport, the capacity of the Le Mans was increased to 844 cc and it was fitted with disc brakes featuring linked operation.

Honda CB750

The original superbike, the Honda CB750, was a landmark motorcycle, influencing the future of large-capacity bikes like no other model. Honda combined a powerful four-cylinder engine with features usually only available as extras, all for a competitive price. Launched in 1969, the CB750 heralded the arrival of Japanese manufacturers in the big-bike market, and initiated a seismic shift in the design, efficiency, and production of large-capacity bikes.

HONDA ALREADY had a reputation for manufacturing motorcycles on a grand scale, with its 1958 50 cc Cub proving an instant worldwide hit. But by the late 1960s the Japanese marque had yet to produce a large-capacity model for export. Drawn to the big-bike market in the US, Honda set about developing a machine that could break into a sector traditionally dominated by US and British marques. The result – the CB750 – was a total revelation. Never before had a standard road machine offered such a specification: an overhead-camshaft four-cylinder engine, five speeds, electric starting, and the first hydraulic disc front brake on a production motorcycle. Suddenly BSA, Triumph, and Harley-Davidson products looked outdated. Motorcycling was transformed. The big, fast Honda set new standards for power, reliability, and sophistication, and threw down the gauntlet to other Japanese manufacturers.

FRONT VIEW   **REAR VIEW**

Rapid growth
Named after its founder, Soichiro Honda, the Honda Motor Company came into being in 1948. Early Honda logos were always accompanied by an illustration of wings - symbolic of the classical winged goddess of Victory. By 1963 the Honda name was internationally known.

Fuel tank design is traditional yet stylish

Engine rev-counter and speedometer angled to be easy to read at speed

Mudguards are chrome, which is also used on other detailing

Deep-padded seat can accommodate rider and pillion

Four carburettors supply fuel-air mixture to the engine

Exhaust system is four-into-four with megaphone silencers

Stopping power
For big-bike owners used to relying on drum brakes for stopping power, the CB750's hydraulic front disc was revolutionary. It provided safe, judder-free deceleration from the bike's high top speeds, with the disc's performance unaffected by water or dirt. From 1975, the model received a disc brake at the rear as well.

SPECIFICATIONS	
Model	Honda CB750 (1970)
Assembly	Hamamatsu/Suzuka, Japan
Production	Not known
Construction	Tubular-steel cradle frame
Engine	736 cc, in-line four
Power output	67 hp at 8,500 rpm
Transmission	Five-speed
Suspension	Telescopic front forks, swingarm rear
Brakes	Disc front, drum rear
Maximum speed	Over 125 mph (201 km/h)

THE BIKE

"Speak to the wind. And listen to the answer. Freedom!" Honda's marketing team promoted this new machine as a bike that broke boundaries. The CB750, originally called the Dream Four, boasted a dazzling array of refinements, while retaining well-proven conventional features, including a cradle frame, telescopic front forks and twin-shock, swingarm rear suspension. The CB750 was the bike that changed the face of motorcycling, crushing the British competition along the way.

1. Tank script **2.** Fork gaiters **3.** Side reflector **4.** Honda wing badge on side panel **5.** Handlebar switchgear **6.** Front brake lever **7.** Front brake disc **8.** Rear shock **9.** 140 mph (225 km/h) speedometer **10.** Passenger footrest **11.** Kick-starter provides back-up **12.** Front wheel hub cone **13.** Exhaust outlets

THE ENGINE

The CB750 was powered by the world's first mass-produced transverse four-cylinder engine, developed using Honda's Grand Prix racing experience. The fuel/air mixture was supplied by four carburettors, and the overhead-cam, four-stroke, 736 cc power plant was smooth and powerful with an exciting tone from the exhaust.

14. Overhead-camshaft engine **15.** Choke lever on carburettor **16.** Alternator beneath circular cover **17.** Chromed exhaust pipes

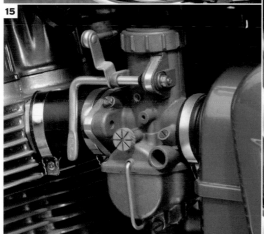

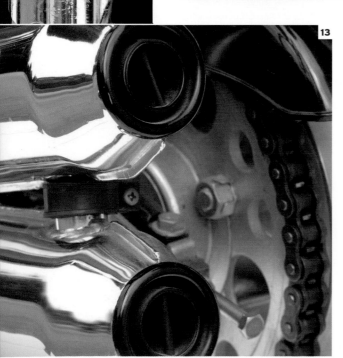

Superbikes (cont.)

The choice for buyers in the 1970s was mainly between the power and sophistication of the Japanese machines and simpler, but better handling, European bikes. The Italian manufacturers Ducati, Laverda, and Moto Guzzi achieved Japanese levels of performance with tuned versions of their basic models, while BMW used superior aerodynamics.

◁ **Ducati 860GTS 1977**

Origin Italy

Engine 864 cc, ohc V-twin

Top speed 118 mph (190 km/h)

To create the 860GTS, Ducati enlarged the capacity of their V-twin engine and commissioned the car designer Giorgetto Giugiaro to style the bike.

◁ **Yamaha XS750 1977**

Origin Japan

Engine 747 cc, in-line triple

Top speed 115 mph (185 km/h)

Yamaha sidestepped the superbike race with the XS750, a heavy, shaft-drive machine that was clearly more touring than sporting, yet not far behind in performance.

△ **BMW R100RS 1978**

Origin Germany

Engine 980 cc, flat-twin

Top speed 123 mph (198 km/h)

This bike had a fairing developed in a wind tunnel, which meant big distances could be covered at speed and in comfort despite the modest output of its engine.

▷ **Yamaha XS1100F 1979**

Origin Japan

Engine 1,101 cc, in-line four

Top speed 138 mph (222 km/h)

Yamaha went head-to-head with BMW for the luxury touring market, offering more power and sophistication but also more weight and mediocre handling.

△ **Honda CBX 1000 1978**

Origin Japan

Engine 1,047 cc, in-line six

Top speed 136 mph (219 km/h)

Hondas had become boring in the 1970s but this bike changed all that, with a stunning, 24-valve, twin-cam, six-cylinder engine that made it the fastest road bike of its time.

◁ Ducati 900SD Darmah 1979

Origin Italy

Engine 864 cc, V-twin

Top speed 114 mph (183 km/h)

With good balance and its unusual 90-degree (V-twin), desmodromic-valve engine integral to a stiff and lightweight frame, the SD was very fast on twisty roads.

△ Kawasaki Z1000 Z1R D1 1978

Origin Japan

Engine 1,015 cc, in-line four

Top speed 136 mph (219 km/h)

Japan's first "custom" café racer, with 1970s sharp-edged styling, black-painted engine, and alloy wheels, was the most powerful Z yet, though sales were sluggish.

▷ Suzuki GS750 1978

Origin Japan

Engine 748 cc, in-line four

Top speed 120 mph (193 km/h)

Suzuki abandoned two-strokes for four-strokes with this machine, building a superb twin-cam four that outclassed the opposition, yet remained a usable everyday commuter bike.

△ Kawasaki Z650C 1979

Origin Japan

Engine 652 cc, in-line four

Top speed 118 mph (190 km/h)

First launched in 1976, Kawasaki added extra chrome, alloy wheels, and pinstriping in 1979, hoping to increase sales – but buyers wanted 750 bikes.

△ Suzuki GT750 1978

Origin Japan

Engine 738 cc, in-line triple

Top speed 123 mph (198 km/h)

The only water-cooled two-stroke ever to make mass production, the GT750 was a fast, comfortable machine, but it lacked handling finesse on the road.

△ Suzuki GS1000S 1979

Origin Japan

Engine 987 cc, in-line four

Top speed 139 mph (224 km/h)

Built to commemorate Wes Cooley and Yoshimura winning the AMA Superbike title in 1978, this faired GS1000 was among the fastest of its day, but was civilized to ride.

◁ Laverda Jota 1000 1979

Origin Italy

Engine 981 cc, in-line triple

Top speed 139 mph (224 km/h)

For a short time the Jota was the world's fastest production motorcycle. It was loud, raw and uncompromising, which was an appealing prospect for many enthusiasts.

Middleweights

In the mid-range motorcycle market, some buyers were still looking for reliable "get-me-home" transport like the dependable Spanish Sanglas, while for others more speed and better handling mattered. European manufacturers refined earlier developments to build fast, but often somewhat crude and unreliable, labour-intensive machines, while the Japanese made perfectly engineered motorcycles: from Honda's smallest-yet 350 Four to Yamaha's twin-cam, four-valve 500 parallel-twin.

△ **Ducati 350 Desmo 1974**

Origin Italy

Engine 340 cc, single-cylinder

Top speed 92 mph (148 km/h)

Fabio Taglioni devised a desmodromic system that opened and closed the valves without springs, to give these singles an exceptionally high performance.

▽ **Ducati 450 Desmo 1974**

Origin Italy

Engine 436 cc, single-cylinder

Top speed 98 mph (158 km/h)

Its supremely powerful desmodromic-valve engine combined with superbly light nimble handling more than made up for the shoddy build quality of the 1970s' Ducatis.

△ **Ducati Silver Shotgun 1970**

Origin Italy

Engine 436 cc, single-cylinder

Top speed 98 mph (158 km/h)

With its glassfibre café-racer body panels painted in silver metalflake, you could not miss this Ducati, nor the sound of its desmodromic engine revving at 7,000 rpm.

△ **MV Agusta 350S Elettronica 1972**

Origin Italy

Engine 349 cc, in-line twin

Top speed 103 mph (166 km/h)

This bike had excellent handling thanks to a lightweight frame that incorporated the engine as a structural member. The 1972 model was equipped with an early form of electronic ignition.

▽ **Triumph T100R Daytona 1972**

Origin UK

Engine 490 cc, in-line twin

Top speed 111 mph (179 km/h)

Named after Triumph's first victory at Daytona Raceway in 1966, this high-performance version of the Tiger 100 was built to beat the Japanese competition.

△ **Yamaha TX500 1972**

Origin Japan

Engine 498 cc, in-line twin

Top speed 110 mph (177 km/h)

This was the first road bike to combine double overhead camshafts and four valves per cylinder on a parallel-twin. It was docile and civilized to ride.

◁ **Sanglas 400E Electrico 1973**

Origin Spain

Engine 422 cc, single-cylinder

Top speed 81 mph (130 km/h)

Sanglas built simple, low-revving, four-stroke singles in Barcelona from 1945 until absorbed by Yamaha in 1981. This electric-start model offered dependable transport.

▽ **Honda CB350F 1973**

Origin Japan

Engine 347 cc, in-line four

Top speed 99 mph (159 km/h)

An overhead camshaft in-line four of such small dimensions was unique at the time. This was a beautifully made, smooth, and quiet machine, though not especially fast.

△ **Benelli 500 Quattro 1975**

Origin Italy

Engine 498 cc, in-line four

Top speed 107 mph (172 km/h)

Under De Tomaso's control, Benelli's Honda-like engine was built by Moto Guzzi. With a disc front brake, good power output, and excellent economy, this was an attractive bike.

▽ **Suzuki GT550 1975**

Origin Japan

Engine 543 cc, in-line triple

Top speed 108 mph (174 km/h)

The 550 sat between a 380 and a 750 in Suzuki's two-stroke triples. This bike is modified with aftermarket bodywork and exhaust, as well as cast wheels.

△ **Suzuki T500 1975**

Origin Japan

Engine 492 cc, in-line twin

Top speed 106 mph (170 km/h)

This first two-stroke to win an AMA National race was also the world's largest two-stroke twin at the time, prone to vibration but worth it for the performance on offer.

Middleweights (cont.)

As the decade progressed, any decent 500cc bike was expected to top 100mph (160km/h), and the really sporty ones 10–15mph (16–24km/h) above that. Though at this stage they were not always getting every detail right, the Japanese marques took great chunks of the mid-range market with their sophisticated, clean, and stylish machines, and a new era began as Kawasaki started building motorcycles in the US.

◁ **Honda CB400F 1975**

Origin	Japan
Engine	408cc, in-line four
Top speed	98mph (158km/h)

Small but perfectly formed, the 400 Four was one of the bikes that helped Japanese makes to dominate the market. It had a delightful engine, great looks, and great performance.

△ **Morini 3½ Sport 1975**

Origin	Italy
Engine	344cc, V-twin
Top speed	97mph (156km/h)

Using the "Heron head" design gave the Franco Lambertini-designed V-twin engine great power and flexibility, easily exploited in this lightweight, great-handling frame.

◁ **Honda CB550 Four 1976**

Origin	Japan
Engine	544cc, in-line four
Top speed	105mph (169km/h)

Considered one of the finest compromises between performance, economy, and handling quality at the time, the 550 Four was an extremely well-integrated design.

△ **Honda CB500T 1976**

Origin	Japan
Engine	499cc, parallel-twin
Top speed	100mph (160km/h)

Quiet, with good handling, the CB500 suffered vibration that a few years earlier would have been acceptable, but not in 1975. This bike has been given a racer look.

△ **Honda CX500 1978**

Origin	Japan
Engine	497cc, V-twin
Top speed	105mph (169km/h)

Honda appeared to try every engine configuration for its mid-range bikes in the mid-1970s. The CX was the most innovative, with a water-cooled V-twin engine and shaft drive.

△ **Ducati 500 Sport Desmo 1977**

Origin Italy

Engine 497 cc, in-line twin

Top speed 106 mph (170 km/h)

Ducati's trademark desmodromic valves were scarcely necessary on a road bike, but added cachet to this rapid, nimble, compact class-leading 500.

△ **Ducati 500SL Pantah 1977**

Origin Italy

Engine 497 cc, V-twin

Top speed 117 mph (188 km/h)

The desmodromic-valve V-twin was a structural element in the Pantah's light but stiff trellis frame, which helped to give it superb handling to match its performance.

△ **Moto Guzzi V50 1977**

Origin Italy

Engine 490 cc, V-twin

Top speed 105 mph (169 km/h)

Under De Tomaso's control, smaller versions of Guzzi's trademark transverse V-twin were introduced, with alloy wheels, good performance, and a shaft drive.

△ **MV Agusta 350S Ipotesi 1978**

Origin Italy

Engine 349 cc, in-line twin

Top speed 94 mph (151 km/h)

The MV 350 was restyled by Giorgio Guigiaro for 1975, with a new frame and modern features. The overhead valve engine remained largely unchanged.

▷ **Yamaha XS400 1978**

Origin Japan

Engine 392 cc, in-line twin

Top speed 105 mph (169 km/h)

Disc brakes, alloy wheels, and stylish paintwork, with a level of equipment equal to many larger machines, made the four-stroke XS400 an attractive buy.

▷ **Kawasaki KZ400 1978**

Origin Japan

Engine 398 cc, in-line twin

Top speed 93 mph (150 km/h)

Kawasaki opened the first "foreign" motorcycle factory in the US to build bikes like this, designed to be an all-round better version of Honda's CB360.

A rider on a Meguro-based W-Series model

Great Marques
The Kawasaki Story

There is often an unusually strong bond between a Kawasaki and its owner. Unlike other Japanese manufacturers, whose output may sometimes feel generic and interchangeable, Kawasaki has pursued a path of innovation and individuality that has created a loyalty between riders and its fearsomely muscular machines.

IN THE LAST FEW YEARS of the 19th century, Shozo Kawasaki established the Kawasaki Shipyard in Tokyo. Success in that sphere resulted in the company branching out into locomotives and aircraft. In the difficult times after World War II the motorcycle was seen as a cost-effective means of transport in financially crippled Japan. At this time Kawasaki began to produce engines for other manufacturers, but by the end of the 1950s the company started full motorcycle production. An assembly plant was built at Akashi, while technical know-how was absorbed through a merger with Meguro, an established name in the field.

Kawasaki badge
(introduced 1968)

Initial efforts were competent, if uninspiring. The debut model wholly built by Kawasaki was 1961's 125 cc, two-stroke B7. The first machine to carry a Kawasaki badge was the B8 of 1963, which was similarly efficient but unexciting. Models such as the long-running B1 of 1966 consolidated the company's reputation for rather mundane machines rather than bikes that reinvented the motorcycling world.

That all started to change, especially in the US, with the 1967 A1, a twin-cylinder, 250 cc bike that was also known as the Samurai. This machine showed that Kawasaki was capable of game-changing revolution as well as steady evolution, but the motorbiking world was not fully prepared for what would come in 1968. The H1 was a 500 cc machine, with fearsome acceleration that reduced competitors to also-rans. Handling could be hard work, but motorcycle journalist Ian Falloon summed up the general fervour, calling it "the motorcycle that every adolescent, including myself, dreamed about".

If it was performance a rider was seeking, there was little need to look any further than Kawasaki's Z1 of 1972. This 900 cc double-overhead-camshaft beast was capable of 131 mph (211 km/h). More than 40 speed and endurance records fell before it at Daytona in 1973. The H1 and H2

were admired for their sheer aggression, but the four-cylinder Z1 was an all-round superior machine, with poise added to its undoubted power. Its nickname – "the King" – was no overstatement.

The decade that followed the Z1 was a golden age for Kawasaki. On the road the KZ1000A and the KZ650 continued the success in 1976. Later there was

All-terrain marque
Kawasaki has a long tradition for producing some of the finest off-road bikes, a fact borne out by numerous motocross and endurance World Championships secured by the marque.

unprecedented world dominance for the racers. The aerodynamically supreme KR250 and KR350 made the respective world championships their own personal property in the late 1970s and early 1980s.

It is often said that getting to the top is one thing, but staying there is quite another, but the six-cylinder Z1300 tourer confirmed Kawasaki's position in the field with power

Pioneering model
Unveiled in 1972, the 903 cc Kawasaki Z1 had class-leading performance and, with its disc brakes, exceptional stopping power. It was one of the world's first "superbikes".

W1

Z1

ZX-12R

KX250F

1954 Meihatsu's 125V bike is powered by the new Kawasaki KB-5 engine.
1961 The first bike completely built as a Kawasaki machine – the B7 – hits the market.
1963 The first fully fledged Kawasaki arrives in the form of the badged B8.
1967 The A1, also known as the Samurai, is introduced.
1968 Kawasaki debuts in the three-cylinder market with the H1, trumpeted as the world's fastest production machine.

1972 The four-cylinder Z1 throws wide open the market for power machines.
1976 The KZ650 is released.
1978 Kork Ballington wins both the 250 cc and 350 cc World Championships in this and the following year.
1980 Anton Mang wins the first of four titles over three years in the 250 cc and 350 cc categories.
1981 Jean Lafond and Raymond Roche win the World Endurance title; the company releases the AR 50.

1983 The GPZ900R becomes the world's best-selling two-wheeler.
1991 Alex Vieira starts a sequence of five World Endurance titles in six years for the marque.
1994 The ZZ-R1100, the world's fastest production bike, is released.
1994 The 900 cc class, traditionally a strong category for the company, proves so again with the release of the ZX-9R.
1996 Production numbers of Kawasaki vehicles hit the 10 million mark.

1998 Sebastian Tortelli wins the 250 cc World Motocross title to build on his 125 cc triumph of two years earlier.
2000 Kawasaki solves the conundrum of reducing weight but increasing power with the ZX-12R "Ninja".
2008 The 1400GTR draws from the ZZ-R1400 of two years earlier as Kawasaki enters the tourer-field once again.
2009 In the VN1700 Voyager, the Harley-Davidson Electra Glide Ultra has a serious rival in the tourer class.

that even eclipsed many cars. Then, into the fiercely competitive markets of the mid-1980s, came the liquid-cooled GPZ900R. The GPZ Series was a reminder of Kawasaki's quality and breathtaking performance, and the 900R helped it maintain this profile for many years. The growing list

"The engineering was **magnificent**, it was all **beautifully made**."

KORK BALLINGTON, 250/350 CC WORLD CHAMPION, ON THE KR500

of Kawasaki classics lengthened with the release of the ZZ-R1100 in 1990. Capable of 175 mph (282 km/h), it took the title of the fastest production model motorbike in the world.

During the 1990s Kawasaki had impressive competition successes. From 1991 the marque took five Endurance World Championships

in six years. In the middle of that run, American Scott Russell edged out England's Carl Fogarty for the 1993 World Superbike Championship. Years of endeavour in the mud-spattered arena of motocross were rewarded in 1995 as the brilliant Belgian Stefan Everts lifted the 250 cc crown.

The ZX-7R of the mid-1990s was often under-appreciated by critics, but its looks, handling, and speed were a big hit with the public. Taking charge of the top end of the market in 2000 was the flagship ZX-12R "Ninja", in

FRENCH CLASSIC
The Kawasaki team of Gregory Leblanc, Olivier Four, and Julien Da Costa celebrate winning the 2010 Le Mans 24 Hours event, part of the Endurance World Championship.

which a formidable power-to-weight ratio was designed for breaking records. With the Z1000 of 2003 and the ZZ-R1400 of 2006, there has been little let-up from Kawasaki. The latter can reach 60 mph (97 km/h) in just 2.5 seconds. This makes it a more-than-honourable heir to the bikes of Kawasaki's power-packed past.

Kawasaki's "Green Meanies" competition bikes and mould-breaking road machines have often been in a class of their own. Although part of the giant Kawasaki Heavy Industries group, the marque is the smallest of Japan's Big Four motorcycle makers, after Honda, Suzuki, and Yamaha, but that hasn't prevented it from being a heavy-hitter at the top end of the market.

Standing Out

For the customer who could afford to stand out from the crowd in the 1970s, there was plenty of choice, including Wankel rotary-engined bikes from Germany, Japan, and the Netherlands. Some marques employed top industrial car stylists in an attempt to steal a march over their opponents; others looked to technology. Sales were not always strong , but survivors are regarded as cult classics today.

▷ **Harley-Davidson FLH Custom 1970**

Origin USA

Engine 1,208 cc, V-twin

Top speed 90 mph (145 km/h)

Harley's restyled FL engine was nicknamed "Shovelhead". Custom make-overs, with elongated front forks, high handlebars, and aftermarket exhausts were fashionable.

▽ **Triumph X-75 Hurricane 1973**

Origin UK

Engine 741 cc, in-line triple

Top speed 114 mph (183 km/h)

This bike was designed for the US market by custom-builder Craig Vetter. Originally a BSA, the striking X-75 was sold with Triumph badging to be the first factory-built custom.

◁ **Triumph T140D Bonneville Special 1979**

Origin UK

Engine 744 cc, in-line twin

Top speed 105 mph (169 km/h)

This attractive D variant of the T140 had cast-alloy wheels, a small tank, high handlebars, and a two-into-one exhaust. Aimed at the US market, the "D" stood for Daytona, USA.

△ **Hercules/DKW W2000 1974**

Origin Germany

Engine 294 cc, Wankel 1-rotor

Top speed 90 mph (145 km/h)

The first motorcycle with a piston-less Wankel-rotary engine was sold as a Hercules in Germany and a DKW elsewhere; the strange air-cooled unit put buyers off.

▷ **Suzuki RE-5 1974**

Origin Japan

Engine 497 cc, Wankel 1-rotor

Top speed 104 mph (167 km/h)

Japan's first rotary-engined bike was typically sophisticated but alien to most motorcyclists' eyes, being top-heavy, and thirsty for fuel. Suzuki dropped the idea after 1977.

▽ Harley-Davidson XLCR 1978

Origin USA

Engine 998 cc, V-twin

Top speed 115 mph (185 km/h)

Derived from the 1,000cc Sportster, the XL Cafe Racer was stylistically inspired by European sports bikes. However, it lacked their speed and handling so attracted few buyers.

◁ BMW R90S 1975

Origin Germany

Engine 898 cc, flat-twin

Top speed 124 mph (200 km/h)

Normally sombre BMW colours were abandoned when the company joined the superbike sales race with a big-engined sports tourer that was both fast and comfortable.

▷ IZH Jupiter 3 1975

Origin Russia

Engine 348 cc, in-line twin

Top speed 72 mph (115 km/h)

The Izhevsk-made Jupiter was expensive but dated, both mechanically and cosmetically. This example was sold in the UK under the Cossack brand.

△ MV Agusta Ipotesi Sport

Origin Italy

Engine 349 cc, in-line two

Top speed 106 mph (170 km/h)

Styled by pre-eminent car stylist Giorgetto Giugiaro, the Ipotesi (Hypothesis) was speedy with sharp handling and braking, but its overhead-valve engine vibrated.

△ Benelli 750 Sei 1976

Origin Italy

Engine 747 cc, in-line six

Top speed 126 mph (203 km/h)

After buying Benelli, Alejandro de Tomaso challenged Japan with a straight six. The engine design is similar to Honda's CB500, but with two more cylinders.

△ Quasar 1977

Origin UK

Engine 848 cc, in-line four

Top speed 110 mph (177 km/h)

Created by Malcolm Newell and Ken Leaman, the feet-forward, roofed Quasar used a Reliant car engine, and had a heater and windscreen wipers. Just 21 machines were built.

△ Van Veen OCR 1000 1978

Origin Netherlands

Engine 996 cc, Wankel 2-rotor

Top speed 125 mph (201 km/h)

Henk van Veen designed a motorcycle around the Comotor (NSU/Citroën) engine. It was larger and more powerful than other early Wankels. Just 38 machines were built.

Fun on Wheels

By the 1970s small-capacity machines needed to be more than cheap, ride-to-work hacks, as second-hand cars were inexpensive and widely available. Manufacturers began to cast around for new markets and different ways to present bikes as a must-have purchase. Off-road minibikes for children were part of the answer; here was an opportunity to get the very young addicted to two-wheels.

◁ Honda ST70 Dax/ Trail 70 1970

Origin Japan

Engine 72 cc, single-cylinder

Top speed 29 mph (47 km/h)

With its tiny, 10-in (25-cm) wheels and folding handlebars, the ST70 was not road legal in some countries, but this minibike with a pressed-steel frame was a lot of fun.

△ Honda CB250 K4 1972

Origin Japan

Engine 249 cc, in-line twin

Top speed 92 mph (148 km/h)

A reliable, economical workhorse, Honda's 250 was restyled in 1968, and proved a perfect learner bike, as well as ideal for everyday transport throughout the 1970s.

▷ Vespa Super 150 1970

Origin Italy

Engine 145 cc, single-cylinder

Top speed 56 mph (90 km/h)

Piaggio's smaller scooters (with 8-in/20-cm wheels) were given sharper styling for the mid-1960s, which carried them through to 1976; over half a million were sold.

△ Lambretta GP/DL 150 1970

Origin Italy

Engine 148 cc, single-cylinder

Top speed 63 mph (101 km/h)

A sporty, new design by Bertone (and a disc brake on 200s) took Lambretta into the 1970s. When British Leyland closed Lambretta in 1972, production moved to India.

△ Lambretta J50 Special 1971

Origin Italy

Engine 49 cc, single-cylinder

Top speed 25 mph (40 km/h)

Introduced in 1964, the J50 was the baby Lambretta intended for women riders. It was stylish and lightweight, but low-powered; similar models were offered with 98 cc or 122 cc engines.

△ Zündapp GS 125 1972

Origin Germany

Engine 123 cc, single-cylinder

Top speed 72 mph (116 km/h)

Zündapp built motorcycles from 1922 to 1984. The two-stroke GS 125 was a successful and attractive trail/enduro bike that also had a good turn of speed on the road.

▷ CZ Sport 175 1972

Origin Czechoslovakia

Engine 172 cc, single-cylinder

Top speed 68 mph (109 km/h)

Czech bike-maker Jawa-CZ traded on its motocross-success record with these machines. However, they tended to be rather noisy and crude compared to Japanese competitors.

△ MZ ETS 250 Trophy Sport 1973

Origin East Germany

Engine 249 cc, single-cylinder

Top speed 82 mph (132 km/h)

East German MZ's immensely powerful, two-stroke engines earned it many race wins. Road bikes were usually heavy and durable, but the ETS was a lively sports machine.

▷ Indian MT5A 1973

Origin USA

Engine 46 cc, single-cylinder

Top speed 25 mph (40 km/h)

The historic Indian name went through several lives. In the 1970s it found itself on minibikes like this 50 cc Italjet-derived, "Trials" machine for children, with 10-in (25-cm) wheels.

△ Yamaha 200 CS5E 1972

Origin Japan

Engine 195 cc, in-line twin

Top speed 85 mph (137 km/h)

A performance leader in its class, this 200 cc was the same size as a 125 cc, and had electric starting. Its two-stroke engine had performance equal to that of a four-stroke 250 cc.

△ Yamaha SS50 1973

Origin Japan

Engine 49 cc, single-cylinder

Top speed 45 mph (72 km/h)

Yamaha equipped the SS50 with bicycle-style pedals that could be locked into position, in order to create a model for 16 year olds, who could only ride mopeds legally on the road.

△ Italjet M5B 1973

Origin Italy

Engine 48 cc, single-cylinder

Top speed 25 mph (40 km/h)

Italjet built a range of mostly 50 cc-engined bikes from 1959, including minibikes like this child's scrambler, for a rapidly expanding leisure market in the 1970s.

Fun on Wheels (cont.)

Sharp styling, bright colours, and increasing sophistication made small-engined bikes and lightweight scooters appealing, while highly tuned, two-stroke-engined sporty machines offered exciting performance although there were pollution issues. Japanese manufacturers added disc brakes and alloy wheels to pep up their cheaper models, giving them the "big bike" look for a "fun" bracket price.

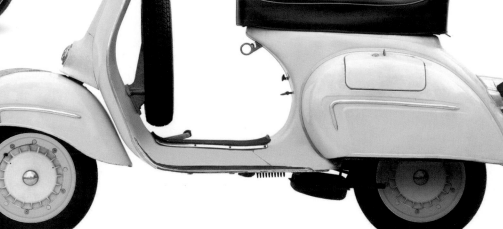

△ MV Agusta Minibike 1973

Origin	Italy
Engine	48 cc, single-cylinder
Top speed	30 mph (48 km/h)

When Phil Read won the 500 cc world title for MV Agusta, the factory commissioned a "racing" minibike for his son, and a limited run of replicas in MV Agusta colours.

△ Puch MS50 1973

Origin	Austria
Engine	49 cc, single-cylinder
Top speed	28 mph (45 km/h)

Puch made dependable, well-engineered mopeds from the 1950s with little change to their basic model from 1956. It has two gears and a twist-grip change.

▷ Vespa Rally 180 US Edition 1974

Origin	Italy
Engine	180 cc, single-cylinder
Top speed	65 mph (105 km/h)

The US version of the Rally 180 had many small additions, from different lights to the inclusion of a battery as standard. The 180 was the first rotary-valve Vespa.

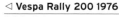

◁ Vespa Rally 200 1976

Origin	Italy
Engine	198 cc, single-cylinder
Top speed	70 mph (113 km/h)

With electric starting, 10 hp in a compact body with a large, comfortable dual seat, and performance to match its stripes, the Rally 200 was one of the most desirable Vespas.

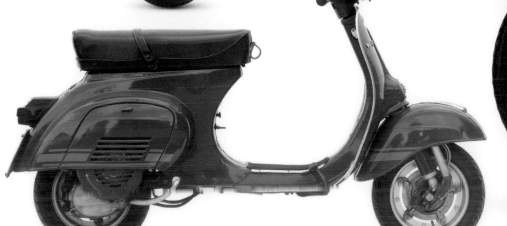

▷ Vespa ET3 1977

Origin	Italy
Engine	123 cc, single-cylinder
Top speed	56 mph (90 km/h)

The final incarnation of Vespa's small-body Primavera model boasted an electronic ignition for improved reliability and a third transfer port, giving 7 bhp instead of 5.5 bhp.

▷ **Harley-Davidson SS-250 1975**

Origin US/Italy

Engine 243 cc, single-cylinder

Top speed 85 mph (137 km/h)

Harley introduced a new range of lightweight two-stroke machines, built at their Italian subsidiary, in the 1970s. The bikes looked good but could not match Japanese reliability.

△ **Casal K196 Sport Moped 1977**

Origin Portugal

Engine 49 cc, single-cylinder

Top speed 38 mph (61 km/h)

Portuguese moped-maker Casal started in 1964, building Zundapps under licence. This slightly sporty offering had a two-speed manual gearchange and back-pedal brake.

◁ **Yamaha XS250 1978**

Origin Japan

Engine 248 cc, in-line two

Top speed 85 mph (137 km/h)

Yamaha introduced the good-looking XS range in 1977 with 250, 360, and 400 cc overhead-camshaft engines and disc brakes. They were capable but not outstanding machines.

△ **Suzuki GT185 1979**

Origin Japan

Engine 184 cc, in-line two

Top speed 82 mph (132 km/h)

This attractive and lively bike was aimed at young riders, though perhaps awkwardly positioned below its 200 cc rivals. It featured an electric starter/ generator and ram air cooling.

△ **Suzuki A100 1975**

Origin Japan

Engine 98 cc, single-cylinder

Top speed 72 mph (115 km/h)

Introduced in the 1960s, this slim, elegant, and usually brightly coloured rotary-valve, two-stroke bike weighed just 183 lb (83 kg), and offered excellent performance.

△ **Cagiva SST350 1979**

Origin Italy

Engine 342 cc, single-cylinder

Top speed 90 mph (145 km/h)

With mopeds and two-stroke fun bikes like this, the Castiglioni brothers became Italy's largest bike-makers within a few years of buying the AMF-Harley factory in 1978.

Mint 400 motocross race, 1971
Also known as the Great American Desert Race, the Mint 400 is an annual endurance race through the Mojave Desert, Nevada. Motorcycles competed alongside cars until 1977, during a period of huge growth in the sport of motocross.

Chrome and Smoke

The great power-to-weight ratio of two-stroke engines was exploited to create a new generation of sports machines with sizzling performance. The Japanese factories were the leaders; they applied race technology and made their products more attractive with chrome plate and bright paintwork. No one cared too much about the exhaust smoke, but the heavy fuel consumption was a drawback.

▷ Suzuki T350 Rebel 1971
Origin Japan
Engine 315 cc, in-line two
Top speed 91 mph (146 km/h)

Suzuki's six-speed two-strokes offered great performance for price, with sales enhanced by racing. In Australia, a T350 beat much larger bikes in the 1972-73 Amaroo six-hour race.

◁ Suzuki T125 Stinger 1972
Origin Japan
Engine 124 cc, in-line two
Top speed 74 mph (119 km/h)

Advertised as a "Road racer you can ride on the street", the Stinger had a high-revving parallel-twin two-stroke, and its styling mixed race and scramble elements.

▷ Suzuki T500 1975
Origin Japan
Engine 492 cc, in-line two
Top speed 106 mph (171 km/h)

The 1968 T500, called both the "Cobra" and "Titan", was Suzuki's first large capacity model. Making rival 500s obsolete, from 1976 it evolved into the GT500 tourer.

◁ Suzuki GT380 1976
Origin Japan
Engine 371 cc, in-line three
Top speed 105 mph (169 km/h)

Featuring Ram Air cooling, Suzuki's 380 cc and 550 cc triples were torquey and smooth. This GT380 is modified with aftermarket wheels, seat, and exhaust system.

◁ Suzuki GT250 X7 1979
Origin Japan
Engine 247 cc, in-line two
Top speed 100 mph (160 km/h)

Descended from the earlier 1960s X6 and later GT250, the 100 mph (161 km/h) X7 was an agile sport bike, ideal for the Café Racer customizing seen on this example.

△ Yamaha CS5 1972
Origin Japan
Engine 195 cc, in-line two
Top speed 84 mph (135 km/h)

Offering terrific performance and good handling for their small dimensions, the little 200 cc two-stroke Yamahas made many friends in the late 1960s and early 1970s.

◁ **Kawasaki H1 Mach III 1973**

Origin Japan

Engine 499 cc, in-line three

Top speed 115 mph (185 km/h)

This two-stroke road stormer produced a formidable 60 bhp and covered a $^1/_4$ mile (400 m) in 12.4 sec. It was a hit in the US, but dangerous for inexperienced riders.

◁ **Yamaha RD400 1978**

Origin Japan

Engine 399 cc, in-line two

Top speed 109 mph (175 km/h)

The RD400 evolved from the racer-like RD350, offering more refinement and cleaner running without losing any of its tremendous performance; it was listed until 1981.

△ **Kawasaki G3SSD 1974**

Origin Japan

Engine 89 cc, single-cylinder

Top speed 65 mph (105 km/h)

Well equipped and beautifully built, the 90 cc SS Series ran from 1969 to 1974, with a rotary-valve, two-stroke engine featuring oil injection, and a five-speed gearbox.

△ **Kawasaki KH400 1978**

Origin Japan

Engine 400 cc, in-line three

Top speed 103 mph (166 km/h)

Kawasaki's air-cooled two-stroke triples were a great success due to their performance and value for money. The civilized 400 stayed in production up to 1980.

▽ **Bultaco Metralla GT 1975**

Origin Spain

Engine 244 cc, single-cylinder

Top speed 90 mph (145 km/h)

Light and lively with 24 bhp from its two-stroke engine, the Metralla was a road bike from a factory that had a strong racing, trials, and motocross pedigree.

△ **Yamaha RD350 1975**

Origin Japan

Engine 347 cc, in-line two

Top speed 106 mph (170 km/h)

Yamaha's rapid 350 cc two-stroke was upgraded for 1973 with reed valves, a six-speed gearbox, and front disc brake, resulting in rave reviews for its race-bred feel.

Off the Highway

Trail riding was the boom leisure occupation in the US and elsewhere in the 1970s, and manufacturers catered for the massive new market by selling trail bikes; street-legal machines with genuine off-road capability. Some riders wanted to take rough-riding skills to a new level in competitive events, so the choice of machinery for motocross, enduros, and observed trials also grew.

◁ **Kawasaki G4TR Trail Boss 1970**

Origin Japan

Engine 99 cc, single-cylinder

Top speed 67 mph (108 km/h)

Switchable high/low ratios giving a 10-speed gearbox, and an aluminium cylinder like its bigger sisters, made this a very desirable little trail bike in the 1970s.

◁ **Honda CT50 Hunter Cub 1970**

Origin Japan

Engine 49 cc, single-cylinder

Top speed 27 mph (43 km/h)

From 1964 Honda built a series of four-stroke bikes with high/low ratio gearing for casual off-road use. It was sold as "Trail Cub" in North America and "Hunter Cub" elsewhere.

△ **Honda XR75 Minibike 1971**

Origin Japan

Engine 72 cc, single-cylinder

Top speed 45 mph (72 km/h)

Primarily for children or used as a pit bike, the four-stroke XR75 minibike was not usually road-legal but was an effective race winner in children's motocross series.

▷ **Hodaka Super Rat 1971**

Origin Japan

Engine 98 cc, single-cylinder

Top speed 54 mph (87 km/h)

Joint US-Japanese company Pabatco, owned by Shell Oils, built trail bikes for the US market. The Super Rat was its first competition bike, and was very successful.

△ **Suzuki TS125 1971**

Origin Japan

Engine 123 cc, single-cylinder

Top speed 68 mph (109 km/h)

With a small two-stroke engine but plenty of punch, the TS125 was also sold in a more serious off-roading guise as the TS 125R Duster.

◁ **Hodaka SS 1973**

Origin Japan/USA

Engine 98 cc, single-cylinder

Top speed 55 mph (89 km/h)

Synthetic oil and minibike guru John Steen took Ace 100 Hodakas, stripped them, and turned them into race winners, with Ceriani forks, Rickman bars, and more.

▽ **Husqvarna Enduro 504 WR 1973**

Origin Sweden

Engine 504 cc, in-line two

Top speed 100 mph (161 km/h)

The 500 cc twin-engine was made by grafting two 250s together. Gunnar Nilsson won the European FIM Cup with one enlarged to 504 cc to qualify for the 500–750 class.

▷ **Husqvarna 390 WR 1979**

Origin Sweden

Engine 384 cc, single-cylinder

Top speed 85 mph (137 km/h)

This fast and rugged two-stroke machine was designed for enduro riding with tremendous torque, six speeds, long-travel suspension, and equipped with lights.

▷ **CZ 175 Enduro DT 1974**

Origin Czech Republic

Engine 172 cc, single-cylinder

Top speed 62 mph (100 km/h)

In standard form the Enduro was a crude, heavy, old-fashioned machine that was widely criticized. However, in lightened DT form it was very effective off road.

◁ **CZ 250 Motocross 1974**

Origin Czech Republic

Engine 246 cc, single-cylinder

Top speed 65 mph (105 km/h)

CZs were at the forefront of motocross from the late 1960s and, despite strong opposition from the Japanese, Jaroslav Falta dominated the 250 cc World Championship.

△ **Yamaha YZ250 1974**

Origin Japan

Engine 249 cc, single-cylinder

Top speed 80 mph (129 km/h)

This hugely successful motocross racer pioneered monoshock suspension. The two-stroke engine gave the boldest riders very strong mid-range and top-end power.

△ **Yamaha XT500 1975**

Origin Japan

Engine 499 cc, single-cylinder

Top speed 82 mph (132 km/h)

Yamaha's first big, four-stroke single "Thumper" was very well received. It won the gruelling Paris-Dakar Rally in 1979 and 1980.

▷ **Montesa Cota 172 1977**

Origin Spain

Engine 158 cc, single-cylinder

Top speed 65 mph (105 km/h)

The Cota was a top trials contender in 250 cc form, while this smaller-engined but similarly agile 158 cc version was more suited to extreme trail riding.

△ **Bultaco Alpina 1975**

Origin Spain

Engine 244 cc, single-cylinder

Top speed 65 mph (105 km/h)

Bultaco won the World Trials Championship for its first five years from 1975, and adapted its winning model into the Alpina to make it suitable for trail riding or enduros.

Jack Marshall on his 1908 TT-winning Triumph

Great Marques
The Triumph Story

The celebrated Triumph marque has come to represent classic motorcycle engineering, boasting a raft of stylish models like Speed Twin, Bonneville, and Thunderbird – names that evoke an era when British bikes reigned supreme. After a brief pause in the 1980s, the rejuvenated company resumed production of distinctive motorcycles that continue to stand out for their looks and powerful engines.

THE QUINTESSENTIALLY BRITISH company Triumph Motorcycles actually owes its existence to the entrepeneurial spirit of two Germans who arrived in England in the late 19th century. In 1895 Siegfried Bettmann began selling bicycles under the Triumph name. He was soon joined in business by an engineer called Mauritz Schulte, and, like other entrepreneurs of the era, they quickly saw the potential of fitting engines to bicycle frames. After finding suitable premises in Coventry, in 1902 Bettmann and Schulte presented their first powered Triumph bike, which was driven by a 2¼ hp Minerva engine.

Triumph soon developed its own powerplant. In 1905 the 3 hp model quickly earned a reputation as a reliable single-cylinder machine, and over the next decade was developed into more powerful versions. Some

"Swooping R" logo
(introduced mid-30s)

of these would be modified into competition bikes, and Triumph made its mark early in the racing arena. In 1908 Jack Marshall took first place in the single-cylinder class of the Isle of Man TT races. The win provided the impetus for domestic growth, with around 3,000 motorcycles produced in 1909. By the onset of World War I in 1914 Triumph was sufficiently well regarded to be called on to supply military-use motorcycles to the British government. The principal machine on order was the Type H, with around 30,000 examples of this sturdy 499 cc single produced for the war effort.

Early in the 1920s Triumph commissioned engine maestro Harry Ricardo to develop a new powerplant. The result was the 499 cc unit which featured four valves in the cylinder head. Fitted to the Model R, it increased the bike's performance to such a level that it set several speed records. Later in the decade, the company branched out into car production, but new motorcycles like Triumph's first twin-cylinder model in 1933 showed that two-wheeled transportation was still very much the core of the business.

Nevertheless, the general economic downturn hit the company hard, and in 1936 Triumph's motorcycle division was taken over by Jack Sangster, who had previously turned around the Ariel motorcycle company.

The new owner installed ex-Ariel employee Edward Turner as design chief. This would prove a pivotal move, as the engineering genius immediately revamped the range, introducing the Tiger models with their attractive designs, good performance, and competitive price.

Turner's greatest contribution came in 1937 with the landmark Triumph T100 Speed Twin, arguably the most

1934 Triumph TT race team
Triumph's riders line up for the 1934 Isle of Man TT. From left to right: Tommy Spann, Jock West, and Ernie Thomas.

> **"Ain't no finer thrill,** You **ain't lived** until, You climb aboard a **Triumph Bonneville."**
> STEVE GIBBONS BAND'S "TRIUMPH BONNEVILLE" TRACK, 2007

influential British motorcycle of the 20th century. The engineer's ability to fit two cylinders into the space usually occupied by one proved to be so revolutionary that it shaped twin-cylinder motorcycle design for the next few decades. Here was a 500 cc parallel twin that was lighter, faster, and better looking than any previous machine of this capacity and configuration.

Having developed this seminal twin-cylinder engine, Triumph briefly turned its attentions to making side-valve models for the military in World War II. Early in the war in 1940 German bombs destroyed the

Triumph factory in Coventry. But two years later a new plant had been built at nearby Meriden.

Postwar production concentrated on twin-cylinder machines, beginning a prosperous era when Triumph made the most sought-after bikes in the world. Turner enlarged his 500 cc engine to 650 cc, creating the 1950 Thunderbird and a line of derivatives expressly aimed at American riders who found the 500 cc engine too small. The new model's image was given added kudos when Marlon Brando rode a Thunderbird in the cult 1953 biker movie *The Wild One*. Though Triumph had been sold to

Perfect tourer
Triumph was keen to promote its models as being the best of British, and a perfect way of exploring the countryside.

Type R Fast Roadster

Speed Twin

T120 Bonneville

Daytona 955i

1902 Triumph releases its first motorized model, a 2¼ hp bicycle utilizing a Belgian-made Minerva engine.
1908 Jack Marshall wins the Isle of Man Tourist Trophy single-cylinder race on a Triumph.
1921 The Model R with a Harry Ricardo-designed engine hits 75 mph (120 km/h).
1924 The 494 cc Model P is the first of Triumph's mass-produced models.
1936 Jack Sangster buys Triumph. The Tiger 70, 80, and 90 singles are introduced.

1937 The Speed Twin model with radical twin-cylinder design is superior to all rival 500 ccs, providing a blueprint for postwar British motorcycle makers.
1942 After the Coventry plant is bombed, Triumph are able to occupy a new factory at Meriden.
1951 BSA buys Triumph, although the marque is run independently.
1953 The T110 Tiger model is released.
1954 The 650 cc Tiger 110 joins the range.
1956 A Triumph-engined vehicle sets a new

land-speed record at the Bonneville Salt Flats in the US.
1958 Twin-carburettor T120 Bonneville is unveiled, to become Britain's best-known motorcycle.
1963 *The Great Escape* features Steve McQueen on a Triumph twin.
1969 Launch of the 750 cc Trident, with a three-cylinder engine.
1973 Norton-Villiers-Triumph is formed.
1979 The T140 Bonneville is unveiled, the last Triumph exported to the US in quantity.

1983 Triumph closes its Meriden plant.
1990 The reborn Triumph Motorcycle Company unveils six new models with capacities 750 cc–1,200 cc.
1994 The Speed Triple is unveiled.
1995 T595 Daytona is released with three cylinders and fuel injection. The Hinckley plant is devastated by fire but rebuilt six months later.
2004 The Rocket III model features a 2,293 cc powerplant, the largest production motorcycle engine to date.

BSA in 1951 it remained an independently run marque, and as well as large machines the company rolled out smaller models like the 149 cc Terrier and 199 cc Tiger Cub. In 1956 the marque received worldwide publicity when it was involved in setting a new land-speed record. On the Bonneville Salt Flats in Utah, USA, Johnny Allen reached more than 214 mph (345 km/h) in a streamlined vehicle powered by a 649 cc Triumph engine. This led to the release of

Screen idols
Steve McQueen made his iconic attempt to leap to freedom over the barbed wire borderfence on a Triumph TR6 in the 1963 film *The Great Escape*.

the T120 Bonneville in 1958. This speedy 650 cc twin became Britain's most famous motorcycle. During the 1960s output rose to 50,000 bikes a year, most for export.

The decade also saw ever-larger Japanese machines entering the market, a threat that was partly countered by

Triumph's 125 mph three-cylinder Trident in 1969. Nevertheless, Triumph's BSA owners were in financial difficulty, and after incurring substantial losses a new company was formed in 1973 featuring three British manufacturers: Norton-Villiers-Triumph (NVT). A 750 cc Bonneville had been launched, but when NVT attempted to close down Meriden, a large proportion of the workforce occupied and blockaded the factory. Production stopped until a government-backed worker's cooperative resumed manufacture of the 750 cc twins in 1975.

When the cash-strapped coop folded in 1983, house builder John Bloor bought the Triumph name and set up an entirely new

World Class
A world-class British company, Triumph has five manufacturing plants: two in Leicestershire, UK, and three in Thailand.

operation. Triumph Motorcycles Ltd unveiled its first new offerings in 1990, impressing fans with models featuring evocative names such as Trident, Daytona, and Trophy. In the following years a series of new models confirmed that Triumph was back as a world-class manufacturer. In the 2000s a long-awaited modern version of the Bonneville arrived. It was no longer the ultimate speedster, but a versatile rider-friendly machine. The modern twin and its variants have been a huge sales success.

More than half a century ago motorcyclists were drawn to Triumph machines' clean lines, superb handling, and impressive speeds. Now a younger generation appreciates these qualities in the Triumph motorbikes of today.

Racers

On the racetracks, the 1970s saw technology leap to the fore. Manufacturers employed exotic alloys and experimented with monocoque construction in stainless steel, while seeking more power from ever-higher revving engines using multiple valves and camshafts, fuel injection, and forced induction. The Japanese dominated grand prix, but European and US marques battled on and still cleaned up in more obscure competitions.

◁ **Triumph F750 1971**

Origin UK

Engine 741 cc, in-line twin

Top speed 140 mph (225 km/h)

A combined Triumph/BSA factory team dominated US and European 750 cc racing with three cylinder machines in 1971. This Triumph was raced by 1970 US champion Gene Romero.

△ **Norton F750 1973**

Origin UK

Engine 746 cc, in-line two

Top speed 155 mph (259 km/h)

With a stainless steel monocoque chassis, the aerodynamic Norton handled superbly, compensating for a lack of power. Peter Williams rode it to a 1973 Formula 750 TT victory.

△ **Ducati 750SS 1972**

Origin Italy

Engine 748 cc, V-twin

Top speed 140 mph (225 km/h)

Finishing both first and second in Italy's Imola 200 international race in 1972 was a breakthrough for Ducati's early, high-revving V-twin with desmodromic-valve gear.

△ **Harley-Davidson XRTT 1972**

Origin USA

Engine 750 cc, V-twin

Top speed 145 mph (233 km/h)

The faired road-racing version of the factory XR750 was also used in flat-track trim. This machine, with a Fontana front brake, was ridden by legendary US racer Carl Rayborn.

◁ **Harley-Davidson RR250 1976**

Origin USA

Engine 250 cc, in-line twin

Top speed 110 mph (177 km/h)

Developed and built at the Aermacchi factory, water-cooled twins defeated Yamaha in 250 cc and 350 cc races taking the Italian Walter Villa to four world titles.

Drag Racers

Born in the US, motorcycle drag racing spread to Europe in the 1960s. During the 1970s top contenders used doubled-up engines to get maximum power for ¼-mile (400-m) sprints from a standing start. Nithromethane fuel, massive rear tyres, quick-shift transmissions, and superchargers were fitted to elongated frames. Maintaining control on the drag strip took consummate skill and incredible bravery.

▽ **Norton Hogslayer Dragster 1975**

Origin UK/USA

Engine 2 x 880 cc, in-line two

Top speed 180 mph (290 km/h)

Tom Christenson dominated American dragstrips in the 1970s on this twin-engined machine, christened "Hogslayer" for its ability to beat Harley-Davidsons.

▷ Jawa Briggo Speedway 1975

Origin Czech Republic

Engine 599 cc, single-cylinder

Top speed 110 mph (177 km/h)

Top riders Neil Street and Barry Briggs revolutionized speedway in the 1970s with four-valve conversions for Jawa engines. The Briggo was sold by New Zealander Briggs.

△ Honda RCB1000 1976

Origin Japan

Engine 941 cc, in-line four

Top speed 175 mph (282 km/h)

In 1976 Honda dominated European and World Endurance racing with this bike derived from the CB750 but with double overhead camshafts and many innovations.

△ Suzuki RG500 1978

Origin Japan

Engine 498 cc, square-four

Top speed 175 mph (282 km/h)

Suzuki adopted the unusual square-four layout with a separate crankshaft for each cylinder. Barry Sheene won world championships on factory versions of the RG500 in 1976 and 1977.

◁ Yamaha YZR 500 OW48 1979

Origin Japan

Engine 500 cc, in-line four

Top speed 175 mph (282 km/h)

Yamaha developed the YZR 500, which went on to win many Grands Prix from 1973 onwards. By 1980 the OW48 had an all-new aluminium frame, helping Kenny Roberts win his third World title.

◁ Yamaha TZ250 1977

Origin Japan

Engine 247 cc, in-line two

Top speed 130 mph (209 km/h)

Yamaha experimented with water-cooled heads for the 250 cc and 350 cc Grand Prix in 1972 and fitted them to the the TZ in 1973, which was updated annually until 1986.

▷ Kawasaki KR250 1979

Origin Japan

Engine 250 cc, in-line two

Top speed 150 mph (241 km/h)

This two-stroke tandem-twin Grand Prix racer was very successful, winning World Championships for Kork Ballington in 1978 and 1979, and for Anton Mang in 1981.

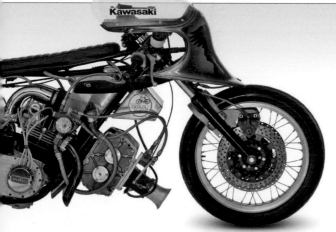

◁ Kawasaki 2400 cc Dragster 1977

Origin UK/Japan

Engine 2 x 850 cc, in-line two

Top Speed 220 mph (354 km/h)

Bob Webster bolted two Kawasaki 850 cc engines together and added a supercharger, hitting 150 mph (241 km/h) at the climax of a 7.75 sec 1/4 mile (400 m) sprint at Santa Pod in Northampton.

△ Weslake Hobbit Dragster 1978

Origin UK

Engine 2 x 850 cc, in-line two

Top speed 210 mph (338 km/h)

John Hobbs built the fearsome Hobbit with two Weslake engines and two Shorrocks superchargers. Steadily improved from 1975 to 1979, it could run an 8.2 sec 1/4 mile (400 m).

Classic Style

In the early 1970s the contrast between Japanese and British motorcycle manufacturers became abundantly clear. While their machines looked superficially similar and were built along well-established lines, a closer look revealed superior levels of sophistication in Japanese engines, mechanical components, and the equipment supplied: the fate of the British industry was clear.

▽ Harley-Davidson FX Super Glide 1971

Origin USA

Engine 1,213 cc, V-twin

Top speed 108 mph (174 km/h)

By combining the FL frame with the XL Sportster front forks, Harley created the Super Glide as a "production custom"; it sold better later, with less radical rear-end styling.

◁ BSA B25SS Gold Star 1975

Origin UK

Engine 247 cc, single-cylinder

Top speed 80 mph (129 km/h)

BSA was struggling against Japanese rivals when it built this model. It was let down by the antiquated engine – BSA motorcycles were soon to become history.

△ BSA A65 Thunderbolt 1971

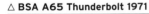

Origin UK

Engine 654 cc, in-line twin

Top speed 104 mph (167 km/h)

The single-carburettor Thunderbolt was not a bad bike, despite a tall seat height due to its frame design, which incorporated the oil tank in the top tube.

▽ Honda CB350 K4 1973

Origin Japan

Engine 326 cc, in-line twin

Top speed 110 mph (177 km/h)

The overhead cam, parallel-twin CB350 became the highest-selling motorcycle in American history with over 300,000 sold between 1968 and 1973. Six gears featured on the K4 Super Sport.

▷ Jawa 350 Type 634 1974

Origin Czech Republic

Engine 343 cc, in-line twin

Top speed 80 mph (129 km/h)

Built from the late 1940s right through into the 21st century, the parallel-twin, two-stroke-engined Jawa was sold in huge numbers throughout the world.

▷ **Norton Commando Interstate MkIII 850 ES 1975**
Origin UK
Engine 829 cc, in-line twin
Top speed 120 mph (193 km/h)

Battling with Japanese entries in the superbike market, Norton enlarged the Commando's parallel-twin, strengthened the running gear, and added electric starting.

△ **Benelli Tornado S 1975**
Origin Italy
Engine 643 cc, in-line twin
Top speed 105 mph (169 km/h)

A family business making motorcycles since 1911, Benelli targeted the US and UK markets with this traditional but rapid parallel-twin. De Tomaso bought Benelli in 1973.

◁ **Triumph Trident T160V 1975**
Origin UK
Engine 750 cc, in-line three
Top speed 115 mph (185 km/h)

Sloping the engine forward to fit in a larger airbox and adding a rear disc brake and electric starting kept the ageing BSA/Trident on the market for its final year or two.

▽ **BMW R60/6 1976**
Origin Germany
Engine 599 cc, flat-twin
Top speed 99 mph (159 km/h)

The /6 Series BMW twins, launched in 1973, added front disc brakes and a five-speed gearbox to the R60/5's virtues of shaft drive and great balance.

△ **Triumph Bonneville T140J Jubilee 1977**
Origin UK
Engine 744 cc, in-line twin
Top speed 111 mph (179 km/h)

To mark the Queen's Silver Jubilee in 1977, Triumph made 1,000 each of both US and UK spec bikes and 400 Commonwealth special editions, with fancy paint, decals, and extra chrome.

◁ **Yamaha XS650B 1976**
Origin Japan
Engine 653 cc, in-line twin
Top speed 113 mph (182 km/h)

Modelled on the BSA 650 and launched in 1969, Yamaha's big, parallel-twin outlasted the BSA thanks to its leak-free build, electric starting, and twin disc brakes.

△ **Triumph Bonneville T140E 1979**
Origin UK
Engine 744 cc, in-line twin
Top speed 118 mph (190 km/h)

Triumph enlarged the 650 Bonneville in 1973, and fitted front, and later rear, disc brakes. The T140E had electronic ignition and modifications to pass emissions laws.

▷ **Yamaha SR500 1979**
Origin Japan
Engine 499 cc, single-cylinder
Top speed 93 mph (150 km/h)

Well engineered with a leak-free, overhead-camshaft engine, the simple, agile, and relatively light SR500 retained kick-starting and a drum rear brake.

The
1980s

Technology marched on, spurred by intense competition between the Big Four: Honda, Kawasaki, Suzuki, and Yamaha. Sometimes it reached overkill, exemplified by a brief infatuation with turbocharging, but it also produced sound, new machines, from tiny commuters to big and fast superbikes. Harley-Davidson, America's only maker of any size, emerged from lean years with new vigour, and Europeans like Aprilia, BMW, and Ducati were also moving forward. At the same time, a growing interest in classic machinery of the past was beginning to influence design.

Road Sport

During the 1980s manufacturers' ranges became more diverse, with sports bikes taking the inspiration from racing machines. Higher power outputs and the need for more compact engines meant that water-cooling of sports engines became almost universal, and chassis design evolved too. Rear suspension using a single shock absorber, mounted ahead of the rear wheel, became standard.

▷ Kawasaki GPZ 550 1981

Origin Japan

Engine 553 cc, in-line four

Top speed 119 mph (192 km/h)

Five-spoke alloys and a black engine and exhaust marked out the 61 hp GPZ. It was Kawasaki's leading mid-range bike with a Uni-Trak air-assisted rear suspension.

◁ Yamaha RD250LC 1981

Origin Japan

Engine 247 cc, in-line twin

Top speed 98 mph (158 km/h)

A racer for learner riders, the LC's 100 mph (160 km/h) capability stemmed from the power of its reed-valve, water-cooled, two-stroke twin, equivalent to over 140 hp per litre.

▷ Yamaha RD350LC YPVS 1983

Origin Japan

Engine 347 cc, in-line twin

Top speed 117 mph (188 km/h)

Launched in 1981, the liquid-cooled, two-stroke RD350 is legendary for its unique blend of fast and furious fun at an affordable price. The YPVS system introduced in 1983 further improved performance.

△ Kawasaki Z1100 1984

Origin Japan

Engine 1,089 cc, in-line four

Top speed 137 mph (220 km/h)

Kawasaki needed only two valves per cylinder to extract 108 bhp – the highest four-cylinder output of the time – from its 1100, giving it tremendous acceleration.

▽ Yamaha RD500LC/RZ500 1984

Origin Japan

Engine 499 cc, V-four

Top speed 148 mph (238 km/h)

With a water-cooled, reed-valve, two-stroke engine the Grand Prix-inspired 500 was sold with either a steel or alloy chassis depending on the market. Either way it was light, powerful, and stunning.

▷ BMW R100CS 1983

Origin Germany

Engine 980 cc, flat-twin

Top speed 123 mph (198 km/h)

Motorcyclists have always been keen to modify their machines. This BMW is equipped with Krauser cylinder heads, and other performance-handling improvements.

△ Kawasaki GPZ900R/ ZX900 Ninja 1984

Origin Japan

Engine 908 cc, in-line four

Top speed 154 mph (248 km/h)

Kawasaki were late in developing water cooling and four valves per cylinder for their sports machines. Their new 900 was compact, sophisticated, powerful, and well-balanced.

▽ Honda VF400F 1983

Origin Japan

Engine 399 cc, V-four

Top speed 112 mph (180 km/h)

An innovative machine with a 16-valve, V-four engine in a naked-bike style with bikini-type fairing, this bike featured inboard disc brakes and an anti-dive, air-assisted suspension.

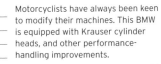

◁ Moto Guzzi Le Mans 1000 1983

Origin Italy

Engine 949 cc, V-twin

Top speed 137 mph (220 km/h)

Moto Guzzi's top sports bike started as an 850 in 1977. One of the original Café Racers, it had low seating, linked brakes, high gearing, and a lovely, balanced feel.

△ Honda MBX50 1984

Origin Japan

Engine 59 cc, single-cylinder

Top speed 42 mph (68 km/h)

Honda targeted the European youth market with the stylish, six-speed, disc-braked MBX50. Its air-cooled two-stroke engine was surprisingly nippy when unrestricted.

△ Honda VF500F2 1984

Origin Japan

Engine 498 cc, V-four

Top speed 132 mph (212 km/h)

Small, beautifully built, and with performance that put most other 500s to shame, the water-cooled twin-cam, 16-valve VF500 had much to justify its high price tag.

▷ Ducati 1000 MHR 1985

Origin Italy

Engine 973 cc, V-twin

Top speed 127 mph (204 km/h)

The MHR (Mike Hailwood Replica) had a 90 hp enlargement of the 900SS V-twin and commemorated Hailwood's 1978 comeback victory at the Isle of Man TT.

Honda RC30

One of the all-time great Japanese sports models, the Honda RC30 was a race replica with a difference: on this bike, private, unsponsored riders could take part in competition – and win. Created for the Superbike World Championship, it helped Honda win the Constructor's Title for three years running from 1988 to 1990. The RC30's record-breaking feats at the Isle of Man TT races earned the bike a cult status that was further heightened by limited production.

RELEASED IN JAPAN in 1987, Honda's RC30 was bred for the racetrack. The new model – also known as the VFR750R – had an excellent pedigree, based as it was on the RVF750, which had dominated prestigious endurance events such as the Le Mans 24 Hours and the Bol d'Or since 1985. Featuring a 748cc water-cooled V-four engine, the RC30 may not have been exceptionally powerful for a bike of its size, but its race components were used so effectively the machine outstripped all its rivals. Honda's competition expertise

was unparalleled and the success of their strategy became apparent when rider Fred Merkel took the Superbike World Champion title in 1988 and 1989 on the RC30, plus four Isle of Man TT race wins in the same years. In the first few years of production, the bike spread into other markets to be warmly received by race teams, privateer riders, and sports bike fans. The bike's last year of production was 1990, by which time Honda had assembled fewer than 5,000 examples of this very special piece of machinery.

FRONT VIEW

REAR VIEW

Winning start
The Honda badge was first seen on racing circuits in 1953, when the marque entered a number of bikes in the Nagoya Grand Prix in Japan, taking the Manufacturer's Team Prize.

Single seat for racing

Windscreen made from sheer plastic for low distortion

Front fork is multi-adjustable

Front brake discs are 310 mm in diameter and 6 mm thick

One-sided swingarm for rapid wheel changes

Low centre of gravity aids handling

Racing chassis
Light, rigid, and strong, the RC30's frame was cleverly tailored to reinforce stress points, while weight was removed from areas on the structure that took less strain. The bike was clothed in a lightweight full fairing, constructed from ultra-thin, fibreglass-reinforced plastic.

SPECIFICATIONS	
Model	Honda RC30 (1988)
Assembly	Hamamatsu, Japan
Production	4,780
Construction	Triple-box, tubular-steel frame
Engine	748 cc, V-four
Power output	122 hp
Transmission	Six-speed
Suspension	Telescopic front forks, monoshock rear
Brakes	Dual-discs front, single-disc rear
Maximum speed	152 mph (245 km/h)

THE BIKE

The RC30 was designed to be ridden hard. Its single-sided PRO-arm swingarm worked alongside the resilient chassis to give the bike a tautness that inspired confidence when cornering at high speed, while the close-ratio, six-speed gearbox offered precision shifting. Fully adjustable suspension and four-piston front brake callipers were further evidence of the model's racing character. By simultaneously designing a stable bike and one with supreme ride quality, Honda had united track and road in a single sensational package.

1. Maker's badge on fairing **2.** Model code on panel behind seat **3.** Twin headlamps **4.** Lights switch on handlebar **5.** Cockpit **6.** Fuel quick-filler **7.** Fuel tank breather **8.** Choke control **9.** Right footrest **10.** Radiator fan **11.** Front wheel, designed for rapid wheel change **12.** Quick-change sprocket **13.** Silencer **14.** Rear lamp

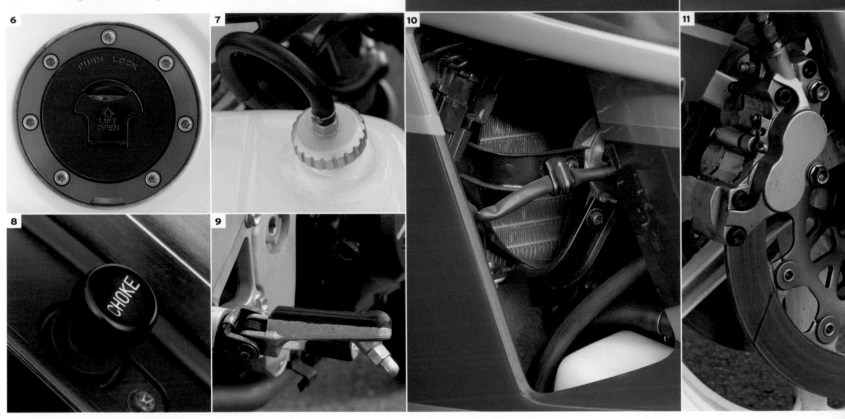

ENGINE

High-tech components featured prominently in the RC30's 16-valve, 90°, V-four engine. The unit's two-ring pistons were connected to the crankshaft by ultra-light, super-strong titanium connecting rods, contributing to the model's impressively low weight of 408lb (185kg). Four 38mm carburettors supplied mixture to the power plant, while the engine was cooled by fan-assisted, lightweight, aluminium radiators. Its reliable engine full of torque made the RC30 a favoured mount for endurance racing. At the Isle of Man TT races, Steve Hislop was the first rider to lap the fearsome Mountain Course at more than 120mph (193km/h) on an RC30 in 1989.

15. Right side of crankcase **16.** Alternator and water pump housings **17.** Idle setting knob **18.** Four-into-one exhaust **19.** Lower radiator **20.** Oil filter **21.** Fairing fastener

Road Sport (cont.)

While ultimate speed freaks still opted for big engines, manufacturers showed that they could offer just as much usable performance from a 750 or a smaller engine, provided the aerodynamics and engine were optimized. Mid-range engines were lighter too, making the bikes easier to handle at low speeds and, more importantly, nimbler and much more manageable on twisty bumpy roads.

▷ **Suzuki GSX-750 ES 1986**

Origin	Japan
Engine	747 cc, in-line four
Top speed	135 mph (217 km/h)

Suzuki rejuvenated its 750 with a box-section frame, full-floating rear suspension, anti-dive, and street-racer styling. Though not the fastest in its class, it was great to ride.

△ **Yamaha FZ750 1985**

Origin	Japan
Engine	749 cc, in-line four
Top speed	145 mph (233 km/h)

Five valves per cylinder helped Yamaha get 100 hp from a 750, while water-cooling helped make it narrower and more aerodynamic, with a drag coefficient of 0.34.

▽ **Honda VFR 700F Interceptor 1987**

Origin	Japan
Engine	699 cc, V-four
Top speed	130 mph (209 km/h)

Devised to beat US import tariffs, this was a short-stroke derivation of the 1983 VF750, the sports bike with racing DNA – from its triple-disc brakes to its water-cooled V-four.

◁ **Buell RR1000 1986**

Origin	USA
Engine	998 cc, V-twin
Top speed	140 mph (225 km/h)

The first new US motorcycle-maker for 60+ years, Erik Buell set out to beat Japanese superbikes with a tuned Harley engine in a light frame with an aerodynamic body.

▽ **Harley-Davidson XLH883 Sportster 1987**

Origin	USA
Engine	883 cc, V-twin
Top speed	100 mph (160 km/h)

Harley's entry-level four-speed cruiser of the mid-1980s was slow, loud, vibrated heavily, and had a tiny tank with a 100-mile (160-km) range; but buyers queued up for it.

△ **Ducati 851 1989**

Origin	Italy
Engine	851 cc, V-twin
Top speed	150 mph (241 km/h)

The new generation Ducati had a 90-degree V-twin engine, but with water cooling, fuel injection, and four valves per cylinder. It was a brutally fast road bike and successful racer.

△ **Suzuki GSX-R400 1989**

Origin Japan

Engine 398 cc, in-line four

Top speed 115 mph (185 km/h)

The first lightweight race replica with an aluminium cradle frame and twin-cam, 16-valve, water-cooled, in-line four, the GSX-R400 was restyled in 1988.

▷ **Gilera Saturno Bialbero 500 1989**

Origin Italy

Engine 492 cc, single-cylinder

Top speed 110 mph (177 km/h)

This compact Café Racer, using the highest quality components to recreate the 1939 Saturno in a modern context, was a light, lively, and stunning-looking bike.

△ **Honda CBR1000F 1988**

Origin Japan

Engine 998 cc, in-line four

Top speed 155 mph (249 km/h)

Good build quality and a comfortable riding position were not enough to endear this bike to road testers, who found it deceptively fast but bland – yet it sold for 10 years.

△ **Honda RC30 1988**

Origin Japan

Engine 748 cc, V-four

Top speed 152 mph (245 km/h)

This machine of the finest quality blends the lightweight, quick steering and fantastic handling of a race bike with excellent ride quality, reliability, and stability.

△ **Honda CBR600F 1989**

Origin Japan

Engine 598 cc, in-line four

Top speed 145 mph (233 km/h)

Introduced in 1987, the CBR's stunning performance made it a class leader. A redesign in 1989 gave it 10 per cent more power and upgrades kept it competitive.

Power Play

As the world became more prosperous in the 1980s, manufacturers played with new technology on their ultimate road bikes, as buyers would pay extra for something really special. Turbocharging was tried (see below); Kawasaki offered a transverse straight-six engine and also introduced digital fuel injection; while Suzuki had a roadgoing two-stroke GP racer. Alternatively, specialists offered frame kits so people could build their own bikes.

◁ **Yamaha XS1100 LG Midnight Special 1980**

Origin Japan

Engine 1,101 cc, in-line four

Top speed 126 mph (203 km/h)

Yamaha went to extreme lengths with the black and gold finish, even down to black chrome exhausts with unified braking to prove this bike was not just about looks.

▽ **Honda CB1100R 1983**

Origin Japan

Engine 1,062 cc, in-line four

Top speed 142 mph (229 km/h)

This was a high-quality sporting machine that was competitive in production racing, but it also made an excellent sports tourer. It was comfortable, fast, and handled well.

▷ **Kawasaki GPZ 1100 1983**

Origin Japan

Engine 1,089 cc, in-line four

Top speed 137 mph (220 km/h)

The GPZ 1100 was upgraded in 1982 with a digital fuel injection and bikini fairing. Kawasaki's fastest bike of the day could be a handful but rewarded the experienced rider.

▷ **Kawasaki Z1300 1984**

Origin Japan

Engine 1,286 cc, in-line six

Top speed 139 mph (224 km/h)

This huge machine was launched as a flagship model but missed the mark. Performance was no better than their 1,000 cc fours, but excess weight meant that it did not handle as well.

▽ **Moto Martin CBX 1260 Special 1985**

Origin France

Engine 1,260 cc, in-line six

Top speed 150 mph (241 km/h)

Built in France, the Moto Martin café racer frame could house the customer's choice of engine and components; this is a Honda CBX, which has been modified for extra power.

△ **Harley-Davidson XR1000 1984**

Origin USA

Engine 998 cc, V-twin

Top speed 115 mph (185 km/h)

Harley's racing boss Dick O'Brien built the first road XR out of his dirt track race-winning bikes in 60 days. More sportster than racer, it was light, strong, and fun.

Turbo Charged

Turbocharging was the latest craze for cars in 1980 and supercharging was normal for drag bikes, so it was no surprise when the Japanese "big four" announced turbocharged bikes in 1982 to 1983. Mid-range acceleration, when the turbo was most efficient, was very quick, but off-boost performance was sluggish and that inflexibility just did not suit motorcycles.

△ **Suzuki XN85D Turbo 1983**

Origin Japan

Engine 673 cc, in-line four

Top speed 128 mph (206 km/h)

Suzuki's turbo ran at low pressure, giving minimal power increase. The 16-in (41-cm) front wheel was meant to improve handling – but that was a gimmick as well.

△ **Honda CX650 Turbo 1983**

Origin Japan

Engine 674 cc, V-twin turbocharged

Top speed 125 mph (201 km/h)

Despite the difficulty of turbocharging a V-twin, Honda launched a CX500 turbo with integrated bodywork in 1981, but soon increased capacity to 650.

△ **Yamaha V-Max 1985**

Origin Japan

Engine 1,198 cc, V4

Top speed 146 mph (235 km/h)

Built like a drag bike with 135 bhp and its fuel tank under the seat, this was the fastest accelerating production bike, capable of a sub-10 sec quarter-mile (0.40 km).

△ **Laverda SFC 1000 1986**

Origin Italy

Engine 981 cc, in-line triple

Top speed 143 mph (230 km/h)

Refined and tamed for the 1980s, Laverda's ultimate air-cooled triple still had a good turn of speed, but was seen more as a sports tourer than a superbike.

△ **Suzuki RG500 1986**

Origin Japan

Engine 498 cc, square-four

Top speed 147 mph (237 km/h)

Suzuki won the 1976, 1977, 1981, and 1982 World Championships with two-stroke RG500s. In 1984 it was finally released as a road bike: light, peaky, and blisteringly fast.

◁ **Kawasaki ZX750E Turbo 1983**

Origin Japan

Engine 738 cc, in-line four turbo

Top speed 146 mph (235 km/h)

Last of the big four to produce a turbo bike, Kawasaki built the best, minimizing turbo lag to give huge acceleration well ahead of conventionally aspirated superbikes.

△ **Yamaha XJ650 Seca Turbo 1984**

Origin Japan

Engine 653 cc, in-line four

Top speed 126 mph (203 km/h)

The second turbo bike on the market after Honda's, the Seca had terrific acceleration on boost, but turbo lag hampered rapid road progress and it only lasted two years.

Test riders pictured with the 125cc YA-1

Great Marques
The Yamaha Story

Having built a reputation for high performance and quality engineering with lightweight two-strokes, Yamaha diversified to offer a large range of bikes from scooters to cruisers. Always forward-looking and technically adventurous, the company maintains a high sporting profile in both track racing and off-road competition.

THE THREE TUNING FORKS in the Yamaha logo are a reminder of the company's background in music. Torakusu Yamaha founded Nippon Gakki to make reed organs in 1887, and his company grew to be one of the world's largest instrument makers.

In 1955 Nippon Gakki president Genichi Kawakami set up the Yamaha Motor Company. Its first bike, based on a 1930s German DKW design, was the YA1, which had a 125 cc, single cylinder two-stroke engine. This was swiftly followed by a 250 cc twin, influenced by the German Adler. Coded YD1, this sturdy machine sold well in Japan's crowded motorcycle market and set the pattern for a long line of two-stroke twins.

Yamaha soon became a leading contender in Japanese motorbike racing and made a foray into US racing

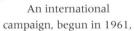

Yamaha badge
(introduced 1964)

in 1958, contesting the Catalina Grand Prix with a 250 cc twin. Official US distribution was set up in 1960 to supply the 250 cc YD2 twin and the exciting YDS1 sports variant. But it was the YDS2 of 1962 that alerted the motorcycling world to the scintillating performance of Yamaha's twin-cylinder bikes.

An international campaign, begun in 1961, reinforced the marque's racing credentials. Within two years, US rider Don Vesco won the 250 cc US Grand Prix and factory rider Fumio Ito won the Belgian Grand Prix. In 1964 Yamaha ended Honda's supremacy in the 250 cc World Championships, when British rider Phil Read took the first of two consecutive titles.

To gain more power while ensuring reliability, Yamaha engineers turned to four-cylinder, water-cooled engines. Britain's Bill Ivy won the 125 cc crown in 1967, while Phil Read collected both the 250 cc and 125 cc titles in 1968. In that year Ivy became the first 125 cc rider to lap the Isle of Man TT circuit at 100 mph (161 km/h) on his V-four with two crankshafts.

From the mid-1960s, Yamaha marketed less exotic track machines for

Weekend getaway
This 1972 poster advertising Yamaha's 125 cc and 175 cc Enduros surely would have appealed to the sense of adventure and freedom of young people of the time.

independent "privateer" racers. The original 250 cc TD air-cooled twin was followed by the 350 cc TR twin and, from 1973, the lightning fast 250 cc and 350 cc TZs.

After new rules restricted the number of cylinders and gear ratios in Grand Prix racing, Yamaha won four 250 cc and three 350 cc world championships in the 1970s. It became the first two-stroke factory to top the 500 cc class when Italian rider Giacomo Agostini took the premier title on a two-stroke in-line four in 1975. Kenny Roberts, who trained on dirt tracks, became America's first asphalt world champion with his 500 cc title in 1978 and gave Yamaha two more titles in the following seasons.

YAMAHA The great machines for '72.

Yamaha forged ahead with innovation. Monoshock rear suspension devised for motocross transferred to road machines in the late 1970s, and racing spin-offs of the 1980s included the Yamaha Power

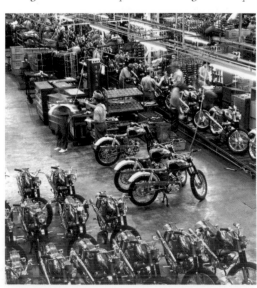

High output
The Yamaha Motor Company started out building 200 bikes a month and became a world leader within 10 years.

> "The most **Western-thinking** of the Japanese makers and always **forward-looking**."
>
> KENNY ROBERTS, YAMAHA WORLD CHAMPION 1978-1980

Meanwhile, the company's ever-widening array of bikes had gained a foothold in world markets. The 250 cc DT1 Enduro of 1968 established Yamaha as a top marque on America's booming off-road scene, while the XS-1 (later the XS650), with a vertical twin-cylinder engine, directly challenged British imports from 1970.

Valve System, which improved two-stroke engine characteristics, and the Deltabox aluminium frame. Catalogued machines ranged from 50 cc step-throughs to 1,100 cc four-strokes and 1,200 cc V-twins with maintenance-free shaft drives. The high-performance road theme persisted with 250 cc, 350 cc, and

DT-1

TX500

RD350

YSZ-R1

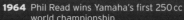
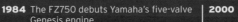

1955	The Yamaha Motor Company is formed; it launches the 125 cc YA1.
1957	Yamaha's first twin-cylinder bike, the 250 cc YD1, is released
1958	Cooper Motors begins to sell Yamaha motorbikes in the US.
1960	The Yamaha International Corporation is founded as the US base; European distribution begins in the Netherlands.
1963	Yamaha's first production racer, the 250 cc TD1, is released; Fumio Ito wins the 250 cc Belgian Grand Prix.

1964	Phil Read wins Yamaha's first 250 cc world championship.
1967	Bill Ivy wins Yamaha's first 125 cc world championship.
1970	Yamaha's first four-stroke, the 650 cc XS-1, is launched.
1977	The 130 mph (209 km/h) shaft-driven XS1100 is introduced.
1978	Kenny Roberts wins Yamaha's first 500 cc world championship.
1980	Yamaha releases the water-cooled two-stroke RD250 LC.

1984	The FZ750 debuts Yamaha's five-valve Genesis engine.
1985	Yamaha's V-Max cruiser begins its 20-year production run.
1987	The EXUP power valve system is introduced.
1992	Wayne Rainey wins his third 500cc world championship in a row.
1994	Yamaha cruisers start to be sold under the Star brand in the US.
1998	The powerful 1000cc YZF-R1 sports bike is released.

2000	Riding a Yamaha YZF-R1, David Jefferies is the first rider to lap the Isle of Man TT road circuit at 125 mph (201 km/h).
2004	Valentino Rossi wins the MotoGP world championship on a YZR-M1.
2007	The YZF-R1 production bike is updated with MotoGP technology.
2009	The new 1700cc VMAX is launched; Ben Spies wins the World Superbike series on a YZF-R1.
2010	Jorge Lorenzo wins the MotoGP series on a Yamaha YZR-M1.

500 cc water-cooled two-strokes, while off-road options ran from versatile trail and enduro models to ferocious YZ motocross racers. Yamaha's 500 cc world championship of 1977 was the first of many motocross titles, and the company won the Dakar Rally nine times between 1979 and 1998.

Two exciting high-performance four-strokes appeared in the mid-1980s. The 1200 cc V-Max cruiser rapidly achieved cult status with the devastatingly strong acceleration of its water-cooled V-four engine. The FZ750 super sport launched Yamaha's Genesis four-cylinder engine. It also sired the FZR line, notably the FZR1000, with an engine featuring Yamaha's pioneering Exhaust Ultimate Power Valve (EXUP) system.

Relentless two-stroke engine and chassis development led to Eddie Lawson winning four world championships between 1984 and 1989, and Wayne Rainey winning three in the early 1990s using YZR500 V-four engines. The 900 cc

MotoGP champion
Spanish star Jorge Lorenzo won the 2010 MotoGP championship on a YZR-M1. Lorenzo follows Valentino Rossi who was champion four times on a Yamaha.

four-stroke YZR-M1, built for the MotoGP formula introduced in 2002, came good in 2004 and 2005 with titles for ex-Honda champion Valentino Rossi.

Race-bred technology fed through to showroom machines, notably the 1,000 cc YZF-R1 launched to acclaim in 1998 with an extremely compact 1,000 cc five-valve engine in a well-balanced chassis. The R1 later gained fuel injection, an uprated Deltabox frame and, from 2007, an improved four-valves-per-cylinder engine. The latest R1 benefits from M1 racer development with a cross-plane crankshaft layout for better power delivery.

Just as sophisticated in their own way are Yamaha's cruisers that have been sold under the Star brand in the US since the mid-1990s. V-twin engine sizes go up to a massive 1,854 cc and Star's ultimate muscle machine is the current 1,679 cc VMAX.

Retro technology
Yamaha's air-cooled pushrod V-twin engine has been used in heavy cruisers since 1999. However, a version of this engine is also used in the Yamaha MT-01 muscle bike.

Design Diversity

A hundred years of motorcycle development had led to a degree of conventionality of design for popular motorcycles, but that did not stop manufacturers in the 1980s from looking for alternative engineering solutions or new niche markets. While some continued to build bikes that had been designed 50 years earlier, others experimented with rotary engines, tilting three-wheelers, and extreme streamlining.

▷ Yamaha XV920R 1981

Origin Japan

Engine 920 cc, V-twin

Top speed 115 mph (185 km/h)

This bike was built for the US market and intended to offer a wide spread of power for sporty touring. A larger capacity 980cc model was sold in European markets as the TR1.

△ Suzuki GSX 1000SV Katana 1982

Origin Japan

Engine 998 cc, in-line four

Top speed 137 mph (220 km/h)

Suzuki Germany commissioned Target Design to conceive a bike for the German market. This 1,000 cc version of that 1,100 was built for one year only for race homologation.

▽ Hesketh V1000 1982

Origin UK

Engine 992 cc, V-twin

Top speed 119 mph (192 km/h)

First shown in 1980 but not built until 1982, Lord Hesketh's indulgent V-twin motorcycle was a status symbol on par with his successful Formula 1 team.

△ Triumph TSX 750 1982

Origin UK

Engine 748 cc, in-line twin

Top speed 119 mph (192 km/h)

US designer Wayne Moulton was commissioned by the Triumph workers' cooperative to design a bike for the US market based on the Bonneville; the cooperative failed in 1983.

▷ Triumph Thunderbird TR65 1982

Origin UK

Engine 649 cc, in-line twin

Top speed 110 mph (177 km/h)

Built by the workers' cooperative, this was a cheaper, economy-oriented version of the 750 Bonneville with a shorter stroke, drum rear brake and points ignition.

△ Greer Streamliner 1983

Origin USA

Engine 185 cc, single-cylinder

Top speed 90 mph (145 km/h)

Jerry Greer and Chuck Guy built this aerodynamic machine with a Yamaha engine for a 3,000-mile (4,828-km) trans-US run, California to New York on 15 gallons (68 litres) at 196.5 mpg (83.53 km/l).

△ Honda Stream 1982

Origin Japan

Engine 49 cc, single-cylinder

Top speed 30 mph (48 km/h)

Honda licensed the design of George Wallis, first sold as the Ariel 3, to build this tilting three-wheeler with a two-stroke engine and continuously variable transmission.

◁ Honda CB250RS 1982

Origin Japan

Engine 249 cc, single-cylinder

Top speed 85 mph (137 km/h)

Honda looked to earlier British singles with this popular twin-exhaust machine, though it had four valves, vibration damping, and, from 1982, electric starting.

▷ Honda XBR500 1988

Origin Japan

Engine 498 cc, single-cylinder

Top speed 108 mph (174 km/h)

Honda wanted to hark back to the traditional British "sports single" using a radial, four-valve arrangement similar to a 1930s Rudge. It was a fun bike, and not too fast.

△ KMZ Dnepr MT11 1985

Origin Russia

Engine 649 cc, flat-twin

Top speed 80 mph (129 km/h)

Based on the 1930s BMW R71, the Kiev-built Dnepr was steadily, if slowly, refined with a swinging-arm rear suspension, overhead-valves, and 12-volt electrics.

◁ Honda Bros Product 2 1989

Origin Japan

Engine 398 cc, V-twin

Top speed 94 mph (151 km/h)

Introduced in Japan as the Bros, this bike was later sold more widely as the NT400. Ideal for new riders, this was a smart, aluminium-framed machine with all-round ability.

△ Norton Classic Rotary 1988

Origin UK

Engine 588 cc, twin-rotor Wankel

Top speed 126 mph (203 km/h)

Norton unveiled its rotary in 1975, but could not afford to build it. However, 300 bikes were built for the British police from 1982 and 100 of these special customer versions were sold in 1988.

△ Honda PC800 Pacific Coast 1989

Origin Japan

Engine 800 cc, V-twin

Top speed 120 mph (193 km/h)

Looking like a super-scooter, the innovative PC800 boasted a water-cooled engine capable of over 100,000 miles (160,934 km), shaft drive, a large boot, and an all-enveloping body.

Mile Eaters

The 1980s brought an economic boom, early retirement for many, and with it the leisure time and funds to buy the ultimate, luxurious cruising motorcycles and set off across countries and continents to enjoy them. While some chose to follow their dream from an expanding range of Harley-Davidsons, others went for slightly sportier rides, or pure luxury from Honda's Goldwing.

◁ Moto Guzzi California II 1980

Origin Italy

Engine 949 cc, V-twin

Top speed 119 mph (192 km/h)

Introduced as an 850 in 1972, Moto Guzzi's big V-twin was mounted transversely. Being Italian, it handled with brio while remaining a great cruising machine.

△ Honda GL1100 Goldwing Aspencade 1982

Origin Japan

Engine 1,085 cc, flat-four

Top speed 103 mph (166 km/h)

A cockpit-controlled air suspension, stereo radio, and vanity mirror were standard fitments on the super-luxury Aspencade, which was still faster than an FL Harley.

▽ Triumph T140AV TSS 1982

Origin UK

Engine 744 cc, in-line twin

Top speed 118 mph (190 km/h)

This was the last of the Meriden-built Triumphs, before the British marque was overwhelmed by Japanese opposition. It had eight valves, an electric starting, and anti-vibration measures.

◁ Honda VF500C Magna 1983

Origin Japan

Engine 498 cc, V-four

Top speed 112 mph (180 km/h)

The compact and powerful Honda V-four engine was used in cruisers as well as sports bikes. The Magna was a sales success in many markets around the world.

△ Honda VF1000F Interceptor 1985

Origin Japan

Engine 998 cc, V-four

Top speed 145 mph (233 km/h)

Impressively fast and sophisticated, with only 6 hp less than the exotic (and much more expensive), race-derived 1000R, the Interceptor was a superb all-rounder.

◁ Honda GL1500 Goldwing 1988

Origin Japan

Engine 1,520 cc, flat-six

Top speed 108 mph (174 km/h)

Honda blew the big touring opposition out of the water with its monster flat-six, a super-smooth engine with lots of power. Its reverse gear was electronically powered.

◁ **BMW K100 1983**

Origin Germany

Engine 987 cc, in-line four

Top speed 137 mph (220 km/h)

After experimenting with a lying-down Peugeot car engine, BMW built its own longitudinally mounted four, with a low centre of gravity and shaft drive, perfect for touring.

△ **BMW K75 1985**

Origin Germany

Engine 740 cc, in-line three

Top speed 122 mph (196 km/h)

After building its longitudinal four, BMW lopped off one cylinder to make a triple, which proved even smoother. It was BMW's cheapest bike in the 1980s.

▽ **Harley-Davidson FLT Tour Glide 1989**

Origin USA

Engine 1,337 cc, V-twin

Top speed 93 mph (150 km/h)

The Tour Glide, with frame-mounted fairing and rubber-insulated engine, was the world's heaviest production roadster; it was difficult at low speeds.

△ **Harley-Davidson FLHT Electra Glide Classic 1984**

Origin USA

Engine 1,337 cc, V-twin

Top speed 100 mph (160 km/h)

Getting ever bigger and more expensive, the FLHT was super-luxurious on a long ride, but a real handful on twisty, hilly roads and heavy in every way, especially on fuel.

▽ **Harley-Davidson FXR Super Glide 1989**

Origin USA

Engine 1,337 cc, V-twin

Top speed 110 mph (177 km/h)

Harley's factory custom model was quicker and more economical than its huge touring sisters, with a lighter gauge frame and its engine rubber-mounted to reduce vibration.

△ **Honda VT1100C Shadow 1989**

Origin Japan

Engine 1,089 cc, V-twin

Top speed 107 mph (172 km/h)

For little over half the price of a big touring Harley, Honda offered its own large cruising V-twin, but water-cooled with multiple valves and plugs for flexibility and speed.

Ice speedway
The sport of ice speedway has a category in which competitors ride bikes with studded tyres. These produce huge amounts of traction, which requires special gearboxes. Four-stroke Jawa motorbikes have dominated the sport.

Dirt Diggers

Motorcycles evolved to stay competitive in the various disciplines of off-road sport. The changes in motocross machines over the course of the decade were obvious, as they went from air to water cooling, from drum to disc brakes, and from twin-shock to single-shock rear-suspension systems. By comparison, bikes used for speedway, or American dirt-track racing, saw little change from the beginning of the decade to the end.

△ **Harley-Davidson XR-750 1980**
Origin USA
Engine 748 cc, V-twin
Top speed 115 mph (185 km/h)

This dirt tracker became the most successful bike in the American Motorcyclist Association's racing history; Harley's racing department built 200 each year.

▽ **Honda CR250R Elsinore 1980**
Origin Japan
Engine 248 cc, single-cylinder
Top speed 65 mph (105 km/h)

Honda's Elsinore motocross bikes were successful and the new, more powerful engine made this model even better, but it needed improved suspension to remain competitive.

△ **GM Speedway 1980**
Origin Italy
Engine 500 cc, single-cylinder
Top speed 90 mph (145 km/h)

In the late 1970s former Italian champion Giuseppe Marzotto designed his own GM Speedway engines with four overhead-valves, running on methanol fuel.

▽ **Godden GR500 1980**
Origin UK
Engine 500 cc, single-cylinder
Top speed 90 mph (145 km/h)

Speedway star Don Godden began making his own frames in the 1970s and developed his own four-valve, overhead-cam engine for the world title-winning GR500.

△ **Honda CR125 1988**
Origin Japan
Engine 124 cc, single-cylinder
Top speed 60 mph (97 km/h)

Part of Honda's range since 1973, the CR125 was always at the forefront of motocross competition thanks to its powerful reed-valve, two-stroke engine.

▷ **Maico Mega 490 1981**

Origin Germany

Engine 488cc, single-cylinder

Top speed 90mph (145km/h)

The Maisch brothers started building motorcycles in 1926 and after the war became famous for bikes like this one. It was not competitive at Grand Prix level, but was popular with amateurs.

◁ **Moto Morini 500 Camel 1981**

Origin Italy

Engine 478cc, V-twin

Top speed 105mph (169km/h)

Built for the growing trail-bike market, using an engine from Morini's road bike, early versions of the Camel, like this one, were surprisingly capable off-road.

▷ **Suzuki PE250X Enduro 1981**

Origin Japan

Engine 246cc, single-cylinder

Top speed 70mph (113km/h)

Suzuki's reed-valve, two-stroke PE model was launched in 1977, with electronic ignition and wide-ratio gearing for enduro events. Weighing just 240lb (109kg), it put out 38.5hp.

◁ **Armstrong MT500 1985**

Origin UK

Engine 481cc, single-cylinder

Top speed 80mph (129km/h)

British Army motorcycles, with Austrian Rotax engines, were made by the specialist Armstrong company. The design was subsequently made by Harley-Davidson, using a 350cc engine.

▷ **MZ GE 250 ISDT Replica 1985**

Origin Germany

Engine 243cc, single-cylinder

Top speed 75mph (120km/h)

MZ's two-stroke engines were powerful. Around 200 bikes of this "kleine serie" were made from 1984 to 1987 as replicas of the factory 1982 International Six Days Trial bikes.

△ **Montesa Cota 304 1987**

Origin Spain

Engine 238cc, single-cylinder

Top speed 75mph (120km/h)

Honda bought out Montesa in 1985; the 304 had its first production disc brake and monoshock rear suspension, enabling Montesa to maintain its competitive edge.

Racers

Although 1980s Grand Prix racing was dominated by thoroughbred two-stroke machines, the emergence of the Superbike class provided a showcase for production-based motorcycles. While Grand Prix continued to be dominated by the Japanese manufacturers, the Superbike class encouraged Italian manufacturer Ducati to bring out their booming, desmodromic valve V-twin to devastating effect; with added electronic fuel-injection, it kept on winning.

◁ **Yamaha YZR500 0W46 1980**

Origin Japan

Engine 499 cc, V-four

Top speed 170 mph (274 km/h)

Yamaha's 500 two-stroke Grand Prix bike switched to a V-four engine layout in 1982, adopting crankcase reed valves in 1984 when Eddie Lawson won the Riders Championship.

△ **Yamaha TZ250H 1981**

Origin Japan

Engine 249 cc, in-line twin

Top speed 130 mph (209 km/h)

The TZ production race bikes were hugely successful and constantly evolved. Exhaust power valves were added for 1981, giving variable port timing for increased power.

◁ **Weslake Speedway 1981**

Origin UK

Engine 499 cc, single-cylinder

Top speed 75 mph (120 km/h)

The four-valve Weslake Speedway engine, in a traditionally skeletal chassis, achieved pre-eminence in the 1970s. Bruce Penhall rode this bike at the 1981 World Championship.

△ **Suzuki RG500 1982**

Origin Japan

Engine 495 cc, square-four

Top speed 170 mph (274 km/h)

This water-cooled, disc-valved, "stepped" square-four two-stroke won Franco Uncini the 500 cc World Championship in 1982, his first year as a Suzuki works rider.

▷ **Kawasaki ZX750 GPz 1983**

Origin Japan

Engine 738 cc, in-line four

Top speed 186 mph (300 km/h)

To everyone's surprise, Wayne Rainey won the 1983 US AMA Superbike Championship on this machine, beating the theoretically superior Honda V-fours.

△ **Kawasaki KR500 1983**

Origin Japan

Engine 499 cc, square-four

Top speed 155 mph (249 km/h)

Debuted in 1980, the two-stroke KR was highly innovative with a monocoque frame and anti-dive forks, but it failed to achieve Grand Prix success.

◁ **MBA 125 1984**

Origin Italy

Engine 125 cc, in-line twin

Top speed 125 mph (201 km/h)

Successful disc-valve, two-stroke racers were built by Morbidelli in the 1970s and won the 125 Grand Prix 36 times. Customer versions of this model were sold by MBA.

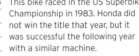

△ **Honda R500R 1984**

Origin Japan

Engine 499 cc, V-triple

Top speed 170 mph (274 km/h)

Freddie Spencer won the 1983 500 cc World Championship on a three-cylinder two-stroke NS500, while the customer version (the RS500) achieved national success.

◁ **Honda RVF750 1986**

Origin Japan

Engine 749 cc, V-four

Top speed 174 mph (280 km/h)

Ultra-light materials such as titanium connecting rods helped Honda keep the RVFs weight down to just 370 lb (168 kg) – without fuel. This is Joey Dunlop's F1 TT winning bike.

▽ **Honda VF750F Interceptor 1983**

Origin Japan

Engine 748 cc, V-four

Top speed 155 mph (249 km/h)

This bike raced in the US Superbike Championship in 1983. Honda did not win the title that year, but it was successful the following year with a similar machine.

△ **Honda NSR500 1989**

Origin Japan

Engine 499 cc, V-four

Top speed 165 mph (266 km/h)

Debuted in 1984, the NSR won 10 World Championships before the Grand Prix rules changed to favour four-strokes in 2002. This is Eddie Lawson's 1989 championship winner.

▽ **Ducati 851 Superbike 1989**

Origin Italy

Engine 851 cc, V-twin

Top speed 195 mph (314 km/h)

Ducati became the dominant force in World Superbike racing with its desmodromic eight-valve, fuel-injected V-twins. This is the road version on which the racers were based.

The
1990s

Aside from Asia and Southern Europe, the use of two-wheelers for essential transport continued to decline, but the industry as a whole offered an evermore diverse range of products. There was a move away from fully enclosed sports machines towards retro styling, with engines proudly displayed. The on/off-road category matured, with more products suited to the rigours of inter-continental adventure. The US-oriented, cruiser class expanded, although Harley-Davidson still dominated. A successful revival of the Triumph marque put Britain back in the frame.

Mike Hailwood leading the 1959 TT race on a 125 cc Ducati

Great Marques
The Ducati Story

Once a maker of tiny clip-on bicycle engines, Ducati has become a leading force in modern motorcycle technology and design. Success has been due to continual involvement in racing development, an enduring passion for creative engineering, and a Latin panache that gives Ducati's bikes their distinctive character.

THE COMPANY'S HISTORY dates back to 1926, when Antonio Ducati and his three sons started a business making radio components in Bologna, northern Italy. Although the company diversified into cameras, shavers, and other consumer products, after World War II it turned its attention to motorcycles, producing a clip-on bicycle engine for Siata, a car-tuning and accessories company in Turin. The 48 cc four-stroke Cucciolo ("Puppy") unit provided basic transport in war-torn Italy and was phenomenally successful. By 1952, when more than 200,000 were in use, Ducati had started to make its own motorcycles and scooters with small engines, as favoured by most of the nation's motorcycle manufacturers. It was the arrival of Fabio Taglioni as technical

Ducati badge
(introduced 2008)

chief in 1954 that put Ducati on the road to glory. A brilliant engineer, he designed a 100 cc single, with an overhead camshaft, that set a pattern for future Ducati models. Potent and sturdy, it excelled in Italy's long-distance road races, and was soon enlarged to 125 cc. A double overhead-camshaft version developed for international racing was further refined by Taglioni's Desmodromic system. This used cams to close the valves as well as to open them, preventing power-loss at high revs. Ducati's first "Desmo" engine won on its race debut in the 1956 125 cc Swedish grand prix and narrowly missed clinching the 1958 125 cc World Championship.

Single-cylinder road bikes were launched onto world markets. Early Ducatis often had crude electrical equipment, a poor finish, and few concessions to comfort, but sporting riders were seduced by their snappy performance and sound handling. Taglioni's singles grew in stages, arriving at their 450 cc maximum by the end of the 1960s, when Desmo engines were offered on premium models.

Ducati entered the superbike arena in the 1970s with a 750 cc model. When building the engine, Taglioni placed two of the proven single

Speed sells
Its racing success with streamlined 125 cc Desmodromic singles was exploited by Ducati when publicizing its products during the mid-1950s.

Mike Hailwood and Ducati
The young racing star sits on a 125 cc single at the 1960 Isle of Man TT. Hailwood would take his 13th TT victory on a Ducati twin.

most radical early work was the all-enclosed Paso 750 of 1986, which, although not a big seller, set the style for sports motorcycles.

As ever, it was racing success that maintained Ducati's reputation. The new generation of water-cooled, four-valve Desmoquattro engines dominated twin-cylinder racing, and in 1988 the road-legal 851 Strada,

cylinders at a 90-degree V angle, creating a slim format often referred to as an L-twin. Its reputation was assured when factory Desmo versions took first and second place in the 1972 Imola 200 race.

Road twin-cylinders were offered in Touring, Sport, and Super Sport versions, at first with 750 cc engines and then 900 cc (actually 864 cc) units. The larger engine further enhanced Ducati's prestige when popular Ducati veteran Mike Hailwood won the 1978 Formula 1 TT.

In the 1980s control of the company passed to Cagiva, a younger motorcycle-maker. Fears that the Ducati brand would disappear were proved to be unfounded when ex-Bimota designer Massimo Tamburini came on board and revitalized the marque. His

Cucciolo

350 Desmo

916

Desmosedici GP8

1926 The Ducati Patented Wireless company is founded in Bologna.
1946 Production of the Cucciolo T1 bicycle engine begins.
1950 65 cc Ducati 60 Sport with pressed-steel frame and rear suspension is released.
1953 98 cc ohv Touring and Sport models are released.
1955 The launch of Taglioni-designed Gran Sport 100.
1956 The first Desmo engine wins the Swedish Grand Prix.

1965 The 250 cc Mach 1 roadster is released.
1969 The first Desmo road machine, the 250 cc Mk3D, debuts.
1970 The Street Scrambler versions of singles are a sales success.
1971 The first road V-twin, the ohc GT750, goes on sale.
1972 Paul Smart and Bruno Spaggiari finish 1st and 2nd on Desmo 750s in the Imola 200 race.
1979 Pantah 500 is Ducati's first production machine with belt-driven cams.

1981 Ducati rider Tony Rutter wins the first of four consecutive TT Formula Two championships.
1985 The Cagiva Group acquires Ducati from the Italian government.
1988 The four-valve 851 Strada gives road riders race technology.
1990 Ducati wins the first of its 16 World Superbike Championships.
1993 First of the best-selling unfaired Monster twins, the M900.
1994 The 916 sports is released to acclaim.

1998 US-based Texas Pacific Group becomes the majority stakeholder in Ducati.
2003 Ducati enters the MotoGP Championship with a V-four engine.
2005 The company is bought by the Italian group Investindustrial Holdings.
2007 Ducati rider Casey Stoner wins the MotoGP World Championship.
2008 The limited-edition 170 hp road version of the Desmosedici Four is a sell-out.
2011 The 1,198 cc Diavel marks a new departure in high-performance models.

with fuel injection, was introduced as a possible World Superbike championship contender. Twin-cylinder 1,000 cc machines could race against four-cylinder 750 cc models in the series, and Ducati's agile bikes were extremely competitive. Frenchman Raymond Roche became the 1990 champion, popularizing the twins and their booming exhausts. A vogue for single-cylinder racing prompted the 1993 Supermono, a high-tech 550 cc racer with svelte styling by Pierre Terblanche. Then came another masterpiece, the 916, designed by Tamburini with the latest 114 hp Desmoquattro engine. Aggressive, yet undeniably beautiful, the 916's stunning looks influenced other leading manufacturers' designs. However, not everyone wanted a semi-racer, which is why the unfaired and rider-friendly M900 Monster accounted for half of Ducati's bike sales in the 1990s.

Throughout the decade Ducati dominated the superbike class, with Carl Fogarty taking four world titles,

Ducati engine
The 90-degree V-twin engine configuration has been employed for four decades, with toothed belts adopted for camshaft drive in the late 1970s.

Doug Polen, two, and Troy Corser, one. The marque joined the MotoGP world series from 2003 with the 990 cc four-cylinder, 16-valve Desmosedici. Essentially a doubled-up L-twin with pairs of cylinders firing together and with a top speed of 215 mph (346 km/h) – the bike took its first victory in 2005. After it was adapted to the revised 800 cc MotoGP formula, the Australian Casey Stoner was victorius in Ducati's first MotoGP Championship in 2007. In 2011, the marque signed Italy's multiple world champion Valentino Rossi as the

basic engine layout and, despite the near-universal adoption of aluminium frames, the tubular steel "trellis" chassis construction remained.

"**Simplicity** has been the **basic principle** of all my designs."
FABIO TAGLIONI, DUCATI'S TECHNICAL DIRECTOR 1954-1989

team's number one, and the development rider of a 1,000 cc Desmosedici for 2012.

Off the track, both Honda and Suzuki unveiled new 1,000 cc, 90-degree V-twin sport bikes in the late 1990s. However, Ducati stuck fast to its

Ducati in MotoGP
Casey Stoner, on the 800 cc Desmosedici V-four, leads Honda's Andreas Dovizioso in the 2010 Japanese round of the MotoGP World Championship on the Twin Ring Motegi circuit.

In 2003 the marque widened its range by releasing a sports tourer, the Multistrada. The Testastretta ("narrow head") 1,098 cc was debuted in 2007 and subsequently grew to 1,198 cc, while the Diavel of 2011, with shattering performance and menacing appearance, defied easy labelling.

From a position of near extinction in the 1980s, Ducati has grown into a world brand so strong that it now sells a variety of prestige merchandise, from watches to men's fragrances. Nonetheless, it continues to be best known for its stylish range of bikes.

Taxi to market, 1992
By the 1990s, affordable motorcycles had become an essential mode of transport for millions of people. Here, one scooter tows a cart laden with people to market in the Kompong Thom region of Cambodia.

After
2000

Electronics brought extraordinary sophistication to 21st-century motorcycles. Driven by the need to reduce emissions, electronically controlled fuel injection became universal. Anti-lock brakes were followed by traction control to prevent rear-wheel slip, plus push-button selection of engine characteristics for different conditions, or even according to mood. Suspension improvements continued to proliferate, sometimes offering a mind-boggling permutation of settings. By the second decade, "clean" motorcycle technology was making great strides.

BMW K1600GT

Touring doesn't get any grander than on BMW's K1600GT model, unveiled to widespread critical acclaim in 2011. Even for a marque renowned for its fine long-distance bikes, its specification level left rivals trailing in its panniered wake. At its heart was a mighty six-cylinder engine which, teamed with a wealth of sophisticated accoutrements providing every possible comfort for rider and passenger, created a ground-breaking 21st-century sporting Grand Tourer.

THE K1600GT's stunning debut came in the nick of time for BMW. In spite of its reputation for building some of the world's finest touring bikes, the marque was facing stiff competition from its Japanese rivals. The K1300GT had gone some way to re-establishing the company's market-leading position in 2009, but the mighty K1600GT enabled the manufacturer to fully flex its engineering muscles once more. This was most clearly expressed through the model's ultra-smooth 160 bhp in-line six engine. Also present was a raft of features that made a K1600GT rider the most pampered motorcyclist on the road. Standard equipment, such as heated seats and grips, and a colour monitor for the on-board computer, could be supplemented by extras – including traction control and an electronic suspension system. Combining power, comfort, and safety in one beautifully designed package, the model – UK magazine *Motor Cycle News'* 2011 Tourer of the Year – took open-road touring to a new level of luxury.

FRONT VIEW

REAR VIEW

Bavarian roots
The blue and white quartered circle in the BMW logo is thought to represent a moving aircraft propeller against the sky. While this reflects the company's background in aircraft engines, the colours are also those featured in the flag of Bavaria, where BMW is based.

Windscreen can be electronically adjusted

Fuel tank with 24-litre capacity

Luggage space in colour-matched pannier cases

Heated seat for rider and pillion passenger

Headlight with pioneering adaptive system

Fairing designed to provide maximum weather protection for rider

Vermilion red metallic is one of two colour schemes offered

Six-speed gearbox and final drive shaft

Suspension is electronically adjusted to suit ride conditions

SPECIFICATIONS

Model	BMW K1600GT (2011)	**Power output**	160 hp at 7,500 rpm
Assembly	Berlin, Germany	**Transmission**	Six-speed
Production	Not known	**Suspension**	Duolever front, paralever rear
Construction	Aluminium bridge frame	**Brakes**	Dual-disc front, single-disc rear
Engine	1,649 cc, in-line six-cylinder	**Maximum speed**	Over 140 mph (225 km/h)

Lighting the way

The adaptive headlight system was a world-first on a production motorcycle. Electronic controls monitored and adjusted the headlight beam so that it remained at exactly the same level, even when the bike leaned through corners.

Freestyle motocross, 2000
Big Air is a crowd-pleasing, freestyle motocross
discipline in which riders perform gravity-defying
stunts high in the air. The bikes used in motocross
are particularly light and manoeuvrable and
have highly developed suspension systems.

Harley-Davidson X8A
Air-cooled Single

The single cylinder, air-cooled power unit fitted to early Harley-Davidson machines is a typical four-stroke design of its time, also favoured by other manufacturers. Its spray carburettor induction, magneto ignition, and cam-operated poppet valve were features that would be seen on motorcycle engines for decades to come. Though not powerful, this 494 cc unit, fitted to the 1912 Model X8A, was rugged and dependable.

F-HEADS

Single cylinder, air-cooled engines were suitably compact and light for fitting to the rudimentary frames of early motorcycles. The combination of an automatic, atmospheric, inlet valve on the cylinder head with a mechanically operated exhaust valve was widely used on early, low-revving, four-stroke engines. On Harley-Davidsons, this configuration came to be known as the F-head, and was seen on both singles and V-twins. The last F-head twins were 1929 models. As engine speeds increased, the automatic valve could not keep up, and inlet valves had to be mechanically operated.

Float chamber
This fuel reservoir supplies the carburettor jet.

Bosch magneto
Its engine-driven ignition sparks the generator.

Fuel pipe

Gear cover
This encloses drive to the magneto.

ENGINE SPECIFICATIONS	
Dates produced	1911 to 1912
Cylinders	One
Configuration	Inclined
Engine capacity	494 cc
Power output	4.3 hp
Type	Conventional four-stroke air-cooled petrol engine
Head	Automatic inlet valve over mechanical exhaust valve
Cooling	Air
Fuel system	Schebler carburettor
Bore and stroke	3.3 in x 3.5 in (84 mm x 89 mm)
Compression ratio	not quoted

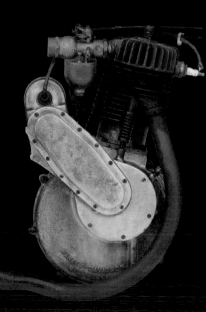

Genesis of the marque
This slightly refined engine unit differs little from the engine that powered Harley-Davidson's first production motorcycle of 1903. All subsequent engines – the majority of them V-twins – from the world-famous company were based on this model.

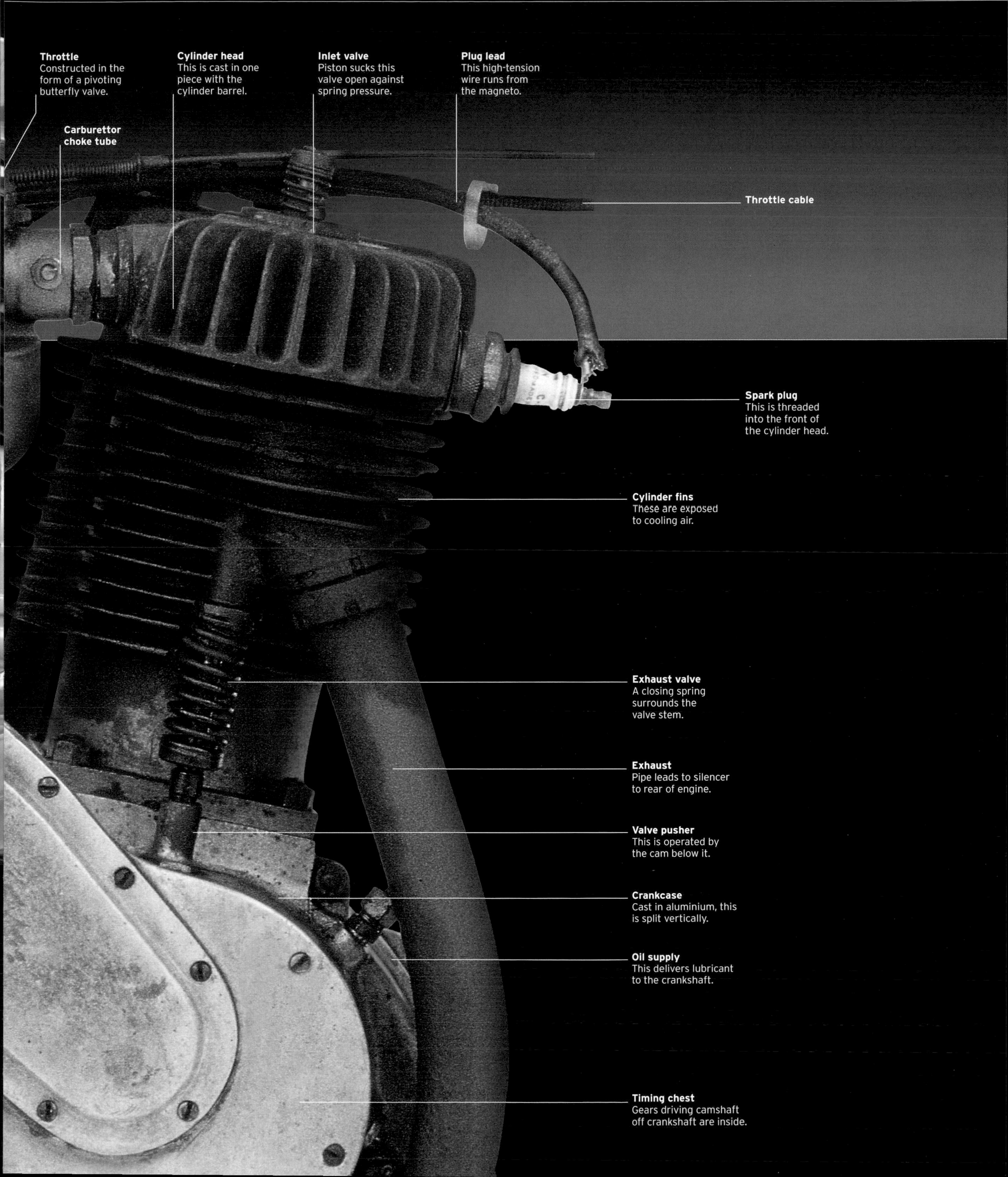

Throttle
Constructed in the form of a pivoting butterfly valve.

Cylinder head
This is cast in one piece with the cylinder barrel.

Inlet valve
Piston sucks this valve open against spring pressure.

Plug lead
This high-tension wire runs from the magneto.

Carburettor choke tube

Throttle cable

Spark plug
This is threaded into the front of the cylinder head.

Cylinder fins
These are exposed to cooling air.

Exhaust valve
A closing spring surrounds the valve stem.

Exhaust
Pipe leads to silencer to rear of engine.

Valve pusher
This is operated by the cam below it.

Crankcase
Cast in aluminium, this is split vertically.

Oil supply
This delivers lubricant to the crankshaft.

Timing chest
Gears driving camshaft off crankshaft are inside.

Vincent Rapide
V-twin

The 1,000 cc V-twin engine made by the small Vincent HRD factory in Stevenage, England, powered the world's fastest production motorcycles. Unlike any other power unit of the 1950s, this engine was the creation of company proprietor Philip Vincent, a design idealist, in collaboration with brilliant Australian engineer Phil Irving.

OFFSET CYLINDERS

Unveiled in 1947 to gain export sales for postwar "austerity" Britain, the Rapide twin engine had an antecedent in Vincent's 1938 1,000 cc twin. However, intensive work during World War II resulted in a more powerful, sophisticated, and tidy-looking unit. The classic "V" configuration of the cylinders, at 55 degrees in this instance, was chosen to minimize the engine's height and width as well as give a relatively vibration-free power delivery. The connecting rods' big-end bearings are placed side-by-side on a single crankpin, so the rear cylinder's bore is offset to the right of the front one.

ENGINE SPECIFICATIONS	
Dates produced	1947-55
Cylinders	50-degree V-twin ohv four-stroke
Configuration	"V"
Engine capacity	998 cc
Power output	45 bhp (34 Kw) @ 5,300 rpm
Type	Conventional four-stroke, air-cooled petrol engine
Head	ohv actuated by pushrods and rocker arms; two valves per cylinder
Cooling	Air
Fuel system	Type 276 Amals carburettors
Bore and stroke	84 mm x 90 mm
Compression ratio	7:1

Compact and strong
Many internal details are revealed on this partially cut-away display engine (red areas). It can be seen that the whole unit, with its built-in four-speed gearbox, is very compact for a 1,000 cc engine. It is also a strong enough structure to support Vincent's "frameless" chassis.

Six-volt dynamo
Driven off the primary chain to charge the battery, a voltage regulator sits on top of the dynamo.

Gear ratio indicator

Selector mechanism
This is part of the four-speed gearbox.

Rear engine plates
These solid plates provide pivot point for cantilevered rear suspension.

Section of kick-start lever

Deep-skirted aluminium piston
This has three sealing rings.

Inlet valve
Valve has an austenitic cast iron seat.

Oil pipe
Oil is fed to the rockers via this pipe.

Valve springs
Placing the springs above the valve operating rockers keeps them cool.

Pivots for the valve rockers
These locate in tunnels within the cylinder head casting.

Cutaway of cylinder

Gear shift lever
This is shown raised through 90 degrees to give a clear view of the cutaway.

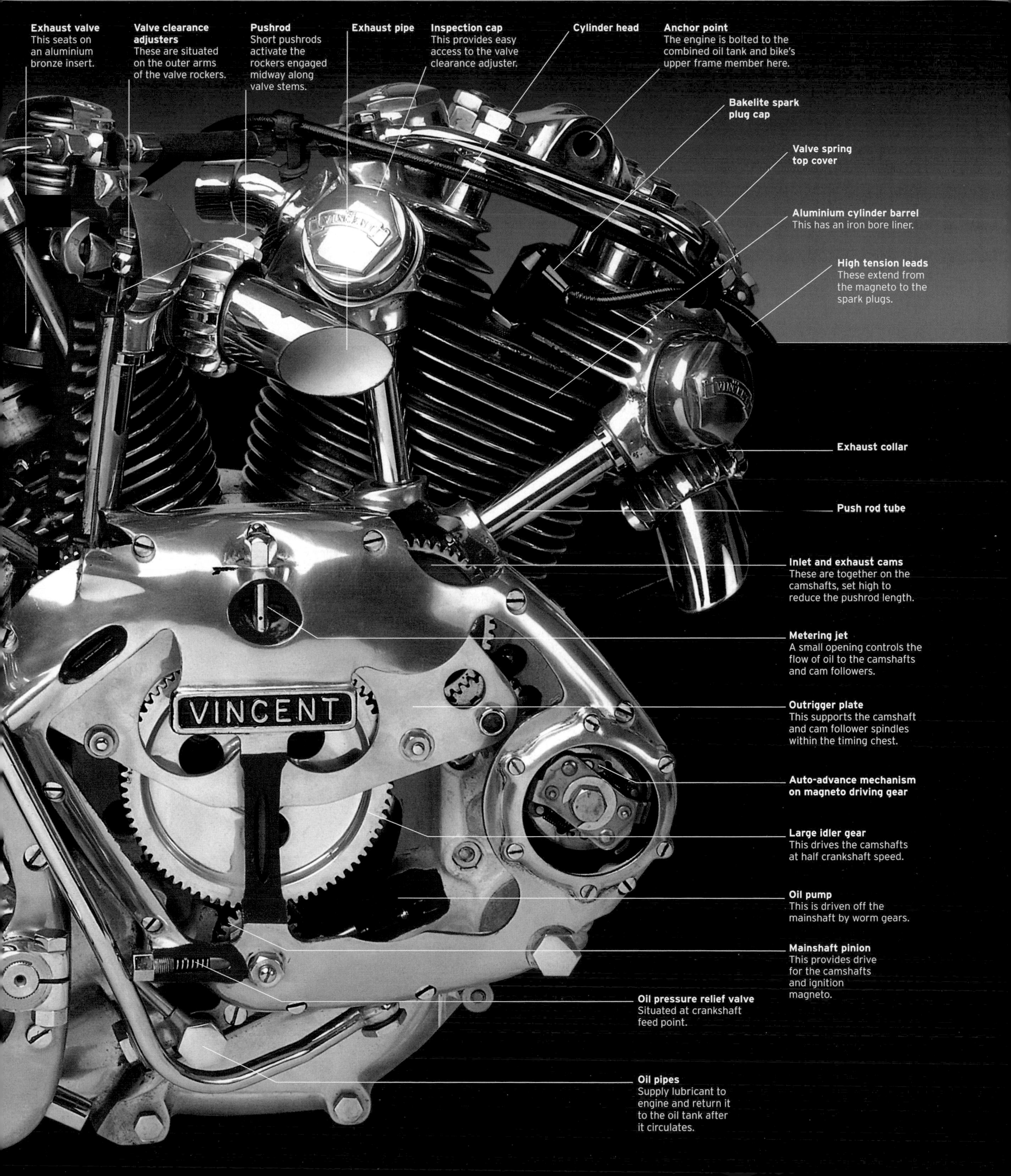

Exhaust valve
This seats on an aluminium bronze insert.

Valve clearance adjusters
These are situated on the outer arms of the valve rockers.

Pushrod
Short pushrods activate the rockers engaged midway along valve stems.

Exhaust pipe

Inspection cap
This provides easy access to the valve clearance adjuster.

Cylinder head

Anchor point
The engine is bolted to the combined oil tank and bike's upper frame member here.

Bakelite spark plug cap

Valve spring top cover

Aluminium cylinder barrel
This has an iron bore liner.

High tension leads
These extend from the magneto to the spark plugs.

Exhaust collar

Push rod tube

Inlet and exhaust cams
These are together on the camshafts, set high to reduce the pushrod length.

Metering jet
A small opening controls the flow of oil to the camshafts and cam followers.

Outrigger plate
This supports the camshaft and cam follower spindles within the timing chest.

Auto-advance mechanism on magneto driving gear

Large idler gear
This drives the camshafts at half crankshaft speed.

Oil pump
This is driven off the mainshaft by worm gears.

Mainshaft pinion
This provides drive for the camshafts and ignition magneto.

Oil pressure relief valve
Situated at crankshaft feed point.

Oil pipes
Supply lubricant to engine and return it to the oil tank after it circulates.

VINCENT

Yamaha YZF-R1°
In-line Four

Since the 1970s the in-line four-cylinder configuration, set across the frame, has been widely adopted for motorcycles. In conjunction with overhead-camshafts, the format can generate high rpm and power output while its frequent power impulses result in smooth running. Over the years, other developments, such as electronically controlled fuel injection and water-cooling, have boosted power from ever-more compact units.

TECHNICAL WIZARDRY

Based on a cross-plane crankshaft with 90-degree firing intervals developed to give linear power delivery on Yamaha's M1 MotoGP racer, the R1 unit also features highly advanced fuelling technology controlled by numerous sensors. A fly-by-wire system provides instant throttle response and electrically powered movement of the air intake funnels ensure that maximum torque is generated at any given engine speed. An upper set of funnels that make the intake tracts longer at low rpm move upwards to effectively make the tract shorter at high rpm.

ENGINE SPECIFICATIONS	
Dates produced	From 2009
Cylinders	four
Configuration	in-line
Engine capacity	998 cc
Power output	152 hp @ 12,600 rpm
Type	four-stroke, petrol engine
Head	double overhead camshafts, four valves per cylinder
Cooling	Water
Fuel system	electronically controlled injectors
Bore and stroke	78 mm x 52.2 mm
Compression ratio	12.7:1

YAMAHA

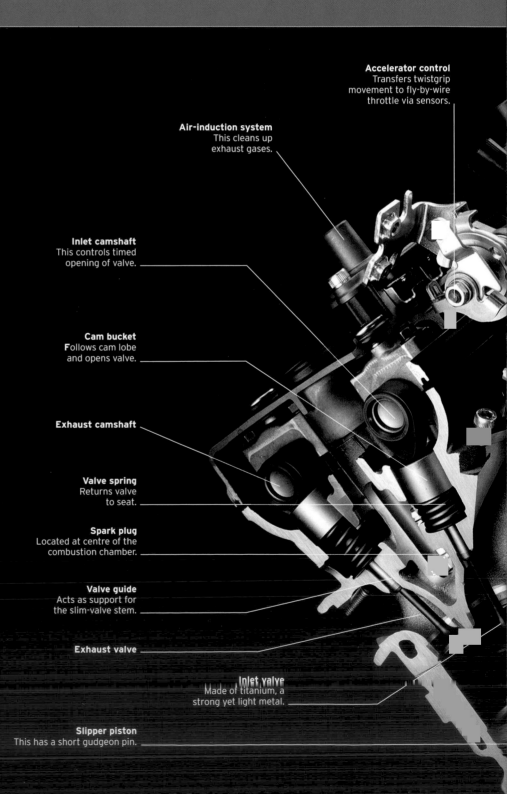

Accelerator control
Transfers twistgrip movement to fly-by-wire throttle via sensors.

Air-induction system
This cleans up exhaust gases.

Inlet camshaft
This controls timed opening of valve.

Cam bucket
Follows cam lobe and opens valve.

Exhaust camshaft

Valve spring
Returns valve to seat.

Spark plug
Located at centre of the combustion chamber.

Valve guide
Acts as support for the slim-valve stem.

Exhaust valve

Inlet valve
Made of titanium, a strong yet light metal.

Slipper piston
This has a short gudgeon pin.

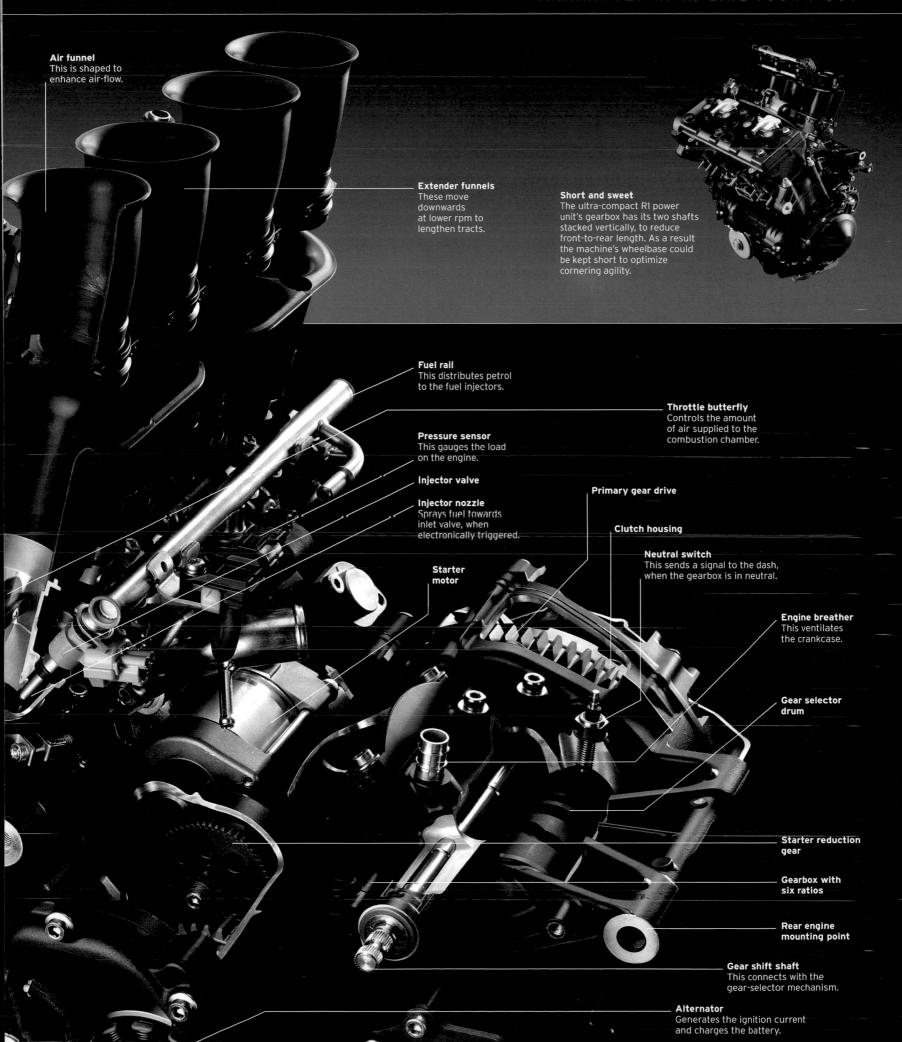

Air funnel
This is shaped to enhance air-flow.

Extender funnels
These move downwards at lower rpm to lengthen tracts.

Short and sweet
The ultra-compact R1 power unit's gearbox has its two shafts stacked vertically, to reduce front-to-rear length. As a result the machine's wheelbase could be kept short to optimize cornering agility.

Fuel rail
This distributes petrol to the fuel injectors.

Throttle butterfly
Controls the amount of air supplied to the combustion chamber.

Pressure sensor
This gauges the load on the engine.

Injector valve

Injector nozzle
Sprays fuel towards inlet valve, when electronically triggered.

Primary gear drive

Clutch housing

Neutral switch
This sends a signal to the dash, when the gearbox is in neutral.

Starter motor

Engine breather
This ventilates the crankcase.

Gear selector drum

Starter reduction gear

Gearbox with six ratios

Rear engine mounting point

Gear shift shaft
This connects with the gear-selector mechanism.

Alternator
Generates the ignition current and charges the battery.

Junior "Baby". **David McMahon:** Rudge 3½HP. **Nigel Hussey:** Triumph 3½HP Roadster. **Phil Crosby:** Humber 3½HP Touring, Rover 500 TT. **21 Alan Hummerstone:** Sun 2½HP. **Ian Anderson:** TD Cross TDC 3½HP. **Micheal Penn:** Sunbeam Single. **Rodney Hann:** Ariel 3½HP Roadster. **23 Rajnish Kashyap:** Royal Enfield 350 Bullet Machismo. **24 Phil Crosby:** Minerva 4½HP V-twin, FN Four. **25 Tony Donnithorne:** Zenith 8/10HP Gradua. **34 Phil Crosby:** Scott Two-speed TT racer. **40 Micheal Penn:** Triumph Model W. **41 Jeff Bishop:** Terrot FT. **Phil Crosby:** BSA Model B. **46 Clive Gant:** BSA Model A. **Don Hunt:** James Model 12. **Pascal Rabier:** Husqvarna T180. **Richard Duffin:** Burney V-twin. **47 Phil Crosby:** Harley-Davidson Model JD. **53 Bill Lennox:** Norton 3½HP. **Phil Crosby:** Norton 500T, Norton Dominator 88. **Wayne Tolson:** Norton F1 Sport. **54 George Harmer and Steven Harmer:** Blackburne 4HP. **Tim Walker:** Duzmo Sports. **57 Ireneusz Tomyslak:** Harley-Davidson Model B. **Steve Willis:** Ariel Model E. **Derek Wickes:** Dot J343. **Ian Kerr:** Norton 16H. **Roger Kimbell:** Sunbeam Model 9. **59 Cenwyn Ap Tomos:** Moto Guzzi Daytona 1000. **60 George Harmer and Steven Harmer:** Clyno 2¼HP, Sun Vitesse. **Micheal Penn:** Hawker Model C. **61 Alan Jennings:** BSA S28. **Phil Crosby:** Henley Blackburne Tourer. **Terry Green:** Triumph Model P. **64 George Harmer and Steven Harmer:** OK Bradshaw, Smart Celle du Salon. **66 Simon Whitaker:** Scott Harry Langman Works TT. **70 Phil Crosby:** Ariel SG. **71 Phil Crosby:** BMW R66. **76 Carl Chippendale:** Norton ES2 Model 18. **Sean Kelly:** Sunbeam Model 90. **77 Phil Crosby:** Brough Superior SS80. **82 David Beckett:** Stylson Blackburne. **John Fairclough:** Cotton Blackburne. **85 George Harmer and Steven Harmer:** Coventry Eagle 250. **Micheal Penn:** OK-Supreme 350. **Trevor Brookes:** Benelli 4TN. **87 Phil Davies:** BMW K1200S, BMW R650GS. **88 Geoffrey Hobbs:** Peugeot P108. **Jim Beckett:** BSA C11. **Martin Carter:** BSA H31 Sloper. **Paul Richmond:** Velocette GTP. **89 George Harmer and Steven Harmer:** Royal Enfield Bullet 250. **Phil Crosby:** Panther 250 Red Panther. **90 Micheal Penn:** Velocette KTT. **94 Phil Crosby:** Velocette MAC-MDD, Triumph 3TW, Triumph 3HW. **95 Phil Crosby:** Norton Big Four, Matchless G3LS, Norton 16H. **105 Phil Crosby:** Norton 500T, Royal Enfield J2. **106 Phil Crosby:** Norton International. **107 Phil Crosby:** Sunbeam S8. **108 Phil Crosby:** Harley Davidson Model JD. **111 George Harmer and Steven Harmer:** VéloSoleX. **113 Phil Crosby:** Triumph Grand prix, AJS 7R, Excelsior JAP

Speedway. **120 George Harmer and Steven Harmer:** Peugeot S157. **121 George Harmer and Steven Harmer:** Lambretta LI 150. **122 Stuart Lanning:** Lambretta LD 150. **126 George Manning:** Triumph T100. **127 Phil Crosby:** Norton Dominator 88. **129 Micheal Penn:** Triumph Tiger Cub. **131 Michael Delaney:** Honda Goldwing GL1500 SE. **134 George Harmer and Steven Harmer:** BSA Winged Wheel. **Jeremy Sykes:** Cyclemaster. **135 Maurice Drew:** Motom Super Sport. **George Harmer and Steven Harmer:** New Hudson Autocycle. **138 George Harmer and Steven Harmer:** James Comet, Excelsior Skutabyk, Express Radex 200. **140 Micheal Penn:** Vincent Comet. **Phil Crosby:** BSA Gold Star. **141 Jonathan E Osborne:** Velocette Mac. **144 Phil Crosby and Peter Mather:** Matchless G3L Trials. **145 Micheal Penn:** Triumph Tiger Cub Scrambler. **156 John Morris:** FB Mondial 48 Sport. **157 Donald Heath:** Greeves 32DC Sports Twin. **162 Micheal Penn:** Lambretta TV175 "Slimline". **Phil Crosby:** Lambretta LI 125. **163 George Harmer and Steven Harmer:** Triumph Tina, Raleigh RM5 Supermatic, Agrati Capri Scooter, Clark Scamp, Motobécane Mobylette. **Paul Tebbit:** NSU Quickly S2/23. **165 Ken Small:** M V Agusta. **Phil Bannister:** MV Agusta Ipotesi Sport. **166 Micheal Penn:** BSA M21, BSA Bantam D10. **167 Andy Baldwin:** Suzuki M15. **Dave Jupp:** Honda CD175. **170 Michael Gower:** Norton Navigator. **Micheal Penn:** Harley-Davidson FLH Duo-Glide. **Rick Lees:** Norton Dominator 99 De Luxe. **173 Adam Atherton:** Suzuki RG500. **Alfred Adebare:** Suzuki Hayabusa GSX 1300R. **Paul Storey:** Suzuki GS750. **174 Brian Chapman and Chris Illman:** Vincent Sprinter Methamon. **175 Brian Chapman and Chris Illman:** Vincent Mighty Mouse. **177 Phil Crosby and Peter Mather:** AJS Stormer. **186 Anthony Tomalin:** Yamaha XS1100F. **Kevin Hall:** Honda CBX 1000. **Michael Price:** Kawasaki NS750. **187 Keith Waring:** Kawasaki Z650C. **Lawrence Aughton:** Suzuki GS1000S. **Neil Comstive:** Kawasaki Z1000 Z1R D1. **Paul Storey:** Suzuki GS750. **188 Phil Crosby:** Ducati Silver Shotgun, Yamaha TX500, Ducati 450 Desmo. **189 Phil Crosby:** Benelli 500 Quatro, Suzuki GT550. **190 Phil Crosby:** Honda CB500T, Honda CB550 Four, Honda CX500. **191 Phil Crosby:** MV Agusta 350S Ipotesi. **193 Alistair Marshall:** Kawasaki Z1. **George Manning:** Kawasaki GS750. **194 Carl M Booth:** IZH Jupiter 3. **Phil Bannister:** MV Agusta Ipotesi Sport. **196 Charlie Garratt:** Honda CB250 K4. **Micheal Penn:** CZ sport

175. **197 Charlie Owens:** Yamaha SS50. **199 Phil Crosby** Suzuki A100, Casal K196 Sport Moped, Yamaha XS250, Suzuki GT185. **202 Dave Jupp:** Suzuki T125 Stinger. **George Manning:** Suzuki T350 Rebel. **Paul Block:** Suzuki GT380. **Peter Hodson:** Suzuki T500. **Wayne Allen:** Suzuki GT250 X7. **203 Mark Taylor:** Yamaha RD400, Kawasaki KH400. **204 Charlie Garratt:** Suzuki TS125. **205 Doug Hill:** Yamaha XT500. **207 George Manning:** Triumph Daytona 955i. **209 Brian Chapman:** Weslake Hobbit Dragster. **Micheal Penn:** Jawa Briggo Speedway. **210 Charlie Garratt:** Honda CB350 K4, BSA B25SS Gold Star. **Ron Perkins:** BSA A65 Thunderbolt. **211 Chris Child:** Benelli Tornado S. **Tom Rogers:** Yamaha SR500. **Tony Thomas:** Yamaha XS650B. **214 Charlie Garratt:** Yamaha RD350LC YPVS. **215 Charlie Garratt:** Honda VF400F, Honda VF500F2. **Steve Mawson:** Honda MBX50. **221 Clive Minshell:** Suzuki GSX-R400. **Paul Turk:** Honda CBR600F. **222 George Manning:** Kawasaki GPZ 1100. **Ian Weston:** Moto Martin CBX 1260 Special. **John Stone:** Michael Tomalin: Yamaha XS1100 LG Midnight Special. **223 Adam Atherton:** Suzuki RG500. **George Manning:** Kawasaki ZX750E Turbo. **225 Charlie Garratt:** Yamaha RD350. **227 Barry Whitehead:** Honda Bros Product 2. **Carl M Booth:** KMZ Dnepr MT11. **John Mather:** Honda XBR500. **Mike Ridley:** Honda CB250RS. **228 Charlie Garratt:** Honda VF500C Magna. **232 Micheal Penn:** GM Speedway, Godden GR500. **234 Les Judkins:** MBA 125. **240 Ian Welford:** Honda VFR400 NC30. **Wayne Tolson:** Norton F1 Sport. **241 Andy Woolley:** Ducati 888 SPS. **242 Cenwyn Ap Tomos:** Moto Guzzi Daytona 1000. **Mark Hatfield:** Bimota Mantra. **243 George Manning:** Kawasaki ZZ-R1100. **Neil Trutwein:** Kawasaki ZX9R. **Nigel Cocks:** Yamaha YZF600R Thundercat. **248 Dave Jupp:** Honda CB50V Dream. **Martyn Roberts:** Triumph Trident 750. **250 Alan Peters:** Honda Goldwing EML Trike. **251 Harley-Davidson:** Harley-Davidson Softail FLSTF Fat Boy. **Justin Watson:** Honda VT 750CT Shadow. **253 Michael Delaney:** Honda Goldwing GL1500 SE. **Rolf Zanders:** Honda XL1000V Varadero. **258 Duncan Whinney:** Triumph Daytona 650. **George Manning:** Triumph Daytona 675, Triumph Daytona 955i. **Phil Davies** BMW K1200S. **Rob Young:** Honda VTR 1000 SP1. **259 George Manning:** Kawasaki ZX-12R, Kawasaki EX250/Ninja 250R, Triumph Speed Triple. **Rob Johnson:** Suzuki G5XR-R 750. **260 Pegasus Motorcycles:** Kawasaki ZX-10R, Kawasaki ZZR1400, Kawasaki Ninja

ZX-6R. **261 Phil Davies:** BMW S1000RR, BMW K1300S. **266 David Driman:** Triumph Street Triple R. **David Farnley:** Yamaha XJR 1300. **George Manning:** Yamaha FZS 1000 Fazer. **John Pitts:** Norton Commando 961 Sport. **Ken Small:** MV Agusta 910S Brutale. **267 Harley-Davidson:** Harley-Davidson Sportster XR1200X, Harley-Davidson Sportster XL883N Iron. **268 G Mann:** Aprilia SL1000 Falco. **Satya Tandon:** Honda CBR 1100X Super Blackbird. **269 David Hall:** KTM 950 Adventure. **Eric Hayes:** Triumph Sprint RS. **George Manning:** BMW R1200RT. **Lloyd Benton and Damien Benton:** Benelli Tornado Tre 900LE. **Mark Band:** Kawazaki Z1000. **270 Alfred Adebare:** Suzuki GSX 1300R Hayabusa. **Michael D Watson:** Harley-Davidson FLHR Road King. **271 George Manning:** Triumph Tiger 800XC. **Phil Davies:** BMW R1200GS Adventure, BMW K1600GT, BMW R1200GS Adventure. **276 Alan Purvis:** Harley CVO Softail Convertible. **David Jones:** Moto Guzzi California EV. **Harley-Davidson:** Harley-Davidson Touring FLHX Street Glide, Harley-Davidson VRSCDX Night Rod Special. **Wayne MacGowan:** Suzuki M1800R. **277 George Manning:** Kawasaki VN900 Custom, Triumph Rocket III Roadster. **Ian Bull:** Triumph Thunderbird 1600. **Roy Dear:** Kawazaki VN1500 Mean Streak. **278 Micheal Penn:** BMW C1200. **Stuart Berenyi:** Suzuki VanVan. **283 G Mann:** Aprilia Falco. **284 George Manning:** Honda Falcon NX4. **Micheal Penn:** IMZ-Ural Tourist. **Nicci Hickman:** Suzuki SV650S. **Pankaj Kumar Jha:** Hero Honda Passion Pro. **Phil Davies:** BMW F800R. **Rajnish Kashyap:** Royal Enfield 350 Bullet Machismo. **285 George Manning:** Can-am Spyder Trike, Triumph Bonneville, Triumph America. **286 Neil Mort:** Yamaha XT660Z Tenere. **Phil Crosby:** BMW F650GS, Yamaha XT660X, BMW G650GS, Suzuki 450z RMX. **Phil Davies:** BMW F650GS, BMW G650GS. **287 Phil Crosby:** Husaberg TE250, KTM 85 SX, Kawasaki KX250F, KTM 65 SX, KTM 350 SX-F. **299 George Manning:** Yamaha FSZ 1000 In-line Four Fazer. **Phil Davies:** BMW K1600GT In-line Six.

Chapter opener images
Before 1920 Norton 5HP V-twin 1906
1920s Martinsyde 680 combination 1921
1930s BSA Empire Star 1936
1940s Harley-Davidson WLC 1942
1950s Lambretta LD 150 1957
1960s Norton Dominator 650SS 1962
1970s Benelli 750 Sei 1976
1980s Suzuki RG500 1986
1990s Honda CBR1000RR Fireblade 1999
After 2000 Yamaha YZF R1 2011
The Engine Harley-Davidson FLSTF Fat boy Engine 2011